GIVE ME THIS MOUNTAIN...

Discover Kingdom Secrets to Standing firm on Gods unfailing promises . . .
Fighting the battle, gaining victory and possessing your Possessions . . .

Dr. ABRAHAM PETERS

Order this book online at www.trafford.com
or email orders@trafford.com

Most Trafford titles are also available at major online book retailers.

Printed in the United States of America.

ISBN: 978-1-4669-5526-4 (sc)
ISBN: 978-1-4669-5525-7 (e)

Trafford rev. 08/25/2012

 www.trafford.com

North America & international
toll-free: 1 888 232 4444 (USA & Canada)
phone: 250 383 6864 ♦ fax: 812 355 4082

FOLLOW YOUR DREAM

Trouble arrives in measures,
and we stack it up real high,
until we're convinced,
we have no reason to try.
If you feel defeated,
you're absolutely wrong,
for if you follow your dream,
you could never lose for long.
Ignore the minor set-backs
that pile up and trouble you,
or you will build a mountain,
out of the stones hurled at you.
The future holds great promise,
your destiny unknown,
but God is always helping,
and you're never alone.
Soar bravely toward your goal.
Let nothing darken the way.
You can change your tomorrow,
if you seek your dream today.
BE THANKFUL ANY WAY . . .

DEDICATION

Dedicated to my beloved covenant partner in ministry, **Prophetess Teresa Yvonne Hay,** for all your great depth of love and commitment towards kingdom advancement and especially making this book project a dream come true. I thank you a million times and may your name be written boldly in gold on the mansion waiting for you in heaven.

ACKNOWLEDGEMENTS

My deepest appreciation and thanks to God almighty for the inspiration, instruction and revelation for this wonderful book.

Many Thanks to a beloved virtuous woman of GOD, **prophetess Teresa Yvonne Hay,** for believing in my calling, vision and ministry. Thank you to Beth Martinez and all her diligent team at **Trafford Publishing House** and the precious people working together as a winning team. may God bless you all more abundantly. Amen.

TABLE OF CONTENTS

ABOUT THE BOOK

My heart's desire for this BOOK is to be a blessing and a benefit to ministers and Bible teachers across the globe. This is a unique Book, as you will see. The sermons in these pages shows the burden in my heart to see people move forward and fulfill their divine destiny. Each sermon is different. Approaches to content, outline, and emphasis vary. These pages will challenge, bless, and inspire. The thread that ties them all together is an unquestioned confidence in the sufficiency and perfection of God's Word, a passion to declare the truth of God's Word, an unashamed surrender to the Lordship of Jesus Christ, and a deep desire to give honor and praise to Him.

This volume is unprecedented in its contents and particularly meaningful to all ages and stages of life. It is especially gratifying to me that rather than provide flimsy excuses to justify your stagnation and moving in circles around the mountain, God charges and encourage us to move forward, fighting the fight of faith by overcoming challenges and possessing your possessions.

"Then we turned around and set out across the wilderness toward the Red Sea, just as the LORD had instructed me, and we wandered around Mount Seir for a long time. Then at last the LORD said to me, `You have been wandering around in this hill country long enough; turn northward

"'Rise, take your journey, and cross over the River Arnon. Look, I have given into your hand Sihon the Amorite, king of Heshbon, and his land. Begin to possess *it*, and engage him in battle. 'This day I will begin to put the dread and fear of you upon the nations under the whole heaven, who shall hear the report of you, and shall tremble and be in anguish because of you.' Deuteronomy 2: 1-3 (NLT) 24-25 (NKJV)

I would encourage you to change your thoughts and control your attitude in conformity with the Holy Spirit. This is the single greatest asset because attitude determines action. Our attitudes determine whether we are going to take responsibility or complain and blame others. (see Numbers 11:4-15.) The choice is always ours and ours alone. No one can influence an individual's attitude. We are the ones who ultimately decide what we are going to think and those thoughts form our attitudes about who we are and what we are capable of accomplishing. This is why the capacity for choosing our thoughts is our greatest power. my prayer is that by reading this book you will change your perception, then can change your thinking, and then only can change your attitudes. If you change your attitudes or outlook, then you can change your outer experiences. By accepting this truth, you will Rediscover your true self by reviewing all of your feelings, hopes, fears, desires, and values to find out what matters to you, not what matters to someone else or what matters to certain groups of people. Not only are we creatures of habit, but we are creatures of social habits, and social habitats. There are times when others' judgments will, if we allow them, creep into our behavior. The more you honestly and clearly explore yourself in relation to your inner desires and values, the more self directed your life will be. To a great degree, you can control your own destiny if you are not afraid to take risks.

INTRODUCTION

The people whose lives are recorded in the Bible are not fictitious storybook characters; they were real people. How they dealt with life issues in their time can help us today. I trust you will be able to grasp some of the rich lessons available from studying their lives and how they overcame challenges and difficulties.

I also hope that reading this book will stimulate a desire in your heart to think carefully about other characters in the Bible not included in this book. As you read of their attitude through adventures and adversities, imagine what they may have looked like or what clothes they might have worn. Try to think of what life lessons they have for you. Another benefit of this book is to show the power of regular Bible reading meditation, audacity of faith and efficacy of prevailing prayers. I highly recommend this beneficial habit. As I wrote this manuscript, I thought over the life messages of each of the persons I selected. If you become a regular reader of God's Word, you too will find understanding and insight into life issues that you will want to share with others.

Friends, Just as the Bible's personalities speak to us, our lives speak to those around us. What we say will have more meaning if it is supported by how we live. Our loudest voice is our actions. What if people a hundred years from now were to examine your life, how you lived, and what you did? What will they learn? What will they write about you to benefit their generation? What is your life saying? Do your good works glorify your Father in heaven? Just as you'll learn from analyzing the stories of people in the Bible, so may your actions illustrate life lessons from which others can learn.

My deepest desire is to inspire and motivate readers to see God as the ultimate mountain mover, as you read this book it is my prayer that your faith will be stirred with audacity and fortitude to become mover of men and mountain by shaking off every challenges on your way to fulfilling divine destiny, taking back what the devil stole from you and enjoying the promise God made to you. Now its time to dare opposition and declare boldly: Give me this mountain . . .

HOW TO BE AN ASSETS AND NOT LIABILITIES

Businesses take an annual inventory of profits and losses, assets and liabilities, what is working and what isn't. Depending on how much we are working on ourselves or changing ourselves, we should take inventory with some kind of regularity as well. An inventory of our liabilities might include personality defects such as intolerance, dishonesty, pride, procrastination, fear, or selfishness, but a personal inventory is not about assessing only our liabilities. We can't forget the *assets* in an *assessment*.

An inventory does not have to be a lengthy list of all that is wrong with us, but rather a look at our assets, uniqueness, strengths, weaknesses, or areas we want to improve. Most importantly, the elements of our personal inventory need to be of such a nature that we can measure and review our progress. If we see a problem repeating itself in a pattern, it will make it easier for us to stop the pattern by recognizing the scenario that triggers the habitual behavior. Wouldn't taking an honest look at your life and taking a personal inventory help you know your Great divine destiny and your greatest happiness? Wouldn't it help you to eliminate your old, undesirable self, which was created by others' expectations, and encourage development of a new, Great divine destiny?

If you build on your assets, even turn your liabilities into assets, then your Great divine destiny will be fully realized. One way to explore and heighten your assets is to examine them through your purpose, which is your passion. You see not only does purpose give you strength, it also rallies your talents to the fore. If you are doing something worthwhile, then you appreciate your true strengths, skills, and talents. By becoming aware of your strengths, you feel more complete, whole, and naturally motivated.

It feels so much better to do what you want to do rather than what you feel burdened to do. If you are using the talents that give you pleasure; you will no longer be looking outside yourself for happiness, because your work and recreation will be fully satisfying, with a positive attitude and would strive for excellence.

If you see yourself as your best or Great destiny, identify all your most motivating talents, and rally them toward some issue or interest you care about. Then you will create work environments that truly fit who you really are, even while working at a job that is unsuited to your greatest talents and abilities. You will be happy and fulfilled when you choose to let go, and let your *real* self out. Personal change always seems difficult, if not impossible, as long as we are focused on what we don't have (liabilities) as opposed to what we do have going for us (assets). The first step is taking a look at our assets rather than our liabilities. Assets are the tools in our favor that we can use to make the impossible possible. The more we focus on our assets, the more power we will have to change our lives and circumstances. Let's take a look at some of our assets.

Spiritual Assets

Belief or lack of belief in a connection to a Higher Power can be a spiritual asset or a spiritual liability. *It is important to understand that we are spiritual beings with a temporary human experience, not human beings with a temporary spiritual experience. The scripture in psalms discloses you are gods, He said further but its unfortunate you shall die like men for failure to take your rightful place.* What this means is that you will outlive and outlast anything that is going on in your life right now. Whether you are tall, short, thin, fat, Asian, Caucasian, European, African, male, female, rich, poor, sick, or healthy, this is only your temporary state. Who you are—your Great divine destiny or human spirit—is permanent and lasting. What is important to understand is that what you *have* and what you *do* is only temporary. Your perception, of who you are mentally, physically, and spiritually, forms your Greatness. This divine destiny is a composite of principles, values, decisions, experiences, friends, heroes, suffering, passion, habits, visions, beliefs, dreams, realities, and goals that are tied to your purpose. Your Great destiny is driven by your life purpose.

Regardless of whether we are clear about our purpose on earth, we can be clear about what we decide to contribute to the world and ourselves. If you have a passion to serve mankind, then this purpose can be tied to what work you choose to do.

If your purpose is tied to what surrounds you, such as you and your family, then your purpose is doing the work that you do is to provide for your family. Nonetheless, there is a purpose behind every goal. In other words, earning a certain amount of money per year is your goal, but your purpose is to create the life you want.

Purpose is what motivates you toward your goals. Therefore, your passion and your spirit are what compel you. Expressing your passion motivates you to be fully engaged in your work and life. Your reason for doing whatever you do can be specifically tied to your goals in your job, even if your job may be somewhat mundane compared to your worldly concerns. For example, if a business is marketing an item to a certain group of consumers, the purpose behind any goal the company sets is to provide the best product that will make their customers more satisfied. This is so that people will prefer their products to some other companies' products and their customers' reasons for using their products will surpass companies whose product designers are simply competing among them for what appears to be the best idea. Having a clear purpose keeps us on track in the right direction and motivates us with a passion.

The human element can never be left out of business. This is why businesses seek innovation from the spirit and passion of their employees. They know that without it, their businesses could not survive and thrive in these highly competitive times. Individually, your passion and spirit make you the best you can be. Your uniqueness is what makes you a valuable contribution to any purpose or organization. Your Great divine destiny is your asset. Your purpose is your Great divine destiny-desiring to express itself.

Values Align Your Purpose with Your Goals

Purpose brings us clarity about where we are going and what specifically we are doing on a daily basis in order to accomplish that end. Commitment to a purpose larger than ourselves gives us meaning.

Purpose make us feel inspired and empowered. We feel like there is always something we can do that can make a difference. Purpose toward something larger is what has driven the great achievers of the world. The larger picture is never merely about larger amounts of money; it is about what we value. Luke 12:15."Then he said to them, "Watch out! Be on your guard against all kinds of greed; a man's life does not consist in the abundance of his possessions." This ancient wisdom of Christ Jesus, tells us that if our desires are based too much on material things because we want to have more than others do, then we may become easily frustrated and angry when we do not get what we want. Those who have visions of grandeur and yet hold those visions with good values and good pleasure can enjoy themselves while they journey toward their ideals. Having a wholesome view, filled with dreams of enjoyment, allows us to be happy along the way.

This is not to say that hard work isn't necessary. At times, we might have to muster up every ounce of our strength to get what we want. There are times when we might need to be like a warrior, fighting to get where we want to go. Only we can know which methods are best at any given time on our journey or mission. Purpose generates strength and courage around our deepest satisfactions.

If our desires are also based on winning, and in turn defeating others, we lose the depth of meaning and strength we need to conduct ourselves successfully and happily. We must certainly take care of overseeing critical details, but we can destroy our happiness by thinking that our value is about winning, which includes an emphasis on defeating others.

Is Your Life about Meaning or Matter?

Then Jesus said to them, "Watch out! Be on your guard against all kinds of greed; a man's life does not consist in the abundance of his possessions." LUKE 12:15.

Is your life about being a consumer? There is little time for meaning when your life is spent in getting, consuming, fixing, repairing, and maintaining physical matter that you cannot take with you when you leave this planet.

Unfortunately, most of us have little understanding of how valuable it would be for us to have meaning in all we do. We should ask ourselves, 'Why am I doing this?" "What do I want to accomplish?" "Why is this task more important than another?" "Why is this person approaching me?"

The last question is good one to ask yourself often, or to ask the person who is approaching you with conversation, especially if he or she rambling on and not getting to the point. You don't have to have a crisis in order to make more meaningful choices in directing your life. A university study of sixty students who had attempted suicide was asked why they did so. Eight-five percent stated that their reason was because their life seemed meaningless. Surprisingly, 93 percent of the students were having good social and family relationships, and they were doing well academically. Many People today have the means to live, but no meaning to live for. When our lives have meaning we are not just enduring life and surviving, rather we will hold an enduring light of true satisfaction and happiness. The only thing we can take with us when we leave this planet is the knowledge or meaning we have given to our lives. The matter, the physical stuff, must be left behind. Our focus should be on those things that will be with us forever. Relationships, love, helping one another, creating a better world, and cooperating with the perfect pattern of our unfoldment as extensions of the one mind as our Greater Inner man has infinite value.

Mental Assets

Mental assets include our attitudes, perception, knowledge, problem solving ability, and style of thinking (linear vs. creative thinking, which is right-brain/left brain thinking). It is no great secret that by controlling our thoughts we can control our attitudes. This is the single greatest asset because attitude determines action. Our attitudes determine whether we are going to take responsibility or complain and blame others. The choice is always ours and ours alone. No one can influence an individual's attitude. We are the ones who ultimately decide what we are going to think and those thoughts form our attitudes about who we are and what we are capable of accomplishing. This is why the capacity for choosing our thoughts is our greatest power.

People go to therapists for weeks, months, and years only to find out that if they change their perception, they can change their thinking. If they change their thinking, they can change their attitudes. If they change their attitudes or outlook, they can change their outer experiences. You can save yourself all that expensive therapy by coming to the same conclusion and accepting this truth. Rediscover your true self by reviewing all of your feelings, hopes, fears, desires, and values to find out what matters to you, not what matters to someone else or what matters to certain groups of people. Not only are we creatures of habit, but we are creatures of social habits, and social habitats. There are times when others' judgments will, if we allow them, creep into our behavior. The more you honestly and clearly explore yourself in relation to your inner desires and values, the more self directed your life will be. To a great degree, you can control your own destiny if you are not afraid to take risks.

Rolling the Dice, Taking Risks

If we think of life as a game, we surely have to take some risks, or we will not get anywhere on the playing board. Life is fair; the game is fair. All is perfect in the end. This you will see by just welcoming, or at least accepting what comes your way and openly and honestly looking at what is really happening to you, and most of all, seeing the purpose of things, the reason why everything happens as it does. The reason why unpleasant things happen is not only because we must make a change that we may be resisting, but also because of the beauty found in the lesson we can learn from the experience.

As the preacher says, "For every season, there is a reason, and a time for every purpose under heaven." Ecclesiastes 3. The word *purpose* and the answer to the word *why* are almost synonymous. It is funny though, that as children we may have often been told not to ask why so much. Yet asking why of yourself and others more often could be quite interesting. For example, just asking a person, "Why did you call?" especially if that person is rambling, could make your time and the time of the caller much more efficient. Asking yourself why you are working on one thing rather than another can make a difference in setting priorities in your time management. "But," you might ask, "if everything has a reason, why would we lose a loved one?" There is always a reason. It may have been best for that person to go on elsewhere, whether you like it or not. After all, who said this world is paradise? Some wonderful people are only here for a short time, or what seems like a short time. Why were they taken from us so early? Why then, would a wicked person be given a long life? Who knows? Since we can't change what happens to us, our only choice for sound mental and spiritual health is to change how we *feel* about what happens. This is something we have control over.

Physical Assets

In order to actualize our thoughts, we must be able to take *physical action* at the appropriate time. This is accomplished through physical energy, movement, sex drive, health, strength, stamina, and fitness. If we are not in balance in any of these areas, we will sabotage our success because we will have to compensate for lacking in these areas of physical well being. Motivation is a combination of physical energy and mental energy. Actually, since the mind controls our physical body, it is our mind that truly drives us to take any action. If our attitude is negative, we won't be motivated to go anywhere or do anything. Motivation is having a positive attitude about doing things that we may not always feel like doing.

When our purpose and passion are tied into our mind-set, we'll do almost anything to get where we want to go. Finally, all we need to do is believe in what we are doing. We can enable this to happen when we realize that we will do almost anything it takes to get what we want.

Only you can motivate yourself. No one can be motivated by others. The important factor is that you are motivated to do the most positive and constructive activities rather than destructive activities such as laziness. To overcome negative motivation, it is essential that you change your awareness of what you desire and how you can achieve it.

Once you focus your desires, you will be motivated to do the right thing for yourself. You must be convinced that any change you make will bring about the gratification of a particular need or desire.

Increasing your awareness of the potential benefits of taking any given action can elevate your motivation. People can attempt to motivate you, they can even threaten you, but unless you desire to make changes and take actions for which you can see rewards, you will not do it, no matter what the consequences might be. Without being aware of it and in touch with your positive inner desires, you could sabotage your own success by making the wrong choices due to lazy and self-destructive motivation.

The criminal, alcoholic, overeater, or drug addict have all gone through the same process and, based on their levels of awareness, decided that addiction is worth whatever price they have to pay for it. Once their awareness changes—usually under tragic circumstances—they realize that the cost of escaping from reality and a self they have come to hate is too high for what they are receiving in return. Their motivation then sets them on a more positive course.

People can only change by the power of the Holy Spirit through their own conscious decisions. Until their awareness is changed, people will not do what you want them to do. You can try every method you can even try to scare them into action, but their action will only be temporary in order to get you off their backs. People will only change when they align their passion and spirit, setting their motivation in gear toward their own positive vision. The story of that prodigal son in Luke 15 makes this point explicit, until he came to himself there was no going back home.

Skills Assets

Along with our personal inventory, we need to review our specific skills in relation to the work we are doing and our basic professional skills, such as communications and interpersonal skills. Make a checklist of your skills and particularly note which areas of expertise you have not brushed up on lately. Continuing education is vital. There is always more to learn; yet we tend to know it all. How are you at handling conflicts, negotiating, persuading, giving directions that someone else can clearly understand, building partnerships and team mates, prioritizing, time managing, and making decisions? Many people do not realize that there are actually seminars specifically on the subject of decision making. Have you ever taken a course in decision making? How about an entire course on listening skills? If you want to double-check and see what skills you might enhance, take a look at a good role model and see what that person does. Ask the role model questions, and then pursue the skills and techniques he or she uses. Have you ever asked someone if you could spend a day with him or her to find out how that person does what they do? This is not something just for students to do; a seasoned professional can do so and, if anything, you will actually impress the person you are interviewing.

The Asset of Persistence with Flexibility—Luke 18:1-8

Then Jesus told his disciples a parable to show them that they should always pray and not give up. He said: "In a certain town there was a judge who neither feared God nor cared about men. And there was a widow in that town who kept coming to him with the plea, 'Grant me justice against my adversary.' "For some time he refused. But finally he said to himself, 'Even though I don't fear God or care about men, yet because this widow keeps bothering me, I will see that she gets justice, so that she won't eventually wear me out with her coming!'" And the Lord said, "Listen to what the unjust judge says. And will not God bring about justice for his chosen ones, who cry out to him day and night? Will he keep putting them off? I tell you, he will see that they get justice, and quickly. However, when the Son of Man comes, will he find faith on the earth?" Luke 18:1-8 NIV.

Persistence receives the category of being an asset on its own. *Nothing in the world can take the place of persistence. Talent will not. Nothing is more common than unsuccessful men with talent. Genius will not. Education will not. The world is full of educated derelicts. Persistence and determination alone are very potent. The slogan "press on" has solved, and always will solve the problems of the human race.*

Although the essence and drive of persistence is the bottom line in accomplishing great things, being persistent to the point of ignorance and stubbornness is just plain stupid.

And disappointingly, we see people and businesses resist adjusting their plan because they think they will lose their plan altogether. Flexibility and quickness are keys to success in these fact-paced times. Nonetheless, the key here is the balance between action and inaction, knowing when to hold 'em and when to fold 'em. During my first efforts as an author of global repute, I constantly examined my capabilities by observing myself and measuring myself against all the qualities I needed to be successful. What I discovered was the most valuable quality I needed was persistence, my publisher a great woman of God Evangelist Dr. Mrs, Deborah Wright would attest to the fact I will call her from time to time and send loads of emails just to keep my contact fresh knowing that we live at different part of the globe separated by Atlantic. I needed the persistence to perform most consistently the tasks that brought me success, and it was important to realize that I should not get too caught up in perfecting other things that were not producing an income. Of critical importance was getting these nonproductive tasks out of the way and performing the tasks that brought real revenue. Sounds like simple prioritizing, but once you get caught up in managing ministry or a business, you can easily lose critical production time that brings you quality results. Entrepreneurs start wearing lots of hats, depending on the growth of the business and available staff. However, being foolishly stubborn and rigid about having your plan implemented *one* way—your way—is not what persistence is about. Problems are not something negative. Problems are our barometers for knowing when and how to change or adjust our course, yet we must keep our eye on the overall vision of what we ultimately want and then persist again.

Welcome on board friends, fasten your seat belt and get ready as I take you on flight to discover kingdom secrets of success and recovery of destiny and all you have lost, taking back possessing your possessions living the greater life you are destined for, becoming a world shaker, mover of men and mountains.

CHAPTER ONE

STANDING ON THE PROMISES THAT CANNOT FAIL

THIS IS THE WORD OF THE LORD . . .

Then the children of Judah came to Joshua in Gilgal. And Caleb the son of Jephunneh the Kenizzite said to him: "You know the word which the LORD said to Moses the man of God concerning you and me in Kadesh Barnea. I was forty years old when Moses the servant of the LORD sent me from Kadesh Barnea to spy out the land, and I brought back word to him as it was in my heart. Nevertheless my brethren who went up with me made the heart of the people melt, but I wholly followed the LORD my God. So Moses swore on that day, saying, 'Surely the land where your foot has trodden shall be your inheritance and your children's forever, because you have wholly followed the LORD my God.' And now, behold, the LORD has kept me alive, as He said, these forty-five years, ever since the LORD spoke this word to Moses while Israel wandered in the wilderness; and now, here I am this day, eighty-five years old. As yet I am as strong this day as on the day that Moses sent me; just as my strength was then, so now is my strength for war, both for going out and for coming in. Now therefore, give me this mountain of which the LORD spoke in that day; for you heard in that day how the Anakim were there, and that the cities were great and fortified. It may be that the LORD will be with me, and I shall be able to drive them out as the LORD said."

And Joshua blessed him, and gave Hebron to Caleb the son of Jephunneh as an inheritance. Hebron therefore became the inheritance of Caleb the son of Jephunneh the Kenizzite to this day, because he wholly followed the LORD God of Israel. And the name of Hebron formerly was Kirjath Arba (Arba was the greatest man among the Anakim). Then the land had rest from war. Joshua 14:6-15.

Zechariah 4:6-14.

So he said to me, "This is the word of the LORD to Zerubbabel: 'Not by might nor by power, but by my Spirit,' says the LORD Almighty. "What are you, O mighty mountain? Before Zerubbabel you will become level ground. Then he will bring out the capstone to shouts of 'God bless it! God bless it!'"

Then the word of the LORD came to me: "The hands of Zerubbabel have laid the foundation of this temple; his hands will also complete it. Then you will know that the LORD Almighty has sent me to you. "Who despises the day of small things? Men will rejoice when they see the plumb line in the hand of Zerubbabel. "(These seven are the eyes of the LORD, which range throughout the earth.)" Then I asked the angel, "What are these two olive trees on the right and the left of the lamp stand?"

Again I asked him, "What are these two olive branches beside the two gold pipes that pour out golden oil?" He replied, "Do you not know what these are?" "No, my lord," I said. So he said, "These are the two who are anointed to serve the Lord of all the earth." Zechariah 4:6-14.

Luke 17:5-6

The apostles said to the Lord, "Increase our faith!" He replied, "If you have faith as small as a mustard seed, you can say to this mulberry tree, 'Be uprooted and planted in the sea,' and it will obey you. Luke 17:5-6

Matthew 17:19-20

Then the disciples came to Jesus in private and asked, "Why couldn't we drive it out?" He replied, "Because you have so little faith. I tell you the truth, if you have faith as small as a mustard seed, you can say to this mountain, 'Move from here to there' and it will move. Nothing will be impossible for you." Matthew 17:19-20

Meet Courageous Caleb:
A Man Who Wholly Followed the Lord . . .

The Holy Scriptures is a rich source of excellent lessons. Romans 15:4 reads, **"For whatever things were written before were written for our learning, that we through the patience and comfort of the Scriptures might have hope." And do not grumble, as some of them did—and were killed by the destroying angel. These things happened to them as examples and were written down as warnings for us, on whom the fulfillment of the ages has come. So, if you**

think you are standing firm, be careful that you don't fall! No temptation has seized you except what is common to man. And God is faithful; he will not let you be tempted beyond what you can bear. But when you are tempted, he will also provide a way out so that you can stand up under it." 1Corinthians 10:10-13.NIV.

When we examine the lives of the spiritual giants of old, many important and profitable lessons can be learned. These lessons encourage us to persevere, bring comfort to our hearts, and cause us to rejoice in our hope. It is the purpose of this book to examine the faithfulness of Caleb and afew others as well as their trials, triumph and reward.

Caleb was one of the twelve spies who were chosen. Each spy was selected because he was a leader among his tribe. (Num.13:1-3).We can conclude from his being selected that Caleb was well respected by the people. Caleb was a man of courage. Caleb accepted the difficult and dangerous assignment to spy out the land. (Num. 13:17-21).Caleb encouraged the people to immediately go up and take the land. (Num13:30-33).Caleb held to his faith and convictions in the face of bitter opposition. (Num. 14:1-10).In their first battle with the Canaanites since their 40 year wandering, Israel did not loose a single man. (Num. 31:48-49). Caleb and Joshua had been right about Israel's capabilities the first time the spies came back from Canaan. Caleb was a man of faith and a man who completely trusted in God. (Num. 14:8) Caleb's faith was the key to his success.

God was very angry with the Israelites because of their lack of faith and their rebellion. God wanted to destroy all of the children of Israel, but Moses interceded. (Num. 14:15-19). God said that Caleb and Joshua would go in and inherit the land. (Num. 14:28-32)

CALEB RECEIVED WHAT HE HAD BEEN PROMISED. (Joshua 14:6-15). In verse 9 of Joshua 14, we find Caleb restating Moses' promise to him regarding the land that would be given to him. At the age of 85 years, 45 years after having spied out the land, Caleb asked for this land. (10-12). According to verse 12, we find that Caleb had the faith and confidence that the Lord would help him to drive out the inhabitants of the land that was promised to him. Caleb said, "It may be that the Lord will be with me, and I shall be able to drive them out as the Lord said." (Josh. 14:12, NKJV). Caleb received what he had been promised. Caleb had been faithful for many years, but he eventually received his promised land. (vss 13-14)

We can learn a lesson in character. Caleb was first and foremost a man of God. Such character is sorely needed in our generation. Caleb possessed the characteristic of courage; he was not afraid of the giants. We must not be fearful or cowardly. (II Tim. 1:7; Rev. 21:8)

Caleb possessed the characteristic of dedication. His life was as a job well done. Caleb was a lot like Paul in this respect. (II Tim. 4:6-8)

Caleb had faith and trusted in God. ". . . The Lord is with us. Do not fear them," said Caleb. (Num. 14:9; Rom. 8:31,37). We, too, are going to face our own giants. We have our own mountains to conquer. These giants will take on various forms: a personal weakness; possibly an addiction of some sort; a difficult task of some kind; a door of opportunity that has been opened, etc.

How can we be strong and courageous like Caleb? The answer is found in Ephesians 3:16 and 6:10-17. We need to wholly trust God and rely on His promises. If we wholly trust in God, then we will be pleasing unto God. (Heb. 11:6)

If we wholly trust in God and seek him, then we will have what we need to conquer any "giants" which come against us. (Matt. 6:33)

By trusting in God and relying upon Him, we will have "all things that pertain to life and godliness, through the knowledge of Him who called us by glory and virtue." (II Pet. 1:1-4,)

COVENANT PATIENCE: Although it does take time, we will eventually receive our promised inheritance. Paul hoped for eternal life promised by Him who cannot lie. (Titus 1:2)

The writer of Hebrews states that we will be of the house which Christ is over if we "hold fast the confidence and the rejoicing of the hope firm to the end." (Heb. 3:6,)

We must have "diligence to the full assurance of hope until the end." We must not become sluggish, but instead, we are to "imitate those who through faith and patience inherit the promises." (Heb. 6:11-12,)

With God on our side, we can face any giant and conquer any mountain. With God on our side, we can face obstacles with courage and confidence.

Let us follow Caleb's example and follow the Lord. We cannot hold back, we cannot doubt, and we cannot waver. Within a few short years, we, too, will receive the object of our hope. (I Pet. 4:19)

It is easy to give flimsy excuses today in an age of compromise and serious pollution of old time faith. let us be sincere by asking ourselves "Shall we follow Jesus like Caleb followed the Lord, despite the hazards?"

What is it to follow Christ despite the hazards? Caleb followed the Lord despite the dangers. He was willing to face the giants in the land—cf. Num 13:33 "And there we saw the Nephilim (the sons of Anak, who come from the Nephilim), and we seemed to ourselves like grasshoppers, and so we seemed to them.'" He was willing to face the wrath of his brethren—Num 14:10 "Then all the congregation said to stone them with stones. But the glory of the LORD appeared at the tent of meeting to all the people of Israel." He was willing to take a mountain from the giants in his old age—Josh 14:10-12 "And now, behold, the LORD has kept me alive, just as he said, these forty-five years since the time that the LORD spoke this word to Moses, while Israel walked in the wilderness. And now, behold, I am this day eighty-five years old. I am still as strong today as I was in the day that Moses sent me; my strength now is as my strength was then, for war and for going and coming. So now give me this hill country of which the LORD spoke on that day, for you heard on that day how the Anakim were there, with great fortified cities. It may be that the LORD will be with me, and I shall drive them out just as the LORD said."'

It is unfortunate today that, Many will serve the Lord only when it is convenient. When it is popular, like the crowds who followed Jesus. When it is safe, like Peter before confronted by the maiden—Mt 26:69-70 "Now Peter was sitting outside in the courtyard. And a servant girl came up to him and said, "You also were with Jesus the Galilean." But he denied it before them all, saying, "I do not know what you mean."" What of us who follow Jesus today? Shall we follow Him only when convenient? Shall we follow Him despite ridicule, persecution, dangers?—Mt 5:10-12 ""Blessed are those who are persecuted for righteousness' sake, for theirs is the kingdom of heaven. "Blessed are you when others revile you and persecute you and utter all kinds of evil against you falsely on my account. Rejoice and be glad, for your reward is great in heaven, for so they persecuted the prophets who were before you."—Shall we follow Jesus like Caleb followed the Lord, despite the hazards?

Certainly the commitment of Caleb to his Lord is commendable. How was he able to be so committed? How might we be so enabled . . . ? How are we enabled to follow the Lord fully? One way is by keeping our eye on Him. Caleb's faith was in the Lord, not himself. He was confident they could take the land—Num 13:30. But that was because he knew the Lord would be with them—Num 14:6-9. Thus his eye was on the Lord! So we need to keep our eye on Jesus—Heb 12:1-4 "Therefore, since we are surrounded by so great a cloud of witnesses, let us also lay aside every weight, and sin which clings so closely, and let us run with endurance the race that is set before us, looking to Jesus, the founder and perfecter of our faith, who for the joy that was set before him endured the cross, despising the shame, and is seated at the right hand of the throne of God. Consider him who endured from sinners such hostility against himself, so that you may not grow weary or fainthearted. In your struggle against sin you have not yet resisted to the point of shedding your blood."

Looking unto Him as the author and finisher of our faith. Considering the hostility He endured, knowing the Father will help us as He helped Him to endure.—Shall we look to the Lord for our inspiration and confidence, like Caleb did?

We can follow the Lord fully by having a different spirit. Caleb was noted for a having a different spirit—Num 14:24 "But my servant Caleb, because he has a different spirit and has followed me fully, I will bring into the land into which he went, and his descendants shall possess it." Different than the spirit in the other ten spies, who were defeatists—Num 13:31 "Then the men who had gone up with him said, "We are not able to go up against the people, for they are stronger than we are."" Different than the spirit in the rest of Israel, who complained—Num 14:1-2 "Then all the congregation raised a loud cry, and the people wept that night. And all the people of Israel grumbled against Moses and Aaron. The whole congregation said to them, "Would that we had died in the land of Egypt! Or would that we had died in this wilderness!" We can be strengthened by a different spirit. Certainly the spirit of a positive attitude will help—Ph 4:13 "I can do all things through him who strengthens me." How much more so, with the Spirit of God helping us!—Ro 8:12-13 "So then, brothers, we are debtors, not to the flesh, to live according to the flesh. For if you live according to the flesh you will die, but if by the Spirit you put to death the deeds of the body, you will live."; Ep 3:16 "that according to the riches of his glory he may grant you to be strengthened with power through his Spirit in your inner being,"—Shall we have a "can do" attitude, knowing we are clothed in the strength of God's might?—Ep 6:10-13 "Finally, be strong in the Lord and in the strength of his might. Put on the whole armor of God, that you may be able to stand against the schemes of the devil. For we do not wrestle against flesh and blood, but against the rulers, against the authorities, against the cosmic powers over this present darkness, against the spiritual forces of evil in the heavenly places. Therefore take up the whole armor of God, that you may be able to withstand in the evil day, and having done all, to stand firm." and Jude 20-23 admonished "But you, beloved, building yourselves up on your most holy faith, praying in the Holy Spirit, keep yourselves in the love of God, looking for the mercy of our Lord Jesus Christ unto eternal life. And on some have compassion, making a distinction (difference) ; but others save with fear, pulling them out of the fire, hating even the garment defiled by the flesh."

Friends, let us seek to discern to glean from the example of Caleb a motivation to follow the Lord fully. It leads to a fuller life. Consider how God was able to use Caleb: As a leader in Israel—cf. Num 13:2,6; 34:18,19. As a servant of God, first to spy out the land, then to divide it—Num 14:24a. As an example of faith and courage—Num 13:30; 14:8,9. As a reminder of God's justice—Num 14:29-30.

As an inspiration of service, even in old age—Josh 14:6-12.

How useful will we be, if we follow Jesus fully? We can be an example in youth—1 Timothy 4:12 "Let no one despise you for your youth, but set the believers an example in speech, in conduct, in love, in faith, in purity." We can be useful to the Master—2 Timothy 2:20-22 "Now in a great house there are not only vessels of gold and silver but also of wood and clay, some for honorable use, some for dishonorable. Therefore, if anyone cleanses himself from what is dishonorable, he will be a vessel for honorable use, set apart as holy, useful to the master of the house, ready for every good work. So flee youthful passions and pursue righteousness, faith, love, and peace, along with those who call on the Lord from a pure heart."—Don't we want to be useful to Jesus?

It leads to a fulfilled life. Consider how Caleb was fulfilled in life: Only he and Joshua were blessed to enter Canaan—Deuteronomy 1:35-36. He received the land around Hebron as an inheritance—Josh 14:6-14; 21:12. His land had rest from war—Josh 14:15. What kind of fulfilled life does Jesus offer those who follow Him fully today? One that experiences love which passes knowledge—Ep 3:19 "and to know the love of Christ that surpasses knowledge, that you may be filled with all the fullness of God." One that experiences peace which surpasses understanding—Philippians 4:7 "And the peace of God, which surpasses all understanding, will guard your hearts and your minds in Christ Jesus." One that experiences joy inexpressible—1 Peter 1:8 "Though you have not seen him, you love him. Though you do not now see him, you believe in him and rejoice with joy that is inexpressible and filled with glory," One in which our daily needs are provided—Mt 6:33 "But seek first the kingdom of God and his righteousness, and all these things will be added to you."—Don't we want to have a fulfilled life?

Let the example of Caleb inspire you to follow the Lord fully in your life . . . To follow Jesus all the days of your life. To follow Jesus with all your heart. To follow Jesus despite the hazards. Shall we, like Caleb, follow the Lord fully so we too may have a useful life in service to the Lord? Have a fulfilled life that is blessed by the Lord? Don't forget—Caleb and Joshua were the only two (out of 603,550 men) who survived the forty years of wilderness wanderings and entered the promised land (Num 32:10-13). Their brethren did not enter Canaan, for as the Lord said of them "they have not wholly followed Me". How are we following the Lord? Like Caleb? Or like those who died in the wilderness . . . ?

We all have times when we desire some word from God. We know that this would encourage us. It would help us in our difficulties. Make the will strong. The will is the part of us that makes us able to choose. The Holy Spirit gives us the strength to continue when things are hard. Once I heard a man shared his story of visits to a library. He wants to know what to do about a minor illness. He finds that he seems to have 101 serious diseases! That is not the purpose of this book! Nobody will have all the problems that are in this book. But all of us have bad times. We may have problems. We may feel sad. One trouble often leads to another too. Some of the subjects are very similar. They may go with each other. So, fear and worry may go together. But they are separate here. One situation may not be the same as the reader's situation. Another one will be. There is something else important. We may not have these difficulties ourselves. But we may need to help people who do have them. We should not just study problems that **we** might have. Christians help **other people** with their problems. We will study some of these.

Caleb 'always obeyed the Lord'. (Read Deuteronomy 1:36; Joshua 14:8-9.) Moses sent him, and 9 other men, to look at the land. But most of them were very much afraid. They also made the rest of the people feel their great fear. They 'told the people things that made them afraid . . . '. (Read Joshua 14:8.) Caleb was free from fear. He used his strong trust in God to help God's people. They were full of pain and despair. Caleb wanted them to trust God instead.

This could be important to you. Maybe **you** are not afraid yourself. But the Lord God wants you to help those who are afraid. Yours is a service like Caleb's. You have something to say to people who are afraid. In the present times, people are certainly full of fear. There is the worry about fate and death. There is the worry about two feelings. The feelings are about two lacks. There is the lack of inner satisfaction. There is the lack of meaning to life. The third type of worry is about being guilty and deserving punishment.

People do not always express their fears immediately. Then, their sense of need can be so great that they do speak. They tell someone else about their fears and worries. How great if that 'someone' is a Christian! What an opportunity! We can tell them what we know about God. We can tell them the good news about Jesus.

Surrender means to give oneself completely to God. This is the first thing to take us towards peace. It seems a very plain truth. But people neglect it. Caleb said that the people were afraid. 'But', he said, 'I completely followed the Lord.' (Joshua 14:8.)

Many of the people did not trust in God. (Read Deuteronomy 1:31-32.) The first language of our Old Testament (the first part of the Bible) was Hebrew. The Hebrew word here for 'trust' has a strong meaning. It means 'to put firm confidence in' the Lord. It also means 'cause to expect God's help'. God says many things. He promises many things too. This is a strong appeal to believe what he says. It is an appeal to trust God without any kind of fear or worry. (Deuteronomy 1:21.)

The Bible says that Caleb 'completely followed the Lord'. The Hebrew word here is full of meaning. It describes a man who gives himself entirely and completely to God. He does this because he loves God so much. He wants to serve God only.

Our surrender to God is the only answer to the problem of fear. Remember what Isaiah 26:3 says. 'You, Lord, give him perfect peace . . . because he puts his trust in you.' 'Perfect peace' means that it could not be any better. Someone said: 'I have made God the end of all my fears.' So, I bring all my anxious worries to God. Then I leave them with him. God promises this 'perfect peace'. But it is for those who trust him. It is for those who have confidence in God. They are sure of him. I strongly believe the only fear permissive is the fear of God and any who fear Yahweh will have none else to fear whatsoever.

Caleb certainly had this quality. The reason for his calm attitude is his surrender. (He has given himself completely to God.) Trust leads to being at peace. In the same way, if we do not trust, we do not have peace. There is a reason for this. When we give ourselves completely to God, we make a clear statement. It is this. The responsibility for our lives is not ours. God has total responsibility for our lives.

Caleb was able to make the people calm. (Numbers 13:30.) This was because he had a different attitude. (Numbers 14:24.) He was not like the people. They would not trust God. They would not obey God's rules. Caleb gave himself completely to God.

Perhaps we want to bring practical help to somebody who is afraid. If we do, we must be like Caleb: He was honest about the difficulties. But he was not afraid. Read again the story in Numbers 13:17-33. People can try to escape from fear. They pretend to themselves that there are no difficulties. They might even persuade other people that there are none. But we cannot escape from fear in these ways.

Napoleon Bonaparte lived from 1769-1821. He was a famous soldier and ruler. There is a story about him. It was when he had a serious problem with his army. He would plan on paper how to move his army. He used soldiers and arms that he knew did not exist. His captains reminded him of the facts. The soldiers and arms were not there. Napoleon said to them: 'Do you want to you rob me of my peace?'

We do not want that kind of peace. That is just trying to escape from reality. In the end, it leads to even more despair and pain.

No, Caleb reported the facts. (Numbers 14:7-8.) He did not avoid the problems. It was the way that he gave the facts. This was what was different. The other men saw only the difficulties of the Promised Land. They were depressed, felt sad and filled with despair about them all. (Numbers 13:31-33.) Caleb reported about the good things too. He reminded the people of God's power: Moses asked the men to bring good news. He said 'Bring some of the fruit of the land' (Numbers 13:20). In this, Moses was accepting God's word. (Exodus 3:8.) The land was full of many good things. God had clearly said it. Moses trusted God, and so did Caleb.

We must understand other people's problems. This is most important. You may act as if a person's problems are not serious. You may even pretend that they do not exist. You can never help someone in that way. Listen to what they say with sympathy. Let them know that you care about them. Then try to help them to see their problems as they really are. They need to see the bad things in proportion to the good things.

Often, a person in need does not see facts as they really are. They cannot help this. It is because they are feeling depressed. So, you should show the facts as they are. This is the greatest thing that you can do for them. You cannot do it quickly or in a careless way. Perhaps the person feels that you are in a hurry. If they do feel that, then it gives a definite impression to them. They feel that you do not really care. You do not have sympathy for them in their troubles.

Caleb did not pretend that the giants did not exist. But he was different from most of the men who were with him. He tried to report the good things too.

This leads to an important rule. Fear can come in any new dimension and difficult situation. This rule is a way to attack this fear.

Searching for something positive even in the odd situation that will be useful: Search for something that will encourage. When someone is in trouble, he can only think of the giants. But there are **always** good things too! (Numbers13:23.) You may be afraid. If so, then try to be quiet and speak to the Lord. He can show you good things that he can bring out of the situation.

Moses told the 12 men to gather fruits of the land (Numbers 13:20). This can be picture language for today. Fresh experiences of God are like gathering fruits. They are good for you. You can enjoy them too. They are better than ordinary things.

You can have these experiences even when all is against you. You may feel depressed or lonely. Whatever your troubles, they will seem like giants. At these times, remember something important. It is this. The Lord can use this experience to bring sure help. He can use it to bring you closer to him.

The Chinese have a word that means 'crisis'. It comes from 2 word pictures. One of the words means 'danger'. The other word means 'opportunity'. Every crisis in life has an opportunity. It is an opportunity for us: to grow in the Christian life, to get to know the Lord better and not become bitter, to become more useful in service and help to other people.

In the east African country of Kenya, there is a tribe with the ancient custom and traditional norm and value which require that a young man must kill a full grown lion or lioness before such is allowed to get married to his new bride. How weird or great herculean task it may seem but its has great lesson of proving manhood and sense of security, responsibility and great strength before attaining adulthood.

Caleb recognises something else: Acting in a definite and quick way to defeat fear Caleb says: 'Let us go there **at once**'. (Numbers 13:30.) Remember how God called Moses at the scene of burning bush. God says: 'Now therefore go . . . '. (Exodus 4:12.)

We may have fears and worries. We may feel depressed. These things can easily become worse in our lives. We should aim to overcome them immediately. We can only do this with the help of the Lord Jesus Christ.

Talk to yourself. (Psalm 42:5, 11.) In what may seem as physical or Spiritual Depression. there is the difference between two possibilities. You could let your moods and feelings dictate to you. Or you could talk to yourself in a confident way. 'Why am

I so sad? Why am I so upset? I should wait for God's help.' You may be feeling depressed. If so, do not let that mood control what you say to yourself.

Caleb's friends were very afraid, but Caleb reminds them of their resources, which did not have any limits (Numbers 13:30, 31.) 'We are well able', Caleb says. 'We are not able', say his friends. Ask yourself which group you belong to. One group deserves honour. They are those who are well able. Do not belong to the miserable group of those who are not able.

Caleb's words are important. He said, 'We are well able'. This does not mean that he had confidence in himself. He did not have the wrong idea of their military power either. No. He was emphasising where their power came from. It came from firm confidence in God's power.

Friend, whatever **your** trouble, 'God is able'. The New Testament even speaks about this many times. Some examples are: Ephesians 3:20; Philippians 3:21; 2 Timothy 1:12; Hebrews 2:18; 7:25 and Jude 24.

Maybe you have many troubles, There is something very important to avoid: Avoid always being sad about former troubles. It is easy to think about them all the time. It is not good to do this. It is a very natural thing to do. But it is certainly not a holy thing to do. Numbers 14:1-4. The people were trying to escape their present troubles. They did this by thinking of their past. They showed a serious lack of trust in God. They showed too that they were not grateful. They did this in a terrible way. This passage is like a sad song about the past. But it was false.

Earlier, the same people danced with delight. They sang of God's goodness when he saved them. (Exodus 15:1-21.) Now they can only talk about death. There was: death in Egypt, which they wished they had had. (Numbers 14:2.) death in the desert, which they might have had. (Numbers 14:2.) death in the Promised Land, which they were sure that they would have. (Numbers 14:3.)

You may be in some kind of trouble. You may be feeling very unhappy. Do not return to former sad times. You would just add them to your present troubles. You might do it like this. You say: 'The last 2 years have been awful for me. It began with . . .' This is not God's way to see life.

If you made God the end of your fears at that time, leave them there. He was able to keep you in those difficult days. It is easy to forget this when we only think of the former troubles.

I remember old chorus we used to sing several years ago when I was in the choir,:" when I think of the goodness and all He has done for me my very soul shall shout hallelujah . . . Praise God for saving me . . ." Gloooooooooooooory !!!

Caleb knew the thing that matters most in all of life's experiences: The most important thing is to please God (Numbers 14:8.) Caleb said, 'If we are pleasing the Lord . . . '. Read Hebrews 11:5-6 too. God's people were refusing his authority. They were just thinking about pleasing themselves. Caleb had a much better ambition. His desire was to give delight to God. He appealed to his friends not to refuse God's authority. He reminded them that God loved them (Numbers 14:9).

There is something serious here for us to understand. If we always complain, we show our resistance against God. 1 John 3:22 is very important here. We must obey him and do the things that please him. We must make it our ambition to please him. (2 Corinthians 5:9.)

We can succeed if we know that God is with us, It will be like this whatever our fears and troubles are. Caleb realised this great truth. It gives us courage to continue in every situation of life. 'The Lord is with us', Caleb and Joshua declared. The people still refused to accept this truth. They picked up the stones at their feet. They were going to kill the brave men who appealed to them.

Then something wonderful happened. 'The glory of the Lord appeared.' (The word 'glory' speaks about the power of God. It shows that God is very great. People usually saw it as a very bright light or fire.) Everyone could see that Caleb's words were true. So, the angry crowd dropped their stones.

We can be certain that God is with us every day. So, we can be confident whatever happens to us. God is with us, This makes us sure of God's power in us. Look closely again this by reading what Caleb himself says. He speaks about God's goodness in Joshua 14:6-12. Notice especially what he says in Joshua 14:11-12. 'I am as strong today as I was when Moses sent me . . . . If the Lord will be with me then I shall be able . . . as the Lord said.'

You may have times of great trouble. You may sometimes think that you will never live through them. But God is able to help you. He is also ready to help you.(Isaiah41:10) Let this truth encourage **us** all in our troubles. Then, our experiences may help **other people** in their difficulties.

SIGNIFICANCE OF A DIFFERENT SPIRIT

In life you will face oppositions because there is a divine position on top that God has destined for you. Therefore, it is imperative that you will first possess the Holy Spirit empowerment to help you overcome fiery opponents and daunting oppositions. let me briefly give you a brief synopsis of Joshua and Caleb, of whom the lord God commended that they got a different spirit. and then give you what needs to be learned from their differing positive attitude spirit and how it personally applies to the situation that you are now facing.

God sends Moses into the land of Egypt to rescue and deliver His people from their slavery to the Egyptians. He throws 10 whopper plaques at the Pharaoh in order to get him to release His people from their bondage. God literally parts the Red Sea to complete the deliverance mission. God the Father performs one of the most powerful, supernatural displays of signs and wonders that the world has ever seen to get His people pulled out of Egypt.

Moses tells God's people that God will give them what He calls the Promised Land. It is a land flowing with milk and honey. He will settle His people down in this land and this is where He will then break the Israelites off into 12 different tribes.

However, there is one little catch to this story. Before they are allowed to enter into this Promised Land, they must all first pass a test with the Lord. God allows them to stay in the wilderness for 40 years. He gives them all the basics as far as food and water in order to be able to survive in the wilderness for the 40 years. God purposely tested His people to see if they would hold fast to Him and follow all of His ways while in this wilderness setting. And time after time, they continued to get themselves in major trouble with the Lord.

At one point, God got so angry at their negative rebellious attitude, that He literally wanted to kill them. But Moses went into the gap for his people, pleaded his case before God as to why He should not kill His people, and the Bible said that God then relented and changed His mind—all because Moses stood in the gap and effectively pleaded his case before God.

However, just after a little over 2 years into this 40 year wilderness journey is where they finally blew it for the last time with God the Father. The Israelites sent twelve spies into the Promised Land to check out who the enemy was and to develop battle strategies to defeat them. God was going to allow them to go into the Promised Land, but they first had to defeat and drive out some of their enemies in order to conquer and possess the land. When the spies came back, ten of them came back with a bad report. They said their enemies were giants and that their kingdoms were too well fortified and they would not be able to defeat them.

Now mind you, God had just got done delivering them out of Egypt with one of the greatest displays of His supernatural power the world has ever seen with Him throwing 10 whopper plaques against the Egyptians and then parting the Red Sea to give them safe passage into the wilderness. When God saw all of their negative attitudes, and their lack of faith and belief in Him and His power, He literally threw up His hands and said that was going to be it.

At this point, He tells them that all of the men who are 20 years and older would not enter into the Promised Land due to their lack of faith and belief in Him. He said they would all wander in the desert for the next 40 years until they all literally died out in the desert. God says that their carcasses would fall in this wilderness, and that their sons would be their shepherds bearing the brunt of their infidelity towards God. The spies that went went in to spy out the land did so for 40 days. As a result of this bad report—God pronounces judgment that they should wander in the wilderness for 40 years to match up with the 40 days they had spied out the land for.

Now this is where Joshua and Caleb come in. God then tells Joshua and Caleb that they and the younger generation under 20 years of age would be the ones who would be able to go into the Promised Land because they had "a different spirit and wholeheartedly followed God." They had full faith and belief in God that He could defeat all of their enemies once they went into the Promised Land to conquer and possess it.

Joshua was the leader that eventually led them in. Moses himself was not allowed to go in, and he died and was buried out in the wilderness. Joshua then took Moses' position as leader of the Israelites. Joshua then goes into the Promised Land with his strong faith and belief in God, and then proceeds to literally wipe their enemies off the face of the earth and conquer and possess the land that God had promised their earlier forefathers Abraham, Isaac, and Jacob.

Living Lessons To be Learned From Joshua and Caleb

I believe the Promised Land for today's Christian refers to God's call on that person's life. For the Christian that will fully surrender their entire life over to God the Father—I believe that God will place a specific call or calls on that person's life. However, it may take many years before God releases this person into what their true calling is going to be for Him. Sometimes it may take years of preparation to get ready for this call.

But once this call comes in and you are getting ready to cross over into your Promised Land, many Christians get cold feet at the last minute and walk out on their call. They start to get too focused on all the negative possibilities they will encounter if they take the call just like the 10 spies did with God the Father. Fear starts to set in and they then bail out of the boat.

This is why this story is so powerful. The Israelites lost their one and only chance to go into this Promised Land due to one main reason—fear, and lack of full faith and belief in the power of God to see them through.

They were too scared of the giants and kingdoms they saw in the Promised Land they were supposed to possess—and they did not have enough faith and belief in God that He could conquer and defeat these giants for them. As a result, they lost out on the biggest blessing of their entire life.

After Joshua fully succeeded in all of his missions for the Lord, he makes the comment shortly before he dies that God had **not** failed to give him every ounce of land that his foot had stepped on. God told Joshua that his enemies would be taken out and that he would be given total victory as long as he stayed with God's instructions on how to do all of this. Joshua saw his call completely through, and when he died, he died a man with his call and mission from God completely accomplished and fulfilled.

The two keys to Joshua's success was his strong faith and belief in God, and the fact that he had always "wholeheartedly followed God." I always tell everyone to stay with their leadings from the Holy Spirit. The Bible says that the Holy Spirit will guide us into all truth and teach us all things. He is our personal Guide and Teacher in this life. If God puts a call on your life, but you do not follow His specific instructions and leadings on how to get there, then you will never succeed.

Joshua's story is one of the most dramatic stories in all of the Bible about someone who did it right in God. His story is a perfect example for all Christians on how to properly follow God and the call that He can place on your life.

Friends, this story really applies to where you are at right now with God. You may be getting ready to have your door opened to enter into your Promised Land—into God's true calling on your life. However, you are well aware of the giants and strongholds that you will be coming against if this door opens up for you. Joshua and Caleb saw the same giants and strongholds that you are now seeing. And they gained the hill country, they possessed their possession. He saw all this before going in. God allowed him to see exactly what he was going into before he actually went into it—and God is showing you the exact same thing.

You now have one of two choices to make. You can either let fear and panic set in just like the Israelites did, and lose your one and only chance to enter into your Promised Land—or you can have the same strong faith and belief in God that Joshua and Caleb had—and go in there with a kick-butt attitude that you will be completely victorious

and that you will accomplish everything that God will want you to accomplish for Him.

Joshua and Caleb took their strong faith and belief in God, entered the Promised Land, and achieved **total victory** in God. The Bible says that God is no respecter of persons. What He will do for one, He will do for another. If God is calling you to go through this door, then rest assured that you will have the full power of God operating through you to achieve total victory just like Joshua and Caleb did! As God saw fit to name one of the Books of the Bible after him—**"The Book of Joshua."** I think this was a very fitting ending to what this man accomplished in God while down here on this earth. The Bible said Joshua lived to be 110 years old. Beloved, let God do the same for you as He did for Joshua and Caleb.

OVERCOMING IMPOSSIBILITY THINKING: THE GRASS HOPPER, GIANT AND MOUNTAIN MENTALITY

When we perceive our lives to be on an inevitable path of continual decline, when we think that our situations are impossible and that we are failures, the likely response is to resign our lives to problems and thereby create more problems. Have you ever noticed this? People who have problems seem to create more than their share of problems. It looks like everything is happening to them or that they are very unlucky.

They often appear to be victims of a cruel world where they never have a chance to succeed. In essence, they feel powerless, and this became their reality. The cycle becomes self-destructive because belief keeps creating reality and reality keeps creating belief.

LEAD WEIGHTS OF IMPOSSIBLITY

You shouldn't blame yourself when a series of things go wrong all at once. If you do, you will surely conclude that you are the victim of bad luck and therefore *you are* in unlucky person. Any of us at one time or another could be deluged by what seems to be roller coaster, an unending avalanche of problems. Sometimes a substantial series of problems could have like giant ocean waves wiping us out.

Even the most mentally stable individual can reach a breaking point when too many problems and too much negativity comes his way. The solution is to accept it, not denial, go with it, and then get rid of it. Instead of seeing impossible situations as happening to you, see them all as happening for a *reason*. If you hang on to misery, you create emotional, psychological, and sometimes physical lead weights that pull you down.

Changing the impossible to the possible is a matter of letting go of destructive patterns that restrict any aspect of our lives. The destructive patterns are what I call the *lead weights of impossibility*. Picture if you will a series of lead weights. Each one weights five pounds. For every impossible or negative thought we have about ourselves, we are strapping on one five-pound lead weight. These lead weights prevent us from changing the impossible to the possible because we are weighed down so much that we can hardly move emotionally, psychologically, or physically. We must ask ourselves how much extra weight are we carrying around right now. Even though we have many good qualities, our inability to succeed can be impaired by the lead weights of impossibility. Such things as doubt, guilt, anger, fear, and addictions can hold us down. As we try to move forward, we find it impossible because the weights of negativity are almost unbearable. These weights hold us down and keep us from changing our circumstance. Change is almost out of the question unless we figure out a way to release the lead weights of impossibility.

The mind is a marvelous thing. Though the conscious and subconscious, it can either assist us in creating the possible or convince us that whatever we want is impossible. The end result is determined by how we use our mind. To better understand how the mind works, in particular the subconscious, we must first understand its primary function. Although the subconscious can be used to create the possible and guide us to a successful outcome, its primary function is survival.

Through born instincts and programming, the subconscious mind sets up criteria as to what survival means to us as individuals. For each one of us it is different. Some people are concerned about survival in a relationship, some are concerned with financial survival, and for others, it is physical survival. Anything that opposes our notion of survival is challenged by the subconscious. It immediately focuses on the area of perceived danger and alerts us to take evasive action. In essence, it is always looking for perceived danger, similar to the parent who warns a child of safety hazards.

In order to protect us, the subconscious mind looks at every person, place, or situation as a potential source of danger. Another way to define danger is negativity. The mind is always looking within and without for sources of things that could go wrong and possibly hurt us emotionally, physically, or financially. It is saying, "Watch out! You know what happened last time," or "They told you this could happen." The mind and body react, which triggers our flight or fight response.

Unless we control our thinking, we continue to react in a negative way and we continue the downward spiral, which can produce anxiety, procrastination, or in some cases, severe clinical depression. The worst part is that this becomes a habitual thinking pattern. We must break out of this negative mind-set that our life is not about creating a successful, happy life, but should be spent defending ourselves against all the imaginary and perceived dangers that lurk. If this is the case, then our life is only about protection, not creation.

The bottom line is that our thoughts create our reality. If we are focused on the negative, barriers or the impossible, our subconscious will direct us to people, places, and circumstances to prove that we are right. In order to preserve security, the subconscious always seeks to prove that what we are thinking is in fact true. For instance, If you think that every time you get into a relationship the person will leave you, that becomes your reality. Your subconscious then searches for people to come into your life to fulfill that perception. Whenever you are among a group of people, you will be attracted to that type of person. If you should get into a relationship with that person, he or she will eventually leave you. Then you can say, "See, I knew it. Everyone leaves me." If you think that you are going to be sick, your business will fail, or you will lose your money, your subconscious will assist you in making those assumptions a reality.

THE SPIRAL OF IMPOSSIBILITY

When life's outcomes do not match our wishes, we feel threatened. Our primary focus is on survival, *so we are no longer focused on what we want, but what we don't want.* Our motivation is based on fear, and we move away from what we don't want rather than toward what we do want. Our new goal is survival, and one of the ways we protect ourselves is to defend our current situation and ourselves. We express this by claiming that we are victims of bad economy, of society and other people. Our new intention is *not* to turn the impossible into the possible, but to defend ourselves and attack whatever it is we perceive to be the cause of our failure. Our energy sphere keeps contracting as we feel jealousy, blame, self-justification, anger, fear, or the need to run away. This is what causes depression. Until we are willing to change, we are stuck. my goal in this book is to charge you to stand courageously facing the giants and declare give me this mountain.

HOW TO GET OUT OF THE
THAT PRISON OF IMPOSSIBILITY:
THE PRISON GATE IS OPEN

Every time we blame something outside of ourselves, we are in effect trying to weasel and out of being accountable. Instead of being accountable, we use weasel phrases such as, "They did it to me," "I can't," "I had no choice," "I don't know what to do," "That's just the way I am," "If only . . ." "Nobody told me that," and "If things had been different . . ." These weasel phrases only serve to immobilize us in the present. Weasel statements are all wrapped around one basic belief which is, "I am not the cause, I am the effect." Said another way; "I am the victim."

If you believe this, you share a common trait with most prisoners. Studies of inmates in prisons show that only three percent of all inmates believe they are accountable for what happened to them and why they are in prison. It was their parents, poverty, lack of education, a bad influence, or drugs that caused them to end up where they are. When refuse to take responsibility for where we are, we become imprisoned by our own thoughts. We are locked into the past and cannot escape into the future. The good news is that we don't have to escape this prison of impossibility; we can just walk out the front door once we take responsibility.

Freedom comes when you stop placing responsibility on others for your happiness, success, or financial condition. While this may seem harsh, no one really cares but you. In the greater scheme of things, people are more interested in their lives than they are in yours. They are too busy trying to get out of their own prison of impossibility. If you are waiting for them to help you escape, be prepared to wait for the rest of your life.

This approach can only set up for further disappointments. People can assist us, but we must take the initiative and full responsibility for where we are and where we want to be.

REDIRECTING OUR CREATIVE ENERGY

We know that we can use our mind to create the positive or the negative. Why are we so often driven toward the negative? Basically, it comes down to where we direct our creative energy. Universal energy or intelligence is like electricity running through us as creative energy. This energy is directed through the mind. The energy comes to us as positive energy. Unfortunately, we can also use the same potentially creative energy in a negative manner. This is similar to electricity. We can use electricity to turn on the lights in our homes or use it to electrocute a murderer in the electric chair. We form and mold the energy into creation through the mind. Therefore, we have the choice of creating positive energy as possible energy or negative energy as impossible energy in our lives.

Let's examine the power of creative energy within ourselves and how we can direct it. First, we must understand that our ability to use it is in direct proportion to our belief and understanding that it truly exists. The manner in which you use it determines the results you will experience in your life. Let's look at some examples. In its simplest manifestation, it can be experienced when you walk into a room with people in it. Have you ever noticed a heaviness or troublesome atmosphere, even though no one has said anything or acted out of the ordinary? You just get that *feeling*. This is an *energy field*. The energy field around us changes as we change emotionally, spiritually, and psychologically. The reverse is also true. The energy fields around us affect our psychological, spiritual and physical states. Think of the universe as one dynamic energy field that sustains us. If we think negatively of ourselves, we disconnect from that source of energy. In order to overcome the impossible, you must have a sense that you are bigger than any problem, giant or mountain that you face. The *you* I am referring to is not the you think you ought to be, but your Inner man—*who you are.*

A simple but profound way to think about this energy is to think that you are at the center of a large sphere or ball of energy that expands and contracts like a balloon. When you are negative, upset, angry, or scared, this energy balloon contracts. This limits your power to change.

Alternately, when you are confident, joyful, and compassionate, the energy sphere expands. All the solutions for possibility are open to you. You even look and feel different, not just to yourself, but to others.

All problems in life can be viewed in the context of this contraction or expansion phenomenon. We have been conditioned to deal with life's problems by contracting our power or energy. The process of contraction and depression continues until with each contraction, all opportunity literally disappears from our lives. This is the true definition of depression. We have the ability to re-pattern our way of thinking. To do this, we must learn to relax, trust, let go and let God. Then our energy field is free to expand.

OPERATING WITHIN THE CIRCLE OF POSSIBILITY

We tend to take the path of least resistance. Resistance to change is in direct proportion to our comfort zone. We will call this our *circle of possibility*. Our circle of possibility is created by the thoughts we have been thinking and the things we have done. Anything new that we have not done or thought before makes us feel uncomfortable. Apostle Paul realize this and declared I put the past behind me and forge ahead pressing towards the mark of the high calling in Christ Jesus.

Uncomfortable thoughts or the prospect of doing something we have not done before increases our anxiety level. This in turn makes us feel even more uncomfortable and causes us to believe that what we want to do is impossible. This discouragement, which comes from believing what we want is impossible, often causes us to give up even before we start. When we move past our comfort level, we find the adventure, excitement, and satisfaction we desire. This is what the life of faith is all about walking with God into the unknown glorious future.

Have you ever said to yourself, "I don't want to do that because it makes me uncomfortable?" You're not alone. This is a normal response when most people are confronted with a new situation.

Unfortunately, most people use discomfort as a reason or an excuse for not doing something. To illustrate this, picture a circle around you. You are in the middle of the circle. The circle represents your circle of possibility. Everything outside the circle represents things that you have not experienced . . . things that make you uncomfortable. This also is your circle of protection. Just slightly outside your circle are your goals or even problems that come into your life. When faced with new challenges, opportunities, or obstacles, they begin to intrude upon your circle. The tendency is to rush to the outer limits of your circle and set up defenses. In some cases, you'll pretend that whatever is outside your circle isn't there. The problem is, the very thing you want is usually outside your circle. It keeps banging up against your circle until you make a decision to resolve it or achieve it.

Your desire to achieve it or resolve it prompts you to go the edge of the circle and break through. The only way you can get to it is to break through your circle just enough to bring it within your circle of possibility, taking your destiny in your own hands and possessing your possession.

Once it is within your circle, you can deal with it. Now an interesting thing happens. Each thing you bring inside your circle of possibility expands your comfort zone. In other words, the circle becomes larger and extends beyond your ability to deal with the situation. Now that situation that used to be beyond your limits is within your reach. Not only are you able to deal with it, but you can expand your circle and broaden your horizon.

The degree to which you are happy or not happy is in direct proportion to how much control your circle of possibility has over you. If it has more control over you than you do of yourself, then you experiences unhappiness, anxiety, and depression. There are four factors that cause us to stay within our circle of impossibility: fear, guilt, unworthiness, and anger. Let's look at some examples of the lead weights of impossibility and how they make change seem nearly impossible. Hebrews 12:1 says these are weights that easily beguiled us.

Fear

We stay within our limited circle of possibility because of fear. We often feel fear even when we are just skeptical or fear disappointment. Fear is the mind-talk that prevents you from hearing your intuition. It is probably the most common limiting emotion. The basis of fear is the flight of fight syndrome. Remember that our mind is always trying to protect us. Survival, not success and happiness, are the primary goals.

We fear what we don't know, and that fear keeps us from taking action. Not taking action keeps us ignorant, and ignorance creates more fear. Thus the cycle repeats itself. Any time we venture into the unknown, we will have fears. Everyone has fears. For some of us it's death, public speaking, loss of love, animals, darkness, or flying. After working with thousands of people, it has become clear to me that we create our fears as well as our dreams, and they happen just as we planned them to. He Job the greatest man in all of east had fear was a self-created prophecy. Though he feared God and eschew evil and so attracted all pains and loss he went through.

Many people have a fear of making mistakes. A major lead weight is our bundle of past mistakes. We all have made mistakes, but we insist on playing them over and over in our head instead of letting them go and moving on. Perhaps you have gained weight, lost your job, ruined your health, or had a relationship that was self-destructive. Because of these mistakes, you have convinced yourself that you can never be in shape again, never find another good job, never restore your health, or never find someone to love you.

The good news however, is we have not been given the spirit of fear but of sound mind in Christ Jesus. It is likely In the process of expanding our circle of possibility, we are going to make mistakes. There is no way to avoid them. However, mistakes should not be construed as total and irreversible failures. Mistakes are a buffer zone in your circle where you allow yourself and others an opportunity to make mistakes without judgment. This will allow you to look at mistakes and self-correct rather than wasting valuable energy on what should have happened or what you should have done. Consider all mistakes as feedback, not failures. Instead, keep the lesson and throw away the experience.

One of the biggest fears is the fear of failure. However, there is really no way you can fail in life. Failure is a relative term and a value judgment. What looks like failure to you may not be failure to someone else. If you don't earn $50,000 a year, you may consider yourself a failure.

However, someone else may feel that if they earn $10,000 a year, they are a success. Failure is determined by the rules set up in life concerning success and failure. All we have to do is we change the rules. More importantly, we must not let others make the rules for us.

Recently, I read a list of famous and successful individuals that had been fired from a job at least once. One of them was the talk show host, Sally Jessy Rapheal. She was fired by approximately twenty radio and television stations before she finally found success with her television talk show. She certainly never gave up. The great inventor Sir, Thomas Edison made 10,000 mistakes before he discovered the light bulb. So just think if he gave up at the 9,999th try, who knows how long we would have had to wait for someone else to discover the light bulb! Do you think Thomas Edison feared failure? I tell people, "If you are not making at least ten mistakes a day, you're doing something wrong."

How to Be More Fearless

Psalms 23

The LORD is my shepherd, I shall not want. He makes me lie down in green pastures; He leads me beside quiet waters. He restores my soul; He guides me in the paths of righteousness For His name's sake. Even though I walk through the valley of the shadow of death,

I fear no evil, for You are with me; Your rod and Your staff, they comfort me. You prepare a table before me in the presence of my enemies; You have anointed my head with oil; My cup overflows.

Surely goodness and loving kindness will follow me all the days of my life, And I will dwell in the house of the LORD forever. Psalms23.

I believe that life without fear is not an option that is available to us. I prefer to approach it from this manner: Instead of *fighting* our fears, we can *neutralize* their power over us by just *accepting* them and then taking one small step at a time to overcome them. As simple as it may seem, the only difference between successful people and those who are not successful is their response to fear. Let's face it, we are all afraid.

Successful people are afraid, but they take *action*. They don't get immobilized by their fears.

Think of overcoming your fear as a means of building spiritual and emotional muscle. As you start each day, contemplate your daily plan and envision yourself going through it, especially when you will be taking on new challenges that worry or frighten you. If you are in balance, with the mind, body, and spirit connected, you can overcome your fears.

If your biggest fear is that you will be a failure, I have good news for you. You can never really fail, because you can never fail as a *person*. Your job can fail, your finances can fail, your business can fail, your relationship can fail, but that's not *you*. All those things are outside of you. They can all be changed or corrected. The problem comes when you start believing that you are what you have and what you do. The solution to overcoming the fear of failure is to recognize that you cannot fail as a person. The key is to separate yourself from what you have and what you do.

Guilt—The Gift That Keeps on Giving

It is critical to recognize the insidious nature of this emotion in that it can have such crippling, long-term consequences. In adulthood, the guilt prone person can suffer from underlying; free-flowing guilty feelings even when nothing logical supports their presence. Feelings of guilt can manifest in people's dreams along with guilt's twin—anxiety. Guilt is one of the first and foremost components of an unworkable moral code that needs erasing if a person wants to live a healthy, balanced life.

When we think or act in a manner that produces guilty feelings, our responses to guilt is to promise not to do it again and/or to punish ourselves by feeling bad. We rationalize that when good people do bad things, they are supposed to feel bad. Feeling bad is the price we must pay for violating our beliefs about what good people do. In every area of our lives we have beliefs about how good people should think and behave. When we act that way, it proves that we are a good person.

When we fall short of the ideal image, our unquestioned reaction may be to feel guilty and anxious.

As a child, you were given a standard of perfection to live up to by your parents, teachers, and other role models. As you moved into adolescence, you started adding your own set of beliefs about perfection based on input from your family, friends, peer groups, and the effects of advertising and other well-intentioned sources. As an adult, you try to live according to that model of "good" and "bad", based on those beliefs.

Unfortunately, we rarely question our beliefs about "good" and "bad." If our beliefs came from authority figures such as our parents or teachers, we just assume that what they told us is true. Whether they are true or not, is not the issue. More importantly, we must ask ourselves how these programmed images produce feelings of guilt in our daily lives that affect our self-worth? *The important point here is that we must distinguish between when we should change our actions and when we should change our beliefs about our actions.* If our actions are producing a negative result, the easiest way to change our actions is to change our beliefs first.

We must determine the validity of our beliefs by the infallible word of GOD and asking ourselves questions. Where did I get this belief? Who told me it was true? Did someone tell me in order to control me? Did they really know what they were talking about, or are they just passing their programmed beliefs on to me for my own good?

Instead of feeling badly, we can use guilt constructively by changing our belief so that our energy is not directed toward feeling bad every time we do something or don't do something that others have told us is bad or wrong. The key here is to understand that good people sometimes may do bad things. Bad things can be defined as things that produce a negative result. We must separate the doer (us) from the end result (action). In other words, your actions may sometimes be bad or inappropriate, but you are not a bad person—or a good person for that matter. You are just you, doing good or bad things that produce positive or negative results.

Keep in mind that your Inner man is neither good nor bad, because at the spiritual level there is no judgment. However, your outer man is only human and still has imperfections built on false beliefs.

The most formidable guilt-producing statement you can make is, "I could have done better." That is entirely false. To *know* better is not sufficient to *do* better. Knowledge is unrelated to action and is intrinsically an intellectual process. We know we should not smoke, use drugs, overeat, and hurt ourselves or others, but many do these things anyway. The only way this will change is when we come to the point where we realize the pain of our actions is greater than the price we will have to pay to change them. At that point, we will stop doing negative things to ourselves and to others. Guilt only serves to make us feel bad about our thoughts and actions, and it is a poor replacement for consciously choosing to rid ourselves of undesirable actions.

So, when you do things you feel guilty about, just say to yourself. "Obviously, I have not reached the point where I am perfect. I am only human and I am still learning. I am not going to feel bad, but I am going to use this opportunity to remind myself to do better the next time." If the pain of your actions is great enough, you will not do it again. If you got away with it this time and did not pay the full price for your actions, you will probably do it again. Just keep reminding yourself that the price is getting too high and now might be a good time to change your thinking more quickly so that you take more appropriate action in the future, without requiring pain to compel you.

If guilt is feeling discouraged, feeling punished, and self-punishing, then we can replace it by being productive, reliable, sincere, cooperative, lively, involved, tender, gentle and purposeful. Learn to replace stationary and backsliding guilt with positive forward motion. The more you truly become a friend to yourself, recognize your life's purpose, and engage the Holy Spirit in your daily dealings, the more you will sense that guilt is relaxing its hold in your mental makeup.

Action will increasingly replace stagnant self-flagellation. Guilt can be a convenient replacement for taking effective action and accepting responsibility. It's as though we childishly believe that appropriate suffering releases us from capable, adult behavior. As such, guilt becomes a thinly masked form of selfishness. Guilt is a poor substitute for engaging fully in life. As nothing more than self-blame, it is one of the more fruitless, circular non-solutions in which we invest valuable energy.

Allow yourself to release the hold guilt has on you and move on to more effective, self-loving means of changing your behavior. Hair shirts are out . . . constructive thoughts and concrete actions are in.

Unworthiness.

Self-worth comes from the Inner man. If you know your true nature, you will better recognize and understand the true nature of those around you. The more you know about yourself, the better you will understand yourself and others.

Don't be afraid to let others see a weakness in you. Some people are so horrified at the thought that someone would discover a weakness in them that they will even lie and manipulate in order to cover for themselves. Some people will take this so far that they will even let others suffer consequences for them.

A televised report on human behavior set up the following situation and recorded it on tape. A job applicant was put in a waiting room that contained a table with several party platters of food. The applicant was told not to take any, as the trays were for a celebration to be held later on. A hidden camera showed the woman giving in to her temptation by eating a variety of items. When the prospective employee was asked if she took any of the food, she said, "No." She was asked again because the interviewer stated that they noticed that some of the food was missing. She still insisted she did not take any food. Another employee was brought into the room. This man had stopped in earlier when the applicant was alone in the room. The employee was asked in front of the applicant if he saw her take any of the food. Even though he said he had not, the applicant, when asked, stated that the employee took the food and not herself.

Is your self-worth so fragile and on such a thin foundation that you fear being wrong? Do you have a problem with saying, "Oops, I made a mistake? Sorry?" I hope not. When we try to cover up our flaws, along with the cover-up, we block any chance of demonstrating our undiscovered, innate strengths.

Twelve Surefire Ways to Destroy Your Self-Worth

1. Have a lack of faith in yourself and believe in God.
2. Complain, criticize, blame and bring others down. Constantly compare and measure yourself as "better than" others. Hold others down so they won't get ahead of you.
3. Don't be flexible, be a quitter, and be satisfied with less.
4. Associate with weak people. Work along with people who are going nowhere. Worse yet, let them make up your mind for you.
5. Be a "know-it-all."
6. Be a taker, not a Giver.
7. Use this kind of weak language: "Impossible, tired, problems, unreal, what's in it for me."

8. Talk about all the things that are wrong with people. Talk too much, Taking no action and wait for things to happen.
9. Take a job with no chance for advancement. Leave right at closing time. Do no more. Do only what benefits yourself.
10. Deliberately scatter yourself, spread yourself too thin.
11. Satisfy you lack of self-worth by being a workaholic.
12. Dwell on things not working out, and imagine that they could only get worse.

What You Can Do to Build Your Self-Worth: A Can Do Everything Mentality

Phillipians 4:10-13

I rejoice greatly in the Lord that at last you have renewed your concern for me. Indeed, you have been concerned, but you had no opportunity to show it. I am not saying this because I am in need, for I have learned to be content whatever the circumstances. I know what it is to be in need, and I know what it is to have plenty. I have learned the secret of being content in any and every situation, whether well fed or hungry, whether living in plenty or in want. I can do everything through him who gives me strength. Phillipians 4:10-13.

If we don't feel we are worthy, competent, or deserving, every time we try to embrace the possible, our subconscious says, "Remember, you told me—you are a jerk, no one will ever love you, you can't do anything right, and you're not good enough. Who do you think you are? We know that you are a powerless victim. Don't even try." Then we say, "There is no way I can be, do, or have this." Your subconscious replies.

"Now you are being realistic." Then, when we don't get what we want, we say, "See, I knew it would not work out. I was right all along."

This inner dialogue is more predominant than we think. Many people try to cover it up by appearing confident. Some go to the extreme, bordering on arrogance. In reality, they are merely involved in an attempt to hide the fact that they feel incompetent and unworthy.

Where did all this come from? How did we get this way? Without getting into the usual mind babble about how most of it came from our childhood, suffice it to say that we were not born this way. Our well intentioned parents tried to bring us up to do the right thing.

Unfortunately, through their conditioning, they determined that the best way to do this was to get us to focus on what we were doing wrong. "Don't do this. You can't do that. You're bad. How could you think like that?" The problem with parenting is that, even though we are well intentioned, parenting is really about passing insecurity from one generation to the next. This is because our parents were probably brought up in the same way. Most of us do not examine our beliefs to determine if they are valid or workable. Instead, we just accept that what we believe is true and spend our lives trying to convince ourselves, our children, and others that these beliefs are indeed true. The problem that arises is that we have false beliefs that produce faulty results.

It all starts from our infancy, when our parents mostly warned us of dangers like. "Don't touch that electrical outlet," and "Don't touch that hot iron." Most parents are busy and in a rush, so most of their time communicating with their children involves a bunch of "don't do that" messages intended for their basic human need for safety and survival.

Ideally, parents should spend *most* of their time, no matter how busy they are, building up their children's mind sets with positive messages that reinforce what their children are doing right, not wrong. This includes encouraging their children to do new things well. We need to show them how to try to do new things and take risks, but not criticize their mistakes when they try.

Unfortunately, our early years were likely spent going through a conditioning process that told us that we were basically bad, stupid, incompetent, and sinners. The only way we thought we could prove otherwise, and ever hope to get approval, was to do what others wanted. It was our way of earning our worthiness. We reinforce a pattern that positive or possible thoughts about ourselves would be good, but negative or impossible thoughts are more realistic and comfortable. Every time we have possibility thoughts, we automatically check them against this primary belief that we are not worthy or competent, and the answer comes up, "Error!" Negative or impossible thoughts feel comfortable, and therefore normal and believable.

One thing you can do to build your self-worth is to say "no" to criticism unless you asked for feedback. When people try to criticize you, let them know the manner in which they can approach you with their concern; otherwise, say "no" to criticism. If you want feedback about something you are questioning about yourself, then ask someone whose opinion you respect. However, you do not have to believe what they tell you. It's still your life. You can *consider* someone else's opinion, but must make your own decisions.

Eliminating the Feeling of Unworthiness

Unworthiness can leave us feeling unloved, deserted, melancholy, filled with despair, unimportant, unacceptable, and not cared for. One surefire way to perpetuate feelings of unworthiness is to carry out feeling sorry for yourself to the point of becoming a victim.

We can turn around any feelings of unworthiness by doing some soul searching, self-evaluation, and some self-improvement that ultimately builds our feeling or worthiness. Some of the qualities that we want to achieve to lift us out or unworthiness are excitement, feeling alive, delight, trust, tenderness, being congruent, perception, balance, and feeling at one with people. If we could have more faith in the people around us, and if we could have more faith in ourselves, the world would be a better place.

Anger

Have you noticed that the word *anger* is one letter short of *danger*? Anger always seems to be directed at something: at things, at others, and at ourselves. It is about how we measure up, or actually, how others or we *don't* measure up.

Anger manifests itself in us in a variety of forms. Unfortunately Often, we try to *escape* from it instead of facing it and resolving it.

Some Ways We Try to Escape Anger

We have different ways to avoid anger. One way is to hold our anger inside and try not to feel anything. Then there is the old silent treatment.

A study of marital relationships found that this one behavior pattern makes it nearly impossible to couples to work things out. What these people need to know is that it is safer to argue it out if necessary (with a reasonable partner), than to lose a valuable partner because they refuse to communicate. They should realize that problems can be resolved one way or another if they will at least talk about them.

The overly quiet type often manifests their anger in worst form. They can easily become dangerous when they finally explode or act out their anger. Whenever we hear of a serial killer, and they interview their next door neighbor, we often hear them comment, "He was a quite man." It is safer to appropriately express anger than to withhold it. Withholding anger may temporarily help you to calm yourself down, but the lingering problem is still unresolved. The problem must have a resolution. If there is something you can do or must do to solve a problem, face it and do it.

Otherwise, the silent treatment is sure to cause more problems. Some people try to escape their problems and anger with addictions to alcohol, drugs, sex, etc. They soon learn that their addictions will not make their fears and frustrations go away. Anger builds up over a lifetime unless or until we confront it, and do something to release it.

Humor—Your Most Powerful Ally

One of the powerful tools we can use to break through the barriers of challenging impossible situations is humor. Although I am a serious person, I try to see the humorous side of most situations. In fact, some people are taken by surprise when I make a joke about things that are supposed to be serious. Those who know me well have said that, when it comes to humor, "Everything is fair game with you. Nothing is sacred." It's true. I often use humor as a means of defusing a situation either by shock value or just by trying to put things into perspective.

I remember one time during the recent years of recurrent plane crashes in our nation, I was flying from Lagos to Jos. As the plane was landing, the wheels crashed through the concrete runway. Apparently there was a weak spot or a washout under the runway and it couldn't hold the weight of the plane. Anyway, the wheels went through the runway and literally snapped off! The plane landed on its belly and we went scraping across the concrete. Sparks were flying everywhere and the sound of metal against concrete was incredible. After we stopped, the pilot said we were OK and there was no fire, but we would have to evacuate the plane immediately by sliding down the emergency chute.

Everyone was panicked. People were screaming and crying, but no one was hurt. I don't know why, but at that moment I thought to myself. *Gee, what is everyone worried about? hallelujah . . . We're all alive.* My next statement shocked a couple of passengers because I said jokingly as I was getting ready to jump down the chute, "That's great, now how are we going to get the luggage out of here?"

Sure, it was a serious situation, but I used humor to help defuse the tension seriousness of the situation and to put things into perspective. My message was, "Praise God, We are alive, so why worry except, of course, about our luggage." Throughout this book we are going to discuss some serious issues. I just wanted to warn you that often I will try to put things into perspective through the use of humor, or looking at things on the light side. So, make it a fun journey. Let's try to learn more about ourselves and have fun in the process.

If the following behaviors are indicative of our anger: hostility, hatred, resentment, antagonism, sarcasm, withholding, rejecting, fiery temper, then the following opposite behaviors can free us from it; acceptance, willingness, interest, receptiveness, invigoration, encouragement, appreciation, being tuned in, feeling deserving and forgiveness.

CHAPTER TWO

A VOLUNTEER FOR JESUS . . . A TRUE SOLDIER

The LORD said to Moses, "Send some men to explore the land of Canaan, which I am giving to the Israelites. From each ancestral tribe send one of its leaders." So at the LORD's command Moses sent them out from the Desert of Paran. All of them were leaders of the Israelites. These are their names: from the tribe of Reuben, Shammua son of Zaccur; from the tribe of Simeon, Shaphat son of Hori; from the tribe of Judah, Caleb son of Jephunneh; from the tribe of Issachar, Igal son of Joseph; from the tribe of Ephraim, Hoshea son of Nun; from the tribe of Benjamin, Palti son of Raphu; from the tribe of Zebulun, Gaddiel son of Sodi; from the tribe of Manasseh (a tribe of Joseph), Gaddi son of Susi; from the tribe of Dan, Ammiel son of Gemalli; from the tribe of Asher, Sethur son of Michael; from the tribe of Naphtali, Nahbi son of Vophsi; from the tribe of Gad, Geuel son of Maki. These are the names of the men Moses sent to explore the land. (Moses gave Hoshea son of Nun the name Joshua.) Numbers 13:1-16.

These men were leaders, soldiers and volunteers. In life we may volunteer because of what we receive in return—a sense of gratification, knowledge that we have contributed to a cause, a feeling of belonging to something bigger than ourselves. However, with God we volunteer for a different reason. We offer ourselves to God strictly out of a heart filled with gratitude, because we understand that is appropriate given what He has done for us.

What happens when we make a total and ongoing commitment to Christ?

We read in Romans 12:1, "I beseech you therefore, brethren, by the mercies of God, that ye present your bodies a living sacrifice, holy, acceptable unto God, which is your reasonable service."

Sacrifices were familiar to the Early Church members to whom the Book of Romans was written. These people were accustomed to the Old Testament offerings—the beasts that were brought and offered either to atone for sin, or as an expression of gratitude toward God by the one bringing the offering.

When Jesus came and established the New Covenant, He offered His body as atonement for sin so we no longer need to sacrifice in that way. We bring our bodies instead for that second reason—we offer ourselves to God as an expression of our appreciation to the Lord for what He has done for us. This consecration is different than the way we approached God as sinners. Sinners repent; Christians consecrate. Repentance surrenders that which is bad; consecration offers that which is good.

We came to God as sinners, asking forgiveness for our sins, filled with remorse. We repented and He forgave us of those sins, justified us, and changed our lives. From that point forward, we approached Him in a different manner altogether. We come to Him now with a heart full of gratitude, praying, "Lord, show me what to do. Reach into any part of my life. Show me what You require of me. I'm just glad to be saved, so I bring my life as an offering to You."

As Christians, we are called to consecrate not only today, but every day, for as long as we live and Jesus tarries. Romans12:1 reveals three aspects of consecration.

A voluntary yielding

First, consecration is voluntary. We want to serve the Lord. The Lord has been good to us so we bring to Him our devotion and our allegiance. Nobody demands it of us; we offer it because we love God. That principle is seen in Old Testament times. Under the Levitical law, God commanded the sacrifices that were to be offered to obtain justification. However, other offerings were voluntary, like the burnt offering of the herd. Leviticus 1:3

says, "Let him offer a male without blemish: he shall offer it of his own voluntary will." God could have commanded all offerings, but even under the Law, He wanted individuals to bring Him sacrifices just because they wanted to.

The Apostle Paul, the author of the Book of Romans, admonished these early believers to *present* themselves to the Lord. Elsewhere that word is translated *yield*. For example, in Romans 6:13, this word is used when the people were exhorted not to yield themselves as instruments of unrighteousness unto sin, but to yield themselves as instruments of righteousness unto God.

So the instruction in Romans 12:1 means that we are to *yield* our bodies as a living sacrifice. To yield has to do with relinquishing control. For instance, we could think of it in terms of traffic laws. The law stipulates which driver is to yield to the other driver under certain circumstances. If nobody yields, there will likely be an impact! The difference is that in matters of driving, it is not really voluntary—the requirements are set forth by the laws of the land. In matters of faith, however, the decision to yield is strictly voluntary, and it expresses the idea of putting oneself at the disposal of God. It is not imposed upon us. It is an individual matter, and it is totally voluntary.

The original tense of the verb translated *yield* indicates action. We can relate to that.

When God reaches into our hearts and says, "What about this? Will you give Me this?" it takes an act of our will to respond and make the offering. It is a decisive act, just like the voluntary offerings of the Old Testament times were decisive acts. Back then, the offerer felt a desire within to show appreciation to God, so he took the appropriate animal from his flock and brought it to God.

It required forethought. It required a decision of what to bring, and then it required action to carry that through.

So it is in our hearts and lives. To yield to God requires a decision. Our hearts are moved, and we feel a drawing to offer God something: our energy, our time, our talents.

It is a deliberate decision, made with understanding and without reservations. It does not happen accidently; it is not passive.

Consecration is bringing ourselves in our entirety to the Lord and giving God permission to order our lives. It is accepting His demands. That is what it is to consecrate, and it is totally voluntary.

Giving what is excellent

Secondly, consecration involves excellence—it is about bringing our best to the Lord. Again, we see this pictured in Old Testament times. We read, "And if there be any blemish therein, as if it be lame, or blind, or have any ill blemish, thou shalt not sacrifice it unto the Lord thy God" (Deuteronomy15:21). The people were to bring the best for these types of offerings. Malachi called Israel's offerings into question. He indicted the people, saying that they had offered in their worship to God what was defective. "And if ye offer the lame and the sick, is it not evil? offer it now unto thy governor; will he be pleased with thee, or accept thy person?"(Malachi 1:8).

Obviously you would not offer the governor, someone who is to be honored, an inferior gift. You would not, I presume, serve leftovers to company. You would not say, "Come to my house for dinner," and then just casually open the refrigerator door and look for something that remained from dinner a few nights earlier.

How about our offerings to God? It is only reasonable that we present to Him our very best. We do not give God inferior goods. We do not give God what we have left at the end of the day. We want to give God the best of what we have! The Lord honors us as we do that.

A continual offering

Thirdly, our offerings to God are *living*—they are to be continual. This is in contrast to the Old Testament sacrifices, where the animals were offered once—they were slain as part of the offering. We are living sacrifices, so we are to offer ourselves continually to the service of the Lord. The Lord is pleased with such offerings.

Paul went on to say, "And be not conformed to this world: but be ye transformed by the renewing of your mind, that ye may prove what is that good, and acceptable, and perfect, will of God" (Romans 12:2). The evidence of your continual offering is the way that you order your life. Paul said that believers were not to be conformed to this world, but transformed.

To conform to the world means to accept and assume the "shape" of the world, which is inherently opposed to Christianity. The world is the mind-set that leaves God out. Christianity is the mind-set that has God at the center.

Every decision, every action takes into account the fact that we have presented our bodies as living sacrifices to God. We do not take a job without praying about whether it is God's will or not. We do not engage in any activity without considering if it is what God would have us to do. Of course we think that way, because we have devoted ourselves to God! We are living sacrifices, so every decision we make is wrapped up in prayerfully considering the mind of God.

To be conformed to the world is to ignore God's claim upon our lives. We had no thought of that prior to becoming Christians. Before I was saved, I never gave God any thought when considering where to go to school or what job to take after high school. God's will in those matters never entered my mind. I was shaped by the world, so my decisions were made with the mind-set of the world ingrained in me. But that all changed in a moment of time when I understood, through the mercy of God, that I was to present my life to God.

It is a decisive moment when we are saved and make that initial commitment to God. However, even after we are saved it is possible to get caught up in the current of the world which pulls us away from God. We can forget that yielding our lives to Him is just as important as we progress through our Christian lives as it was the first day we were converted. We do not want to relegate God to being a secondary consideration. We do not want to offer Him that which is inferior. We want to give God our best and we want to do it every day!

If you have never presented yourself to the Lord, we would encourage you to do so now. Yield yourself completely to God. It leads to a beautiful experience! If you abandon yourself to God, presenting your life to Him and submitting control into His hands, you will find that He has a way of shaping lives in ways that are good and wonderful beyond our comprehension.

If you have done that already, present yourself afresh to the Lord today. As you daily lay aside your own desires, putting your energy, resources, and time at His disposal and trusting Him to be your guide, you will find that a life continually presented to God is good, satisfying, and complete!

To conform to the world means to accept and assume the "shape" of the world, which is inherently opposed to Christianity.

When God calls us to follow Him, it is not just a simple, one-time occurrence; it is also a call to ongoing steps of obedience.

Remember Lessons in obedience can pop up in the most unexpected ways.

Anyone who has served the Lord for a period of time knows that situations come along where we find ourselves facing decisions which can affect our walk with God. In those times, He speaks to our hearts and is faithful to remind us that we need to follow Him.

In John 21:15-22, we read how the Lord challenged Peter with the words, "Follow thou me." Like many of us, Peter was in a period of his life where some time had passed since he had responded to the original invitation to follow Christ. At this point, the Savior was not so much inviting him to follow, as He was commanding him to obey. In essence He was saying, "All of these things that we have talked about, all of the words you have heard Me speak, all of the lessons I have taught you can be summed up in these three words: Follow thou me!" The implication was that Peter was to continue to follow by walking in complete obedience.

As it was with Peter, occasionally we all need a fresh reminder, a fresh challenge, just to keep us walking in that same manner.

I believe sometimes the Lord directs us to do things, not so that we can reach out to others, but so that He can reach into us. The words, "What is that to thee? Follow thou me," can be God's way of asking us, "Are you *still* willing to follow Me? Are you willing to take steps of obedience today?"

That simple challenge, "Follow Me," still goes out. God allows situations to come along that require a choice. How important it is that we keep our hearts tuned to the gentle nudge of the Holy Spirit! We want hearts that are quick to respond when He points out something in our lives and says, "Follow Me!" I am so thankful that I didn't try to negotiate with the Lord. I did not try to see how I could get out of doing something that many would have thought was unnecessary. As soon as I realized what the Lord wanted me to do, I began to think, Okay, how am I going to do it? Is there a "MOUNTAIN" in your life? Is there something God is asking you to do, a step of obedience He wants you to take? Please do it. You will never regret it! After all, in light of eternity and our hearts' desire to be all the Lord wants us to be, the lord asked Peter thrice when fishing "do you love me more than this?" it really is . . . just a call to total surrender.

Sometimes the Lord directs us to do something, not so that we can reach out to others, but so that He can reach into us.?

AS A WAITING BRIDE A TRUE SOLDIER IS ALWAYS READY

A wedding is an exciting occasion, especially for the bride and the groom. In Matthew 25, Jesus used a wedding to illustrate a point. The parable was about ten virgins, and the people included in it represent all genders, all generations, all cultures, and all churches. The critical moment in the parable was when the cry at last went out, "Behold, the bridegroom cometh; go ye out to meet him" (Matthew 25:6).

The verses in this account give much information in a few words. Of the ten people in the parable, five were called wise and five were called foolish. Since the story was given to have a spiritual application, the Word of God will help us identify whether we are among the wise or the foolish.

Jesus is coming back for the wise, so we want to be among them. Therefore, we need to know what qualifications the wise possessed. First, they heard the instructions of the bridegroom. However, they not only heard, but they also took heed.

The wise made personal applications to their own lives. They did not neglect their responsibilities. They took their lamps and made sure they were trimmed and filled with oil. They confirmed that they were prepared to go at any moment. When the cry went out at midnight, these five were ready to respond in a positive way.

This is symbolic of us spiritually. If we are going to be wise, we need to do whatever the Lord has told us to do. We are accountable for the truth that we have been given, and we must take heed to the Word of God by obeying it. We want to be certain that everything is ready the moment the Bridegroom, Jesus Christ, comes back for His Bride. The foolish virgins in the parable were those who had neglected something; they lacked oil. In the spiritual application, that could mean a number of problems. Maybe they had a lack of consecration or devotion. Perhaps brotherly love was missing or there was a forgiveness deficiency. It could have been a lack of obedience in some area. The list of possibilities is long, but the five foolish did not have something that they needed, and they were held accountable.

The vessel in the parable represents our hearts, and the oil represents the Spirit of God. Through His Word and His Spirit, God teaches us how we can be wise in our walk with Him and how we can take counsel from Him. God's Word is heart-searching and heart penetrating.

The Spirit of God can cause us to see ourselves in the light of eternity. If we take the Word of God and apply it to our lives, it will be like oil for our vessels.

In order to be part of Christ's Bride, God must change our hearts. It takes the redeeming Blood of the Lord Jesus Christ to wash over each soul and make that person a part of His Bride. I was just a child when I gave my heart to the Lord, but it took the same Blood of Jesus to wash away my sins as it did for a person who had many ugly things in his life.

We can be challenged by looking at a bride and groom of today. Each couple does not do everything exactly the same way, but there are always similarities. Any bride will go to great lengths to make herself beautiful. She wants to present herself in the most lovely way she can. Is that being vain?

Absolutely not! She is preparing for the love of her life, and it is good for her to do her best. The Bride of Christ should feel that way. We should anticipate having the Son of God look at the beauty He has put into our lives. Typically, the bride makes most of the wedding arrangements. She has never entered into marriage before, so she gets a wedding coordinator to help her organize. Every detail, even the smallest, is very important to her.

Spiritually, we want to learn how to be our best for God. We want to be certain that even the smallest matters are handled properly for Him.

Then the moment comes when the bride is ready. She is standing in the entry, waiting for the wedding march. She is going to walk down the aisle toward the bridegroom. When the doors open and she begins to walk, there is an awe that comes over the place. She is the center of attention, and most of all, the bridegroom is looking at her.

When that call comes forth from the portals of glory, "Behold, the bridegroom cometh; go ye out to meet him," I want Jesus to be looking at me. Do you want Him to be looking at you? When a bride walks down the aisle, she has already decided to pledge her love and loyalty. Her heart is ignited with excitement and delight.

But when she stands before her groom at the altar and commits her love forever to him, it is incredibly awesome!

Just so, there is a commitment necessary to be part of Christ's Bride, and making that commitment is an awesome moment. As the story of the wise bride continues, it is not just about emotions. A bride has lots of emotions, but commitments are kept by duty and devotion. The married couple finds this is no fifty-fifty arrangement; each must give one hundred percent, one hundred percent of the time. And the Gospel is not just about emotion or a fifty-fifty arrangement either. It is a full commitment to the Lord Jesus Christ.

We need to give the Bridegroom of our souls one hundred percent of ourselves all the time. If we are doing any less, we are opening ourselves to the possibility of becoming among the five foolish. A new bride wants to do things every day to please her husband. In order to keep love in our marriage, we need to work at it. We can keep our first love for our companion alive, and we can keep our first love for God alive. To do so, we make decisions day by day to give and do our best, and to serve with everything that is in us. We renew our consecrations and commitments. The longer we walk with the Lord and do that, the deeper our love for Him becomes. The more we serve Jesus, the more we want to give to Him.

Jesus Christ has done His part. It is up to us to make certain that we are ready to be among His Bride. We can know without a shadow of a doubt that we are among the wise virgins. If the Trumpet sounds today, we can be ready to meet Him!

Becoming Agents of Change

During my last semester of graduate school, I met a gentleman who was very unusual. He had a deep knowledge of the Word of God, but what made him unusual in my estimation—and I think in the light of the Word of God also—was that he was covered with tattoos on his arms. I did not want to judge him, so I told myself he probably got those before he knew the Lord. If it were me, I would have done the best I could to cover them up, but he seemed to pride himself in showing them off. What caused me to speak up was that one day he came to class wearing a cross in his right ear. We had a break and, as usual, he came to me looking for a deep conversation on the Bible. So I asked him, "What's with the cross and the tattoos? Will you please explain these to me? The last I checked, my Bible says I should not mark my body and I should not bore holes in my ear." He responded by paraphrasing Paul's words in 1 Corinthians 9:20-23, saying, "With the Jews I become a Jew and with the Gentiles I become a Gentile, all to gain them for Christ." When I tried to explain this passage to him, I noticed that he got agitated. He told me that I did not know how to gain souls for the Lord, but I asked, "Who gained whom here? You are supposed to change a sinner to be a believer, but you put on the tattoo to identify with him, so who gained whom?" Christians are supposed to be different. We want to change the world around us, not have the world change us. In Romans 12:2 we read, "And be not conformed to this world: but be ye transformed by the renewing of your mind, that ye may prove what is that good, and acceptable, and perfect, will of God." We are supposed to be agents of change, and to do that, we must first have experienced the change only God can make through salvation. As we continue walking by faith and projecting Jesus in our daily living, those around us will be changed. In life, there are decisions that you have to make. There are costs for your decisions, and also an end result.

In Genesis 39, the Bible says Joseph made a decision. Joseph was far away from his father and the people who knew him, and he had the liberty to do whatever he wanted to do, but he dared to be different. When pursued by his master's wife, Joseph rejected her and said, "How then can I do this great wickedness, and sin against God?" That was the decision Joseph made, and it cost him. He spent years in jail because he refused to act against the will of God. However, the end result was that one day Pharaoh had a dream, and Joseph miraculously interpreted his dream.

Then Pharaoh said, "Where can we find a man as wise as this one? Whatever problem the people have, they will take it to Joseph. Only in my throne will I be greater than him." Being different was not easy, but by standing for God, Joseph was a victor in the end.

Shadrach, Meshach, Abednego, and Daniel are other examples of those who stood for God. They were taken into captivity in Babylon. Common sense tells us that Nebuchadnezzar did not invade Israel, risking the lives of many soldiers, just to bring back four young people.

No, there were tens of thousands who were brought back captive. We have never heard of the names of the other captives, but we know the names of Daniel and the three Hebrews boys. That is because from the very first day they stepped into Babylon, they made the decision to obey the Lord. These Hebrew boys were told to eat food that was not allowed by God, and even though everyone else was eating that food, these four dared to be different. I can almost hear Daniel saying to his friends, "Listen, we are different. We are not like them. We know the Lord our God, and we are going to purpose in our hearts not to defile ourselves with the food of the king." They wanted to make a difference. They wanted to impact the world. They wanted to be agents of change for the glory and honor of their God.

Those Hebrew boys purposed in their hearts not to defile themselves, and it cost them. Because of the excellent spirit that was in Daniel, he was promoted, and then there were some who envied him. They sought everywhere to get rid of him, and because of his righteousness he was forced to sleep among wild beasts. But the Bible says that the angel of the Lord stepped into the den and locked the lions' jaws.

They did not have supper that night, praise God! They went hungry. The end result was that the next day, when King Darius walked to the entrance of that den and called, Daniel's voice was heard from the midst of the lions: "My God hath sent his angel, and hath shut the lions' mouths, that they have not hurt me" (Daniel 6:22). Daniel was later promoted, and his accusers were cast into the lions' den.

Shadrach, Meshach, and Abednego also paid a price for their stand. When a decree was made that everyone must worship the king's image, they told the king, "We are not going to bow down to this image. It is not our way. We are different." The king said he would cast them into the fiery furnace, and defied their God to deliver them. They told the king their decision: "If it be so, our God whom we serve is able to deliver us from the burning fiery furnace, and he will deliver us out of thine hand, O king. But if not, be it known unto thee, O king, that we will not serve thy gods, nor worship the golden image which thou hast set up" (Daniel 3:17-18). They dared to be different!

King Nebuchadnezzar threw them into the furnace, but when he looked, there were four men inside, and the fourth looked like the Son of God. Then he called them out of the furnace, and before all his princes, governors, captains, and counselors declared, "Blessed be the God of Shadrach, Meshach, and Abednego, who hath sent his angel, and delivered his servants that trusted in him . . . there is no other God that can deliver after this sort" (Daniel 3:28-29).

They dared to challenge the king's edict. They dared to only serve their God. And the king believed because three young men dared to be different. What a testimony!

You might think that sinners do not look at you, but they are looking, believe me. They know that you are different.

The way to winning souls is not to be just like the sinner, but to make the sinner want to be just like the Christian.

I remember when I was young and worked as elementary music school teacher. Usually, the kids would come hang out with me, and after I finished work, we would stay and talk bible stories. There was another young man who worked there as a coach. What I did not know was that he noticed the way my little friends and I had bible studies and sang hymns. One day, after a few folks had come and gone, he said to me, "I envy you guys. I wish I could stop drinking." He wanted to be like us but he was bound by sin. You see, you are to be a witness for God, and those who do not believe—even those who may laugh at you—sooner or later will have to understand that you are a servant of the living God because of the testimony you keep for Him.

When I got saved at my parent's local assembly, the First Baptist Church Kaduna and baptized at the age of twelve, our community had very few saved young people. I was ridiculed in school, but I made up my mind that I was going to go on with the Lord, and He has been with me every day since I decided to serve Him. I can look back and see how His hand shaped my life, leading me even through things I could not understand. If you are going through adversity, God is not going to leave your side. When you make a decision for God,

He will honor you. Make up your mind that you are going to serve Him and be true to Him. Purpose that you want the world to be changed because of your living, not have your lifestyle change to please the world. Then God will be pleased with you.

Christians are agents of change. Joseph, Daniel, and the three Hebrew boys brought about change because they decided to stand on God's side. They decided not to bow down, and you also must not bow to the things of this world. You are here to change this world for the glory and honor of God. You are not to be conformed to this world.

You are not to be changed by the world, but God calls you to change the world. We want to make an impact for God. If you ask God, He will give you the power to do just that.

You might think that sinners do not look at you, but they are looking, believe me. They know that you are different.

The way to winning souls is not to be just like the sinner, but to make the sinner want to be just like the Christian.

CHAPTER THREE

HEADED IN A NEW DIRECTION— TAKING A NEW DIMENSION

The LORD our God said to us at Horeb, "You have stayed long enough at this mountain. Break camp and advance into the hill country of the Amorites; go to all the neighboring peoples in the Arabah, in the mountains, in the western foothills, in the Negev and along the coast, to the land of the Canaanites and to Lebanon, as far as the great river, the Euphrates. See, I have given you this land. Go in and take possession of the land that the LORD swore he would give to your fathers—to Abraham, Isaac and Jacob—and to their descendants after them."

"'Rise, take your journey, and cross over the River Arnon. Look, I have given into your hand Sihon the Amorite, king of Heshbon, and his land. Begin to possess it, and engage him in battle. This day I will begin to put the dread and fear of you upon the nations under the whole heaven, who shall hear the report of you, and shall tremble and be in anguish because of you.' DEUTERONOMY 1:6-8 NIV Deut 2:24-25 NKJV.

Any obstacle can appear to be insurmountable if we focus on it. However, if we look to the God of Heaven, whom we serve, there is nothing insurmountable! For that reason, we come to throne of grace with high expectations, not intimidated by any hindrances as we approach God. We know that we serve a God who has promised good things to those who seek Him, and He will fulfill those promises. we are to claim the promise of God in spite of obstacles, and possess our possession.

Caleb was eighty-five years old, and the land of Canaan still had not been possessed. Forty-five years earlier, the Children of Israel had made a relatively short trip from Mount Sinai to the border of Canaan. There, it had come into the mind of the people to send out spies to see if the land was what God had promised it would be.

This had not been God's plan, but Moses approved it at the people's urging. God told Moses to choose a man from each tribe to go and spy out the land, so twelve men traveled through the land for nearly six weeks.

As they viewed their promised inheritance, they thought, This is a good land! There are vineyards planted and wells dug. There are grapes and figs and pomegranates; it is indeed a fertile country, a land flowing with milk and honey. That was the description God had given, and Canaan was all that God had said it would be.

Nevertheless, when the spies came back after forty days, ten of them gave an evil report. They described the attributes of the land, but added, "We saw the children of Anak there." The children of Anak were giants, both in size and in fierceness. When that discouraging report filtered through the congregation, the people feared to go up and take the land as God had instructed. In fact, they began to complain and accuse Moses and Aaron.

They stayed up all night and cried in their tents, lamenting the fact that they had been brought to this point where they would certainly be defeated.

Two of the twelve spies, though, did not share that sentiment. Rather than looking at the problem, Caleb and Joshua recognized the possibility!

They knew that God was able to give the victory. They did their best to calm the people and encourage them to believe they were well able to take the land with God's help. They said, "Let us go up at once and possess it."

They had no intention of faltering or turning back. The people refused their encouragement, and God was angry. He condemned the nation to forty years in the wilderness.

Forty-five years later, as the land was being divided among the tribes, Caleb said to Joshua, "Now therefore give me this mountain, whereof the Lord spake in that day; for thou heardest in that day how the Anakims were there, and that the cities were great and fenced: if so be the Lord will be with me, then I shall be able to drive them out, as the Lord said." In response to Caleb's petition, we read that Joshua blessed him "and gave unto Caleb the son of Jephunneh Hebron for an inheritance" (Joshua 14:12-13).

Typically as people get older, they tend to forget. However, Caleb had no memory problems even though he was eighty-five-years old at this point. He reflected back to those events that had transpired so many years earlier, and they were clear in his mind. He remembered how they had searched out the land. He remembered the fierce Anakims in particular. He recalled that when they had come back, a conversation had taken place between him and Moses. Caleb had let it be known that when they went in and conquered that land, the area where the Anakims lived was the region that he would like to inherit for the children of Judah.

In the intervening years, Moses had died. However, Joshua apparently had been aware of that conversation, because at this point Caleb reminded him of it. In essence, he said, "Remember, Joshua, when we went up and spied out the land? The others gave an evil report, but our hearts beat together. We saw the possibilities of that land and you remember hearing Moses tell me that I could have that land for my people. So now I want you to give me this mountain."

The land of the Anakims was not the easiest land to inhabit. In fact, it may have been the most difficult! It was not a region that one walked into, but rather a region that one climbed *up* to. Lots had been cast to determine where each tribe would have its inheritance, but it appears that Caleb's request trumped the casting of those lots. He wanted the mountainous land that was inhabited by giants! He was not fearful of what existed there because he had a promise from God that it was his.

We get the feeling that Caleb was not really interested in the real estate as much as he was interested in the fact that God had promised it to him. He wanted the promise fulfilled. He had not wanted to wander through the wilderness for decades, almost within sight of the land of Canaan, and not be able to go in. But in his heart, as he followed that pillar of fire by night and the pillar of cloud by day, he purposed to see the day when he would conquer the land of the Anakims and destroy those giants. He was determined to take possession of what God had promised him.

Focus on God

We too will face challenges and obstacles on our spiritual journey. Between us and our ultimate goal will stand some giants and high-walled cities. However, we do not want to focus on those things, but on God who looks down upon those things. God gives us promises too. For example, the Lord states that He is not willing that any should perish but that all should come to repentance. The idea that one person can be saved but someone else cannot be saved simply is not factual, for God's Word says that "whosoever will" may come (Revelation 22:17). That is a promise!

Caleb did not see the challenge before him as an obstacle, but rather as an opportunity. We get the feeling that Caleb was not really interested in the real estate as much as he was interested in the fact that God had promised it to him.

God can make a way

The Spirit of God moves in the hearts of individuals in different ways and at different times, but He enlightens every man who comes into the world.

Each of us has a special invitation to salvation. We have a place reserved in Heaven for us. It is God's promise, and it is obtainable. And while it may seem difficult for us, it is easy for God. That is why we must come to a place of surrender to Him—to a point of realizing we cannot take the land unless He helps us. But no matter what obstacle or challenge we face, and no matter how high our mountain may appear to be, God can provide a way over it. God can put into our hearts a determination to say like Caleb, "Give me this mountain. Give me my share of what God has promised to me. Help me to move forward to higher ground." Sometimes we magnify our problems. That is what the Children of Israel did: they magnified the problems and minimized the possibilities. Friends, I want you to focus on the possibilities of **Gods promises and prophecies fulfillment.** We could wander through the challenges of life like the Children of Israel wandered through the wilderness for forty years, but let us purpose not to do so. Instead, we must look forward to taking a mountain. God is well able to lead us into territory we have never explored before, let alone possessed.

The land of Canaan was called the Promised Land for a reason. It was promised to Abraham and to his descendents, but it was also a land that held promise compared to the land of Egypt where the Israelites had lived in bondage. In many ways that parallels the Gospel. We wander in sin in a dry and barren land where we have no hope and no victory, and we come to the threshold of the promised land of the Gospel. We see possibilities there that the world cannot offer. The Gospel offers forgiveness and justification when we come to Jesus repenting of our sins and surrendering to Him. We can have a life of peace and fulfillment, and the ability to live from that day forward without sinning. We cannot get that in the world!

We may achieve momentary happiness, but the joy that Jesus offers is something that is lasting. There is an underlying peace that will withstand whatever the world sends against us.

So we must not be deterred from seeking the experience of salvation. We certainly want to benefit by the blessings the Gospel affords as we travel through this life, but even more than that, eternal life is at stake! We must make Heaven our home.

A land of promise

The Gospel is a land of promise, the Bible speaks of being sanctified wholly, and teaches that we can be entirely sanctified in heart, mind, and body. Every aspect of our newly saved life is to be consecrated to the Lord. That is how one gets sanctified: by presenting his or her entire life as a living sacrifice to God. the baptism of the Holy Ghost is the experience of the Third Person of the Trinity, the Holy Spirit, coming into a sanctified believer's life to give that individual power for God's service. When the heart is sanctified and made holy before God, the believer should seek God in prayer for that promised gift. Speaking with other tongues, the heavenly understandable language is the evidence that signifies the Spirit has descended.

There is no mountain too high, no challenge too great, and no obstacle so insurmountable that God cannot carry you through it or over it.

Possibilities for you

What possibilities in the Gospel lie before you today? Salvation can be yours. Sanctification can be yours, if you are saved and have fully consecrated your life to God. If you are sanctified, you can be filled with the Holy Spirit. Is that the desire of your heart? If so, you can have the boldness to bow at the altar of prayer and declare to God, "Give me this mountain." There is no mountain too high, no challenge too great, and no obstacle so insurmountable that God cannot carry you through it or over it.

When we approach God we can have confidence that He will take every obstacle and make each one a stepping stone to higher ground. We can take the land!

Whatever your need is, you can drop to your knees and declare it to the Lord. Dig in! Seek God and He will sanctify you. He will fill you with the Holy Ghost. These are promises of God and they are obtainable today.

Are you in any desperate situation? Yet when the crisis is past, it is easy to push the snooze button and not make good on the promise. Now is the time to make matters right with God.

Christians, too, need to stay alert. Very soon, Jesus Christ is going to return for His Bride. The warning has been given; we need to be ready for that day. We want to be listening for the sound of the trumpet, and waiting to answer that call.

It is important for us to understand that God is with and around us. As I saw this transpire, the impression was made on my heart that God was among us, and He cared for us in the simple matters of life. He knew where we were and what was happening in our lives. Indeed, God does know and care about every detail of our lives. The Psalmist said, "Thou knowest my downsitting and mine uprising, thou understandest my thought afar off" (Psalm 139:2). God comes down to our level and knows our needs. He wants to prove Himself strong to each one of us.

At times we may look at our circumstances and wonder if the Lord is with us. Rest assured, He sees us! He knows our hearts' desires. He is not limited and can help when it seems there is no help. We can trust Him to keep His hand over us and be with us every moment.

A NEW DIRECTION

In the days before radar, sonar, and GPS, the captains of ships set a course and kept on it by watching landmarks. They would go by a depth or the location of the sun, moon, and stars. If the weather was foggy or cloudy and they couldn't see the landmarks, they had to wait until they could. When they were traveling, they had to be diligent.

A small deviation from the proper course might not be noticeable at first. However, if it was not corrected, they could end miles from their destination and perhaps be lost.

Spiritually there is a course, and it will end in a safe haven for those who follow it diligently. It is a perfect course designed by God. It is the course that draws people to the point of salvation. Then, little by little, comes more understanding and maturity. God gives callings, and there are duties to be done. We never want to run from those; we want to stay the course.

As Christians, we need to be diligent, like the ships' captains. We could veer off just a little bit and think we are still in good shape, but a little slippage, a little digression to the left or right can put us into dangerous territory. We must make sure that we are on the course for Heaven.

Paul knew about that when he told the Ephesians, "Be no more children, tossed to and fro, and carried about with every wind of doctrine, by the sleight of men, and cunning craftiness, whereby they lie in wait to deceive" (Ephesians 4:14). He wanted these people to mature spiritually and to keep going in the direction God wanted them to.

This course was set from the foundation of the world from the onset of time. Abel found the course; he made an offering unto God that was pleasing and accepted. We can do that today also. If we are careful to follow the directions given in the Bible, the Lord will be with us and guide us. He will help us stay on course until we reach our destination of Heaven.

Staying On Course—Trusting In God

When we take hold of something that has power in it, we know it! There is power running through the Word of God, and when we really take hold of it, we will know it! Hebrews 4:12 tells us, "For the word of God is quick, and powerful, and sharper than any two edged sword, piercing even to the dividing asunder of soul and spirit, and of the joints and marrow, and is a discerner of the thoughts and intents of the heart." The word *quick* in this verse means "alive." *Powerful* means it is "active, effectual, operative." The living Word of God is mighty in convincing man of sin. It searches the heart, enlightens the mind, and discloses truth. *Alive and Powerful!*

Take hold of God's Word and allow it to work in your life!

Consider the Author of the Word of God. We find a description in Isaiah 57:15: "For thus saith the high and lofty One that inhabiteth eternity, whose name is Holy; I dwell in the high and holy place." God is the most high. God is the most exalted above all beings. His dwelling place is eternity. His name is Holy, for He is holy above all. Isaiah 55:8-9 states, "For my thoughts are not your thoughts, neither are your ways my ways, saith the Lord. For as the heavens are higher than the earth, so are my ways higher than your ways, and my thoughts than your thoughts." How much higher are the heavens than the earth? We cannot comprehend such vastness!

God inhabits eternity. He is way out beyond the solar system, beyond the Milky Way, beyond the galaxies, and we read that His thoughts are that much beyond our thoughts.

When we begin to ponder that, it staggers the imagination to realize how awesome God is, how wonderful His Word is! We need to make sure that we give the Word of God the reverence and respect it deserves.

God's Word is alive

God's Word is alive. In 1 Peter 1:24-25, we read, "The grass withereth, and the flower thereof falleth away: but the word of the Lord endureth for ever."

When I think of something living, this words of wisdom from Job readily **comes to mind "For there is hope of a tree, if it be cut down, that it will sprout again, and that the tender branch thereof will not cease. Though the root thereof wax**

old in the earth, and the stock thereof die in the ground; Yet through the scent of water it will bud, and bring forth boughs like a plant. (Job 14:7-9.) Though thy beginning was small, yet thy latter end should greatly increase. Job 8:7. Sometimes, the seed of the Word of God in a life seems to lie dormant for many years. The testimony of Raymond Rolland is an example. For the first thirty years of Brother Ray's life, he was in this Gospel. However, during WorldWar II he let the love of God slip out of his heart, and he was away from God for forty five years. One day Brother Ray said that he was walking across his living room floor and he fell flat on his face. He suddenly became unable to walk. Seven doctors examined him, but they could not find anything wrong with him, except that he couldn't walk.

Then the Word that had been sown so many years before in his life became alive again. God told him, "I made you this way. You wouldn't stop and listen to Me. Now what are you going to do?" Brother Ray knew what he had to do. He had not walked for a year, but he hobbled with the help of a cane out to his car and drove to church on a Tuesday night. When he arrived in the parking lot, he got out of his car and walked into the church.

God had healed him right on the spot! When the altar call was given, he said, "I didn't walk down the aisle. I ran down the aisle!" He said it took him all of about thirty seconds to get saved. That is the power of the Living Word! Our mortal bodies, which were once vigorous, may grow old and lose all vitality, but the Word of God is always fresh and new and full of force. Brother Raymond Rolland proved that. He was an old man when he came back to the Lord, but once the Word came alive in his heart again, he had a shout for the battle that lasted until the Lord took him Home.

God's Word has a purpose

The words recorded in Scripture have a purpose. In Isaiah 55:11, we read, "So shall my word be that goeth forth out of my mouth: it shall not return unto me void, but it shall accomplish that which I please, and it shall prosper in the thing whereto I sent it." God's Word is going to do the very thing that He sent it to do. In Acts 8, we read of a time when the Early Church was under great persecution. As a result, the believers were scattered abroad and went everywhere preaching the Word of God. Philip the Evangelist went down to the city of Samaria, and preached Christ to the people there. We read, "And the people with one accord gave heed unto those things which Philip spake, hearing and seeing the miracles which he did. For unclean spirits, crying with loud voice, came out of many that were possessed with them: and many taken with palsies, and that were lame, were healed. And there was great joy in that city" (Acts 8:6-8).

Philip was not presenting some new philosophy to the people of Samaria. No, he simply came and preached the Gospel message. The Word of God went forward, the people heard it, and they began to apply it to their lives.

Scripture says that "with one accord" they took heed to it. When God's Word goes forth out of Heaven, God said it will not return to Him void. He had a purpose there in Samaria. He had something that He wanted His Word to accomplish, and it accomplished that purpose. It prospered. You can imagine the people there in Samaria going to those services, hearing the message, and then going home and telling their families and neighbors about the mighty power of God. The Word began to spread because it is operative, it is active. And there was great joy in that city!

God's Word has an everlasting effect

Paul told the Romans that "faith cometh by hearing and hearing by the Word of God." When we come under the sound of that Living Word, it begins to have an effect. In Acts 24 we read of Felix and his wife, Drusilla, listening to Paul concerning faith in Christ. It says that as Paul reasoned with them of righteousness, temperance, and judgment to come, Felix trembled. That Word was operative, and the words that Paul spoke to Felix were divinely inspired. Felix trembled under them and it was not because of Paul's natural speaking ability. It was the Spirit of God through His Word reasoning with Felix. When God begins to reason with you, you will know!

God's Word continues to work

The power of God's Word does not stop working in our lives at salvation. God continues to deal with us through His Word. God's Word encourages us to make consecrations. His Word will help us see our need for sanctification, and the baptism of the Holy Ghost. That Word is active and working all the time. We hear it through the reading of the Bible, testimonies, preaching, our Sunday school lessons, and the still small Voice that deals with our soul. That Word is active.

In the Book of Hebrews we find a solemn warning: "Let us labour therefore to enter into that rest, lest any man fall after the same example of unbelief" (Hebrews 4:11). The Children of Israel had not mixed the Word of God with faith, so it did not profit them. We do not want to follow Israel's example of unbelief as we hear the Word of God go forth. we have to take what we hear and mix it with faith. We need to move beyond being hearers only and become doers of the Word.

That Word of God is alive and it is powerful, but if we want to have great joy like they experienced in Samaria, we need to respond to the Word of God. We want to heed the Word of God as it speaks to our hearts. We want to respond to it, mix it with faith, and obey it. Let us purpose in our hearts to take hold of the power in that Living Word of God!

The assault we see on the institution of marriage is evidence that the culture of holiness is endangered. Though challenged in courtrooms and communities around the country, a holiness culture upholds the New Testament teaching that marriage is between one man and one woman for life—the way God designed it from the beginning of time. Not man and man or woman and woman, no ! that's evil from the pit of hell.

Using Biblical references, we discussed the necessity of careful communication, commitment, and having good times together. When the principles of holy living are applied, a married couple's home will be peaceful and pleasurable. Even conflicts that arise can be used in a productive manner to enrich and strengthen the marriage.

Though assaulted, the institution of marriage is in no danger of extinction.

As long as Christians determine to value and preserve God's culture of holiness, marriages will be strong and beneficial to society as well as to family members. one definition of the word *culture* is "the concepts, habits, skills, and institutions of a given people in a given period." In the Old Testament, the primary example of a culture is that of the nation of Israel.

God had delivered the Israelites out of the bondage of Egypt and had established them as a special people in the midst of nations that were very different from them. We read in Deuteronomy 7:6: "For thou art an holy people unto the Lord thy God: the Lord thy God hath chosen thee to be a special people unto himself, above all people that are upon the face of the earth."

The people were not holy in the sense that their sins had been forgiven and they had subsequently experienced entire sanctification, whereby their carnal nature had been eradicated. They were holy in the sense that they had been separated by God from other nations and set apart that He might use them to glorify His Name.

In the New Testament, Peter used Old Testament types to instruct early believers. He said, "Ye are a chosen generation, a royal priesthood, an holy nation, a peculiar people; that ye should shew forth the praises of him who hath called you out of darkness into his marvellous light" (1 Peter 2:9). This passage was not addressed to the nation of Israel.

Peter was speaking to newborn Christians of both Jewish and Gentile backgrounds, telling them, "Ye are . . . chosen." Just as Israel was chosen from surrounding nations to glorify God, so Christians are called out from the surrounding culture to live lives that glorify Him.

This distinction is available to whosoever will. All of us are called to come out of sin and darkness to serve God. Those who take advantage of that call by answering it become members of a unique group of chosen ones.

Peter said that this called-out group was "a royal priesthood." The word *royalty* brings to mind a monarchy where those of that ruling family have certain rights and privileges.

Those who belong to the royalty of Christianity have rights and privileges also. Peter also spoke of Christians as being "a peculiar people." One meaning of *peculiar* is "distinguished from others." The same terminology is applicable to Christians today.

Holy living will not survive automatically—we must strive to preserve the way of life that has been handed down to us.

We are distinguished from others because we have availed ourselves of the salvation provided for us through the precious Blood of Jesus Christ.

We look back to the time of Exodus and Deuteronomy and see that in the midst of corrupt nations, God designed that there be a segment of society which reflected His glory.

And that is true in these times as well. God has designed that there be a called out, chosen segment of society that will glorify His Name. We might describe that segment of society as a "holiness culture." When we consider cultures, we often think of ethnic cultures.

It is not unusual for ethnic groups to strive to preserve what is unique to their cultures. Not long ago, I read a news report about how rapidly the languages of the world are disappearing. According to the linguistic expert who authored the article, there are over seven thousand languages in the world today, and they are disappearing at the rate of one every other week. He noted that half of those seven thousand languages were never written down; they were simply conveyed verbally over generations.

The concern is that when a language dies, a culture dies. So more than a language is lost; a way of **life** is lost. As a result, linguistic experts are striving to save those languages and cultures, and refer to them as "endangered." There is another culture that could be referred to as endangered, and that is the holiness culture. While society generally gives its blessing to preserving a linguistic or tribal culture, we do not see that same passion to save a holiness culture. Most cultures are proud of their identities and take what measures they can to see that their unique characteristics and teachings are preserved and passed on to the next generation. We thank God for a holiness identity, but it will not automatically be preserved. There are few in this world today generations who speak its language. If we fail to preserve it and pass it on to future, we ultimately will lose not only the language, but also the way of life. God has called us to do all we can to protect and pass on a holiness way of life. If we do not get the passion, determination, and energy to do so, it will not happen on its own.

We must strive to preserve it! No wonder Jude wrote that we should "earnestly contend for the faith which was once delivered unto the saints" (Jude 3). We need only to look at the last century of the holiness movement to see that many of those who once stood for a holiness way of life have abandoned it. That downward tendency is typical of all religions. It is difficult to pass a belief system along to the next generation. The bar is often lowered until finally the "language" and the way of life are gone. We thank God that those who came before us in this Gospel had a determination to preserve it, and they passed it on to those who followed after them, until it was given to us. Now we, too, have a responsibility to pass it on.

When we speak of holiness, we refer to two aspects. The first aspect is holiness in a moral sense. This takes place when, after we are saved and come to God to be sanctified, He eradicates that sinful nature and gives us an experience whereby we know the old man has been destroyed. The actions, thoughts, and deeds of our lives then spring from a pure heart. We are still human, but we are holy in the sense of heart purity. Carnality has been destroyed, though our humanity remains, so that leaves room for growing spiritual maturity.

The second aspect is holiness in a ceremonial sense. Before we can be holy in a moral sense, we must be holy in a ceremonial sense. We read in Exodus 40:9-13 how the priests set apart and anointed the articles for service in the Tabernacle. That is the second meaning of *sanctified*—to be "set apart." The altars that are placed across the front of our sanctuary are holy in the sense that they have been dedicated to God.

The pulpit that we preach from is holy in the same sense. These items have no moral quality in themselves, but they are "sanctified," or "holy," because they have been set apart to be used in God's service. The opposite of the Old Testament Hebrew word translated *holy* is *common*. God told Moses to take those common items, separate them from the other common items, and dedicate them to God. Moses did so, and at the end of Exodus 40, we read that a cloud covered the tent and the glory of God came down. This was a witness that God had accepted the setting apart of these articles for Him. At that point, all those artifacts could be pronounced ceremonially holy.

Moses had also set apart Aaron and his sons for service to the Lord. They were sanctified, not in terms of the inner man, but they were consecrated to God. They were set apart to a special calling: that of the priesthood. The step of setting apart is what we do when we come to God after we are saved and want to be sanctified. We set ourselves apart and dedicate ourselves. When we fully dedicate ourselves to God for His use and His glory, God does His part by sanctifying the heart. Then we are morally pure as well as ceremonially pure. The idea of being both ceremonially and spiritually sanctified provides the basis for our culture of holiness. There were aspects about this culture that I immediately noticed when I got saved In the days of old for early believers, it is very obvious that those were holiness people. They believed in a holiness culture. They believed in a careful way of life. Do We still do? Industries in those days promote what they call a "culture of safety," implementing measures to keep those on the job site safe. They may even announce that they have had no accidents or casualties for a certain period of time. Guidelines and efforts to insure safety have merit! They have proved beneficial.

The culture of holiness is designed to promote spiritual safety. The guidelines have merit and have proved beneficial to thousands over the years. Once we see the value of that culture, we will appreciate it. A focus on prayer is part of the holiness culture. The Bible does not command us to have mourners' benches, as they used to be called.

However, altars of prayer are part of our culture and we have benefited by them. We want to preserve that aspect of our culture so that we can continue to benefit by them.

The culture of holiness includes a sense of modesty that applies to both men and women. The young men are not arrogant nor brash—they have a good time, but their behavior is appropriate. The young ladies carry themselves in a modest manner. They are evidence that women can be attractively modest without looking like they stepped out of a previous generation or even the previous decade. People of a holiness culture are careful rather than careless in how they act, how they dress, how they speak, and where they go.

Some will say that it is only what is in the heart that counts. However, the exterior is a reflection of what is in the heart. We want to have that inward adorning of a meek and a quiet spirit—a humble and modest spirit. When we do, it will show outwardly.

That modest appearance and demeanor is not just at church. We do not have one standard for church and another when we walk out the door. This is a holiness way of life! It is a culture! It is not mandated by any church, but it is a call from Heaven to our hearts.

The culture of holiness cannot be separated from its traditions. It is not surprising that a sinful society devalues the idea of a traditional family or a traditional marriage. However, it is disappointing when modern Christianity devalues Bible doctrines behind the traditional way of holiness.

The Apostle Paul knew that every society would have that downward pressure, so in his writings he was consistent in his admonishing to a holy way of life. In 2 Thessalonians 2:15 we find these words, "Therefore, brethren, stand fast, and hold the traditions [transmissions, precepts, or ordinances] which ye have been taught, whether by word, or our epistle." Notice the phrase, "by word, or our epistle." That means what has been taught either verbally or written down. If we let that language die, the culture dies. Wholesome teachings are transmitted from grandmother to mother to daughter to the next daughter, from father to son and the next son. The generations come and go quickly, and we must be sure that each succeeding generation receives the holiness message that was given to us. We must pass it along.

In 1 Timothy 6:20, the Apostle Paul said, "O Timothy, keep that which is committed to thy trust." What Paul was referring to was not money or valuables that an armored car could transport from one location to another, but something of even greater value. Just as the driver of an armored car has a responsibility to make sure that things of value are conveyed properly, Paul was telling the younger man, Timothy, "I want you to convey that which has been committed to you— these teachings—to the next generation." In a later epistle to Timothy, Paul instructed him, "But continue thou in the things which thou has learned and hast been assured of, knowing of whom thou has learned them" (2 Timothy 3:14). This verse was repeating the same point. The word *continue* means "to stay, abide, dwell." That is our assignment too. That is our God-given mandate. We must keep on upholding the culture we have been given.

If the enemy of our souls can cause us to doubt the value of our rich heritage and this holiness culture, he can more easily get us to depart from it. God has called us to abide in it, to continue in it, and to pass it along to those who will follow it. This way of life is worthy of being preserved! It is highly regarded by those who have experienced the blessings that accompany it. There are many benefits that accrue to those who embrace this holiness culture. Families have grown up in it and been blessed by it. God has blessed it, and we want to appreciate it.

Not everyone will embrace it; each individual has freedom of choice. But whether others embrace it or not does not influence our commission. We know what we have heard. We know what we have been taught. We know what our mission is. And we know that those who follow this holiness culture will be blessed.

Let us be faithful to our charge to preserve this holiness culture, and to offer it to whosoever will!

This is true of saints of old, They believed in a holiness culture. They believed in a careful way of life. Today, have we compromised or We still do?

SETTING LIFE GOALS

Luke 14:28-35. "Suppose one of you wants to build a tower. Will he not first sit down and estimate the cost to see if he has enough money to complete it? For if he lays the foundation and is not able to finish it, everyone who sees it will ridicule him, saying, 'This fellow began to build and was not able to finish.' "Or suppose a king is about to go to war against another king. Will he not first sit down and consider whether he is able with ten thousand men to oppose the one coming against him with twenty thousand? If he is not able, he will send a delegation while the other is still a long way off and will ask for terms of peace. In the same way, any of you who does not give up everything he has cannot be my disciple. "Salt is good, but if it loses its saltiness, how can it be made salty again? It is fit neither for the soil nor for the manure pile; it is thrown out. "He who has ears to hear, let him hear." LUKE 14:28-35. SETTING LIFE GOALS WITH PURPOSEFUL STRATEGIC PLANNING.

Your goals don't start in the brain; they start in your heart. If you set goals from a personal perspective in the six major areas of your life, you will find your purpose will be tied into your career and all your daily activities. You can break these goals down into long-term and short-term goals and knowing your values and purpose can set priorities. The six major areas are:

CAREER: What do you want to accomplish as far as your work is concerned?

FINANCIAL: Realistically, how much money do you want to have?

PHYSICAL: What program for physical fitness do you want to develop?

MENTAL: In what areas of your life do you wish to study and obtain more knowledge?

FAMILY: What relationships do you want to have and maintain with your family?

SPIRITUAL: What are you striving for spiritually?

Set your goals with a vision of the new and improved you. Don't get caught up in the trap of living in the past. Recognize your current reality and then move on. It's OK to dream of good and reasonable things happening in your life. Let the dreams roll into your thoughts. Do you know people who seem to actualize their dreams often? Look at how their positive thinking works for them. A little optimism is fine, but keep your feet on the ground at the same time. It is only when dreaming takes us away from what we need to do on a daily basis that we could get into trouble, and I think most of us regularly hear, loud and clear, the constant reminders of all our basic and essential responsibilities.

Have reasonable expectations. Give yourself a frequent reality check. If you are faltering, admit it and find out why. Your present tasks and responsibilities are the most important things you have to do. There is a universal principle that states that you will not be given greater opportunities in life until you have proven that you are more capable than your present work demands. Failure to perform your present actions efficiently and successfully will delay success and may actually set in motion a situation that will cause you to go backward. Do not try to escape from the present for a better future that does not yet exist. Do what is important, and then eliminate or delegate the rest.

EXPAND YOUR HORIZONS ALONG WITH YOUR SOUL

Hold on to your negative thoughts and your world will unfold as those values, inner beliefs, attitudes, and perceptions become reality. Change your thoughts, and your world will unfold in new and more positive ways. In other words, if you don't change your beliefs, your life will be like this forever. Is that good news?

Fortune favors the bold. Wishful thinking will not make your dreams come true. Bold action will. He who hesitates is lost. You won't ever have to be a loser again if you take bold action. If you want to be free, realize that your resources are unlimited. Your mind controls your limitations or freedom from limitations, so don't let your limitations control your mind. If you think the latter, you have declared yourself a prisoner, and you will be a prisoner. Once you are fed up with that kind of thinking, you can move yourself into a kind of freedom greater than you have ever known before. You will remain where you are only as long as you wish.

You don't have to be superman to break through your barriers, overcome giants, taking over the hill country. As you may know, a certain sports shoe manufacturers ad says, "Just do it!" Get that paint brush in your hand and sit down with your canvas. This is your life. You are the artist and creator of your future. All you need to do is to paint the picture of your life on your imaginary canvas. Paint it the way you want it with positive brush strokes of faith audacity and watch it begin to unfold.

Expanding your Inner man requires awareness, wisdom, courage, and action. The more we know, the more we realize that there is more to learn. That's the true adventure of life.

You can do it with the following ten steps to actualizing your divine destiny:

1. Identify what is not working for you and choose to get rid of all that undermines your success. Know your current reality.

2. Get in touch with your Inner man, your soul, your values, your purpose, and align your true essence with your talent.

3. Clarify your vision by aligning your values and purpose with your goals. Everything you do, no matter how mundane, has meaning, a purpose.

4. Check your vision against all your personal assets. Conduct a reality check, for delusion is the enemy of the winner. Be realistic about your assets and liabilities.

5. Check your skills. Get more information, seek advice from others, and get more training. Continuing education is vital.

6. Be self-aware and observant. Honestly check your mind set for neediness, greed, fear, jealousy, and self-righteousness. Improve your mind, with counseling if necessary. Emotionally detach from all that is negative. Also, avoid being too emotionally attached to the result you want.

7. Be dynamic and innovative in how you create what you want. Remember, purpose is why you want something, goals are specifically what you want, and creating what you want is how you will accomplish getting what you want.

8. Recognize which are winning patterns and which are losing patterns. Recognize failures, correct them, and get on course—an adjusted course. An airline pilot is constantly changing the setting of his controls of the aircraft in order to remain on course to get to the final destination. If he gets word that there is an overbearing storm, he will instantly change his course. When the red flags of warning are there, it is time to change promptly.

9. Set up your own rules for success and failure and know that possibility thinking will bring you what you want no matter what challenges arise. You have the power to make the impossible possible.

10. Solidify your commitment to yourself and others. Always stick to your word. Consider a win/win environment for all who are around you. You don't have to gobble up others to get what you want. As you build your own success, build your Self along the way, for this is your most finite purpose on earth. The purpose of life, after all, is to live it, to taste experience to the utmost, to reach out eagerly and without fear for newer and richer experience.

Have you ever heard the joke about a man, who kept praying every day, "Please God, please, let me win the lottery, oh please." On and on, day after day, he kept praying, and finally God said, "Hey Joe! Buy a Lottery Ticket!" Eastern philosophy tends to believe that everything is predestined, and that you have little to do with what happens. Western philosophy tends to be in overdrive about making things happen. Some particularly tend to think they can control everything. To get it right, it takes a balance between these two philosophies.

We are born with our own innate capacity to create our own life dynamics. No one has the same capacity as another. Clearly we are as different as our fingerprints. No one else can make things happen for us.

Not even talent agents can make the talent, they discover the talent. You can discover your own talent and then market it in your life. Discovering our own talent (or further discovering it) involves expanding your divine destiny as opposed to your environment conditioning. Our gateway to expanding our sense of our Inner man is affected by how we perceive what is outside us, within us, and all around us. Our ability to create is constantly affected by our sense of connectivity to the Holy Spirit.

Our personality has been developed by all the outside stimuli that make us has a contracted sense of self. Below you will find a list of influences that affect our sense of self. They either make us constrict ourselves unfavorably, or we can build them up in order to expand our Inner man.

SURE GATEWAYS TO EXPANDING/EXERCISING YOUR INNER MAN

Outside You
Sense of Safety

FROM: Fear of taking risks, of rejection, of self-rejection

TO: Focusing on where support can come from, and supporting yourself with positive affirmations: PSALMS 121.

Sense of Self-Protection

FROM: Letting others bring you down or interfere

TO: Self-nurturing, allowing yourself to be nurtured, setting boundaries with others: PSALMS 91.

Sense of Strength

FROM: Feeling overwhelmed, controlled, weak, helpless, like a victim

TO: Seeing all problems as perfect messages that you can resolve, knowing your Great divine destiny strengthen/renew Inner man is your power. ROMANS 8:28

Within You
Sense of Compassion/Love

FROM: Not loving yourself and others, feeling all used up, drained that all you do is drudgery.

TO: Loving yourself, others, and loving what you do. JOHN 13:35.

Sense of Identity and Autonomy

FROM: The self that everyone else created for you, being jealous of others as a mask to keep you from embarking on your own endeavors.

TO: Recovering your self-identity, your Great divine destiny, by getting in touch with your inner self, knowing that everything that happens has a purpose: 1JOHN 4:4.

Sense of Power

FROM: Giving your power away to others who criticize, control, blame, or cause chaos; having no vision.

TO: Following your Still little voice of the Holy Spirit and letting him guide you fearlessly, from anger and separation to synchronicity, freedom to dream. ISAIAH 41:10-20.

Around You (Universal)
Sense of Possibility

FROM: Resistance, impossibility, and rigidity

TO: Going with the flow, being Meek, receptive and creative—PSALMS 22:26,chp 25:9,chp 147:6. ISAIAH 29:19.

Sense of Connectedness

FROM: Fearing to take risks, having to be perfect

TO: Resourcing Universal Intelligence for all your needs. LUKE 1:37, PHILIPIANS 4:13&19.

Sense of Abundance

FROM: Sense of lack, limitation

TO: Sense of unlimited resources that are attainable. PSALMS 23. ISAIAH41:17-20.PHIL4:19.

Sense of Faith

FROM: Disbelief, "should" or "have to" thinking, lack of belief in self

TO: Knowing that universal intelligence is abundant. HABAKKUK 2:4, ROMANS1:17, HEBREWS10:38.

Remember, whatever we give our attention to, we create more of. By giving attention to your sensitivity to of your Inner man connected to the Holy spirit, you will expand the capacities of your divine destiny. This will allow you to handle with confidence and power any barrier or giant and all impossible mountain like situations you many encounter.

CHAPTER FOUR

UNDERSTANDING THE POWER OF YOUR THOUGHTS AND IMAGINATION

Genesis 11:1-9

Now the whole earth used the same language and the same words. It came about as they journeyed east, that they found a plain in the land of Shinar and settled there. They said to one another, "Come, let us make bricks and burn them thoroughly." And they used brick for stone, and they used tar for mortar. They said, "Come, let us build for ourselves a city, and a tower whose top will reach into heaven, and let us make for ourselves a name, otherwise we will be scattered abroad over the face of the whole earth." The LORD came down to see the city and the tower which the sons of men had built. The LORD said, "Behold, they are one people, and they all have the same language. And this is what they began to do, and now nothing which they purpose to do will be impossible for them. "Come, let Us go down and there confuse their language, so that they will not understand one another's speech." So the LORD scattered them abroad from there over the face of the whole earth; and they stopped building the city. Therefore its name was called Babel, because there the LORD confused the language of the whole earth; and from there the LORD scattered them abroad over the face of the whole earth. **GENESIS 11:1-9 NASU**

Proverbs 23:7

For as he thinketh in his heart, so is he: Eat and drink, saith he to thee; but his heart is not with thee. KJV

Genesis 6:5-10

The LORD saw how great man's wickedness on the earth had become, and that every inclination of the thoughts of his heart was only evil all the time. The LORD was grieved that he had made man on the earth, and his heart was filled with pain. So the LORD said, "I will wipe mankind, whom I have created, from the face of the earth—men and animals, and creatures that move along the ground, and birds of the air—for I am grieved that I have made them." But Noah found favor in the eyes of the LORD. This is the account of Noah.

Noah was a righteous man, blameless among the people of his time, and he walked with God. NIV

Jeremiah 17:5-14

Thus saith the LORD; Cursed be the man that trusteth in man, and maketh flesh his arm, and whose heart departeth from the LORD. For he shall be like the heath in the desert, and shall not see when good cometh; but shall inhabit the parched places in the wilderness, in a salt land and not inhabited. Blessed is the man that trusteth in the LORD, and whose hope the LORD is. For he shall be as a tree planted by the waters, and that spreadeth out her roots by the river, and shall not see when heat cometh, but her leaf shall be green; and shall not be careful in the year of drought, neither shall cease from yielding fruit. The heart is deceitful above all things, and desperately wicked: who can know it? I the LORD search the heart, I try the reins, even to give every man according to his ways, and according to the fruit of his doings. As the partridge sitteth on eggs, and hatcheth them not; so he that getteth riches, and not by right, shall leave them in the midst of his days, and at his end shall be a fool. A glorious high throne from the beginning is the place of our sanctuary. O LORD, the hope of Israel, all that forsake thee shall be ashamed, and they that depart from me shall be written in the earth, because they have forsaken the LORD, the fountain of living waters. Heal me, O LORD, and I shall be healed; save me, and I shall be saved: for thou art my praise. Jeremiah 17: 1-14 KJV

CHANGING IMPOSSIBILITY THINKING TO POSSIBILITY THINKING

It is obvious that impossibility thinking severely limits our lives. All the problems you face in life are caused by your perception. This perception has formed a Created Self that includes personality traits that are both positive and negative. If you want to change any situation from the impossible to the possible, you must first change your perception of *who you are* rather than what you do, or what you have. What you do and what you have is the result of how you perceive your Created Self. The more you tune into who you are—your Greater Self—the less you will have to rely on your Created Self.

Have you ever waited on God and thought, Lord, is it working? Did You even hear my prayer? Did it do anything? Did it go anywhere?

Recently, I have been listening over and over to one of my favorite old hymns, "Sitting at the Feet of Jesus." It brings me a picture of a quiet, peaceful place where I can learn more of Him. It creates a longing in me to be like Mary, sitting at Jesus' feet, listening, learning, trusting. The song says, "Give me, Lord, the mind of Jesus; Make me holy as He is." That is my prayer—to have the mind of Christ so that I can sleep in the middle of a storm, with the waves tossing around me; to have confidence that everything is under our Father's control and I have no need to fear. I want to claim the promise of peace Jesus gave to His disciples: "Peace I leave with you, my peace I give unto you: not as the world giveth, give I unto you. Let not your heart be troubled, neither let it be afraid" (John 14:27).

In a world where the news industry makes money on our fears and anxieties, how can we claim that promise Jesus gives? When financial analysts keep us coming back to learn what calamity they predict will happen next, how can we have the peace "that passeth all understanding"?

Paul the Apostle, who went through extremely trying and difficult times, gives us the formula to fight anxiety and agitation. In Philippians 4:8 he writes, "Finally, brethren, whatsoever things are true, whatsoever things are honest, whatsoever things are just, whatsoever things are pure, whatsoever things are lovely, whatsoever things are of good report; if there be any virtue, and if there be any praise, think on these things."

Do you have trouble keeping your thoughts positive? These steps will help you find peace no matter what is going on around you.

Here is the key: our thought life is what produces most of our anxiety. We struggle with regrets about our past, and fears about what may or may not happen in our future. The battle for peace is fought in our minds. Considering this, what habits can we develop that will help us follow Paul's instruction to control our thought life? One strategy that can be helpful is to remind ourselves that our gracious God is in control. When we do that, we are able to relax. We remember that we are the disciples Jesus loves and we were made in God's image. He wants good for us, and He has promised good to us. When difficult things happen in life, we can remind ourselves that God is working out something positive, whether to shape us or someone else.

These thoughts bring "praise" when we "think upon" them. Another habit that helps bring peace is to fill our hearts with beautiful, inspiring thoughts. Do you have trouble coming up with positive thoughts?

Think about Scripture. Memorize it; pray it; meditate on it. When I find a Scripture that speaks directly to me, one that gives me confidence or direction, or that reminds me of God's great love and power, I write it in a journal that I can read daily. These Scriptures may come from a devotional, a sermon, or a friend. If we keep them close, and display them where we will see them again and again, it keeps something "pure" in our memories to "think upon."

A different way to fill our minds with uplifting thoughts is through music that inspires, encourages, and reminds us of a God who is awesome. God often speaks to us through music, and learning inspirational, testimonial, and worshipful lyrics is a wonderful way to fill our mouths with praise and our hearts with thoughts that are "true" to "think upon."

I've found that God also speaks to me through others. Friends, ministers, and family members will often say something profound, give wise counsel, or tell me something edifying.

Many times I will read something that is so encouraging that I feel it is from God. I try to remind myself of these heavenly messages. I write them down and read them often to keep them in my memory. They have become something "lovely" to "think upon." Paul admonishes us to think on "good reports." We do that by taking advantage of every opportunity to share positive events with others. This will encourage them and also remind us of how good God is. Many of us have daily answers to prayer that we forget too soon. We can remember them if we write them down and share them with others. Ask friends to share their "good reports" with you so you can rejoice with them. These things are "true" and "just."

In rehearsing the answers to prayer you have received from God, also remember the difficult things God has brought you through. Recall the trials that God has used to teach and admonish you, and allow Jesus to redeem these hard things by using them to encourage someone else. Let others know how He has lifted you up and encouraged you. Repeating these events will keep them in your memory and give others a "good report" and something "honest" to "think upon." As we take positive steps to follow Paul's advice, let's not forget the discipline required of ourselves. In 2 Corinthians 10:5, the Apostle speaks of "casting down imaginations, and every high thing that exalteth itself against the knowledge of God, and bringing into captivity every thought to the obedience of Christ." Sometimes I find I must ask God to help me harness my thought life and capture imaginations that are time-wasting and negative. We can all use self-discipline to avoid indulging in contemplation of negative events that may never happen.

These are thoughts that can steal our peace and often bring discouragement. We must develop the habit of turning our minds from the negative to the positive, "bringing into captivity every thought." If we take Paul's advice to "think on these things," we will soon find Jesus' promise of peace fulfilled in our lives. That is not to say discouraging things will never happen, but we will have the formula for inner peace. As we cast down imaginations and capture our thoughts, we can renew our minds by focusing on the good God has promised us. We can develop confidence that God is in control, and experience His promise of peace.

Think about Scripture. Memorize it; pray it; meditate on it. Just as plants grow without being seen, so the Gospel works in ways that may be invisible. *Results Will Come!*

We may forget, we may be on our way, we may be distracted by this or that, but the Gospel is still growing, working, and producing, just as it was intended to do. While the Gospel will continue moving forward whether or not individuals respond, we do have the opportunity to choose to be a part of it. We can put effort into it and see results in our personal lives.

Another example from gardening illustrates that point. As a child, vegetables were not my favorite food, but I did like fresh peas, straight out of the pod. One year I decided to grow my own little pea patch. Mom figured that if I wanted a pea patch so I could eat fresh peas, she was all for it. That was one way to get vegetables in me! However, I found that growing peas was not like growing those wildflowers.

I had to prepare the soil, make trenches, and plant each seed exactly the right distance apart. Then I covered them over and watered them. This time, my attention was focused on that little garden spot. I was watching it every day and tending to it as necessary. I wondered, Where are the peas? When is something going to happen? One day, up came the peas. I had a great little garden there and I enjoyed those peas!

Have you ever had that experience in prayer? Have you ever waited on God and thought, Lord, is it working? Did You even hear my prayer? Did it do anything? Will this mountain move? Did it go anywhere? Be assured, the Gospel is always working. It is a good thing to pray and pray again! But the first prayer you need to pray is lord take away barriers within me, mountain of unbelief doubts and lack of discipline determination and devotion.

In Mark 4:26-27, we find these words about how the Gospel grows: "So is the kingdom of God, as if a man should cast seed into the ground; and he should sleep, and rise night and day, and the seed should spring and grow up, he knoweth not how."

The Gospel of Jesus Christ is always growing, working, and accomplishing its purpose. It goes forward whether individuals respond to it or not. Some people who come into contact with the Gospel may notice it briefly. Some may "visit" it occasionally.

They get more interested in God because of an event in their lives; something comes along and stirs them, so they come to church, or read passages in the Bible, or ask a question. Some people are indifferent to the Gospel. Others seemingly are completely oblivious or even reject it outright. When the seed of the Gospel has been planted, it begins working. It is not dependent upon our efforts. We are told to "pray without ceasing," but even Christians who have the best of hearts before God are still human. We are subject to many cares and distractions. A lot of things demand our attention.

We have physical limitations—we get tired. We sleep. This is all a part of life. Thank God, the Gospel is not subject to our moods. It is not subject to whether it is day or night. It is not subject to whether we are feeling energetic or poorly, or whether we are alert or distracted. The Gospel is always working!

It is accomplishing what it does, just like that seed in the ground. It does not stop growing when we go to bed. It does not quit growing when we are not thinking about it. It just keeps right on.

The Gospel is always there. It is being productive for you; it is being productive for me. What can you depend on at any moment of your life? The Gospel! No matter what circumstances you find yourself in, all the promises and the power of God are in effect, working all the time. You can depend on them.

The Lord said the kingdom of God is like the seed that a man cast into the ground. We may not understand all the intricacies of the growth cycle, but we do not have to understand for it to work. Similarly, once that Gospel seed is planted, it grows. The phrase in verse 2 7, "and the seed should spring and grow up, he knoweth not how," makes me think of an experience In Acts chapter 12, we read of another time when prayer was working behind the scenes. Members of the Early Church were praying for Peter, who had been imprisoned.

James had been slain and now Herod had taken Peter and was going to kill him too. God's people gathered to pray about this crisis, but they easily could have wondered, How is the Lord ever going to deliver Peter? He is down there in the dungeon, behind bars and gates, with guards all around.

How is it ever going to happen?

While they were praying, God was working. The angel of the Lord came to Peter in the middle of the night, and led him out, through gate after gate. He walked through the streets of that city, and came to the door of the house of Mary, where the prayer meeting was going on. The people inside were still praying, and Peter was standing outside, knocking on their door. The Gospel works!

Today, perhaps you are still waiting for answers to some of your prayers. Maybe you have wondered, Lord, is it working? Is anything happening? Have faith: the Gospel is still working!

Plan on it. Trust it. Thank God for it. As you continue to watch and pray in patience, the results will come.

Decision Dilemma

Choosing a college was one of my first experiences with a major life decision that felt overwhelming. I had recently turned eighteen, and as the burden of decision-making transitioned from my parents to myself, the weight of selecting the right school was heavy on my mind. I knew the college I attended would have important and long-lasting effects on my life—the people I would live among for four years, the professors and students I would work with, my future career, and more things I could not foresee. Yet I had no idea what direction to take. More than anything, I wanted the Lord to lead my decision, so I earnestly prayed about it and waited for an answer. And waited . . . and waited.

To my disappointment, God never said, "Thou shalt attend Oxford or Harvard University," or any of the other schools where I had applied. I thought God would be forced to give me an answer in April of my senior year, when schools send acceptance/admission letters, but instead I learned that I had been placed on three waiting lists. It was anticlimactic to say the least. Month after month I waited on God, all the while wondering why He did not just tell me what His plan was. My consecrations were in place and I was willing to go to schools in the Northwest, Midwest, or East Coast, or none at all, if that was what God said to do. But He did not tell me to do anything. It was not until late July (only about a month before my classes would begin) that I knew for sure which University college I would attend. Based almost entirely on the financial aid package my family could afford, I enrolled at a university near my hometown. Later, through several events and answers to prayer, God made it clear to me that this was where He wanted me, but I still wondered, Why didn't He just say that in the first place? For a while after that experience, I continued to be frustrated by important decisions. I thought that if I drew close enough to God, then He would start telling me what He had planned for my life. However, that was not the way God led me to find the right Room accommodation a beloved brother in Christ and experienced Pastor Olu Ibitomi, major, job, or anything else. Instead, I would pray, worry and wait, and then at the last minute, something would come up that was clearly God's plan. The more I saw God come through for me, the less I fretted over my decisions, but I still wanted to know how I could get a little more advance notice from Him. Just as I was becoming accustomed to the idea that God may not ever give me much notice on important choices, I read the story of how God led Samuel to anoint Israel's first king, Saul. The account in 1 Samuel 8-9 tells how the Israelites decided they did not want judges to rule them through God's leading anymore; they wanted a king. Although it was not God's plan, He agreed to give them a king because they were so determined to have one.

This meant that the nation faced a huge decision: who should be their king? The new ruler would have tremendous power— he could tax them, confiscate their property and possessions, and lead them to war. They had to choose just the right person. As I read, I was so surprised to find out that God revealed this critical choice to Samuel "a day before Saul came."

I could not believe it! The Prophet Samuel—the holy man of God—got one day's notice? At that moment, I had a realization. If the Prophet Samuel was not always "in the loop" on future events, then no one is. And I will not be either. What a relief! This means we do not have to seek God's direction until He spells out the answer to every question we have; we can just take our concerns to Him and trust that He will answer—in His time and way. We may not know what will happen until the day before we need the answer, or even later, but we know God is faithful and He will provide an answer.

Shortly after reading about Samuel, I read another Biblical account that gave more insight about God's leading. In 2 Kings 6, the Syrian king was trying to capture the Israelites but could not because God used the Prophet Elisha to warn about the attack. When the king of Syria discovered it was Elisha who had thwarted his efforts, he sent an army to surround the city where Elisha lived. The next morning, Elisha's servant awoke early and was alarmed to find the city surrounded. In distress he said, "Alas, my master! how shall we do?" At this point in the story, I thought Elisha might have been wondering why God did not mention the army outside his door a little sooner. However, Elisha was not worried at all. His response was, "Fear not: for they that be with us are more than they that be with them."

Here again, a man who was extremely in tune with God had no idea what God's plans were, and he was not in the least concerned about that. The reason for his calmness comes in the following verses, when God opens the eyes of Elisha's servant and he sees a heavenly host ready to defend them. Elisha was not worried because he knew God was in control. Whether God chose to tell His plan to Elisha or not, he knew he could trust God.

We also do not need to worry when we are not sure what to do in a particular situation. Human nature makes us want to have specific plans for the future, but it is far better to simply know that God is in control. As a prospective college student, I was under the impression that it was my Christian duty to seek God until He told me what to do in important decisions, but now I understand that we are not the ones who determine what information we need from God; He does that. As we seek His will and trust in Him, He tells us what we need to know. Remember, neither Samuel nor Elisha fretted about their uncertain situations, and it was not because God had explained exactly how things would turn out. They did not know the details, but they did not worry because they knew the outcome: God's will would be done. If we pray until we know that, we will not worry either.

Becoming Addicted to Ministry: The activities which consume our time energy, and financial resources can be spiritually beneficial.

In our society today, the word *addiction* has negative connotations. People become addicted to many things. Alcohol, tobacco, drugs, gambling, the internet, pornography, television, and hobbies are probably the most common. Addictions can consume people's lives, energy, and financial resources, and often are harmful to their health or well-being. That activity or substance becomes a habit that they cannot control. It is amazing to see what people are willing to do to satisfy an addiction.

I heard of a woman who spent every cent she could get on gambling and video lottery games. The situation became so bad that her husband sold their house, thinking that relocating would help her. After the sale, he put $25,000 in the bank. She obtained access to that money and spent every last dollar of it. Then she went from person to person to get loans. In time, the couple was so deeply in debt that she was ready to take her own life.

People need deliverance from such addictions, and thankfully, Jesus Christ can liberate them. Yet, might it be possible for an addiction to be good? Consider what Paul the Apostle wrote: "Ye know the house of Stephanas, that it is the firstfruits of Achaia, and that they have addicted themselves to the ministry of the saints" (1 Corinthians 16:15). The "ministry of the saints" is a good thing! The household of Stephanas may have been among Paul's first converts in the Roman province of Achaia.

Apparently, when they received the Gospel, they did so with open hearts.

They sold out to the L ord. There was nothing outside of the Gospel that was important enough to cause them to give up this treasure they had found.

And as a result, their desire was to minister to others. Paul said they had addicted themselves to the ministry of the saints. While we do not know exactly what he meant, it sounds as though they were hospitable; their house was open. They had church and prayer meetings in their home. If someone like Paul came, they received him with open arms. Perhaps there were various members in the household—father, mother, sons, daughters, grandparents, and servants—and seemingly, they all embraced the Gospel.

That is how the Gospel starts in a location and also how it grows. Somebody fully commits to God and becomes addicted to the extent that serving the Lord means everything to him or her. When the Gospel wave of Revival came to our community, my parents embraced it, and it became the best thing in all the world to them. We had a large family—ten or twelve of us lived at home at one time. But if ten or fifteen visitors came to town for any Gospel Revival service, our home was open. Food and money were not too plentiful, but because my parents were addicted to the ministry of the saints, they were always ready to house guests.

What does it mean to become addicted to the Gospel? It means being willing to give up anything the Lord requires because there is nothing else that can satisfy. In this chapter, Paul gave five imperatives that will help us.

He said, "Watch ye, stand fast in the faith, quit you like men, be strong. Let all your things be done with charity" (1 Corinthians 16:13-14).

To "watch" means to be on the alert. We need to keep our guard up. Paul could have been referring to a sentinel in a military garrison, who is supposed to be alert and watching for the enemy. He dare not let down his guard, fall asleep, or be distracted. He needs to be diligent in his watching, and so do we.

"Stand fast in the faith" speaks of unity, of a battalion of soldiers standing shoulder to shoulder. Paul realized there was a need for unity in order to have spiritual success. To be victorious, we need to stand together in the faith. If there is a breech, the enemy will come in, because he wants to separate and divide us. Standing fast means not giving an inch to the enemy, not yielding or ceding victory. This requires oneness of spirit. The word "quit" in the phrase "quit you like men" means to behave in a brave and manly manner, not acting in a cowardly way.

We need to "be strong" because we do not want to lose heart or turn from the fight when the enemy comes in like a flood. We want to hold our ground, exercise spiritual stamina, and find strength by depending upon the Lord and one another.

Then Paul said to "let all your things be done with charity." That is another key element for success in the Gospel. We must love each other as brethren. Let everything be done with love in our hearts for each other.

The Apostle addressed these words to the church in Corinth. Many of the people there were Gentiles who came from pagan beliefs. Their backgrounds contributed to the problems within the church, such as order in their services, deception, and division among them. However, after Paul addressed these issues, he ended this epistle on a positive note. He told them the actions necessary for success, for victory, for growth, and for prosperity in the Lord. And his words are timeless! We need to take these same steps if we are to defend ourselves against the enemy who is aggressive and full of trickery.

Paul was saying to stand shoulder to shoulder; be watchful, brave and courageous; stand your ground without giving in; fight for what you believe in; and do it all out of love. These actions will help us be addicted to the Gospel.

Paul used the house of Stephanas as an example because he wanted others to be like them. He went on to say, "Submit yourselves unto such, and to every one that helpeth with us, and laboureth" (1 Corinthians 16:16).

Someone once said there are many workers in the church but not many toilers. There is a difference between *workers* and *toilers*. Those who work sometimes are like a flame that flashes up and then quickly goes out. But those who toil are there through thick and thin, rain or shine. Busy or not, they are there. These are the people who keep things going. Who comes out to prayer meeting? It is the same ones all the time; we can be sure they will come. If they are not there, we know that something is wrong—they must be sick or some unforeseen circumstance has come up.

This is true for cleaning the church, helping with a construction or maintenance project, and many other aspects of Gospel activities. If we each do our part, the work of the Gospel rolls along much more smoothly.

Having a spiritual addiction is good for us. People will sell the shirts off their backs to satisfy harmful habits. What would it mean if Christians had that strong of a spiritual addiction to the ministry of the saints and to the work of the Lord? Maybe we would have an addiction to prayer or to church attendance. Would that be bad?

Maybe we are too taken up with other things. The enemy of our souls poses temptations in any way he can. He is sly, and he will try to get us absorbed by things that will be detrimental to our spiritual lives. We need to be careful and watchful.

We want to keep in mind what it means to be addicted to the Gospel. If we follow God's instructions that Paul mentioned, we can be strong and victorious in the Lord. We can be addicted to the ministry of the saints. It's a good addiction!

All of us are on a spiritual journey, and along the way, we have places where the Lord steps in and, in a remarkable way, gives us the help we need; figuratively, where the lord gives you that mountain. In 1 Samuel 7:15-16, we are told of a physical journey—a circuit—that the prophet Samuel made regularly. We read, "And Samuel judged Israel all the days of his life. And he went from year to year in circuit to Bethel, and Gilgal, and Mizpeh, and judged Israel in all those places." Mizpeh was a place of great significance to Samuel. That is where he had erected the stone he called *Ebenezer*, or "a stone of help," as a memorial to how God had helped the Children of Israel.

More than twenty years prior, at that very location, Israel had gone out against the Philistines expecting that they would conquer, but instead were conquered.

Four thousand of their men had been killed in battle. The people at that time were corrupt and superstitious in nature, and they felt if they would take the Ark of the Covenant of the Lord with them into battle, its presence would guarantee victory. Instead of beseeching God to go before them, they arrogantly sent for the Ark and two priests to carry it out before them. However, possessing a symbol of God does not ensure His presence, and again Israel was horribly defeated. This time, thirty thousand of the Children of Israel were slain in battle, and the Ark was taken. The Ark of the Covenant was in the possession of the Philistines for a time, but a plague followed wherever it went within that land. The Philistines wanted to rid themselves of the plague, so they determined to send it back to Israel. They put the Ark on a new cart pulled by oxen. The oxen left their newborn calves and, lowing as they went, headed in the direction of Israel—a remarkable circumstance which proved to the Philistines that God was the One who had plagued them. The Ark eventually was taken to Kirjath-jearim, where it languished for twenty years.

After spending twenty years in a state of defeat and subjugation, the Children of Israel began to long after God once more. They knew the Philistines were coming out to battle against them again and they were afraid. The prophet Samuel exhorted the people to return to God, and they heeded his words. Their confession, "We have sinned against the Lord" (1 Samuel 7:6) was crucial to God working for them. They took definite steps, putting away their strange gods—those foreign, idolatrous practices that they had substituted for the genuine worship of God. Then they prepared for the Lord's presence by drawing water and pouring it out before the Lord, perhaps symbolizing that there was nothing left of themselves.

God saw their repentance, and undertook in a miraculous manner. On that same plot of land where thousands of men had been slain and the people had been scattered by the Philistines, God gave them the victory. In gratitude, Samuel erected a stone there as a memorial. We read, "Then Samuel took a stone, and set it between Mizpeh and Shen, and called the name of it Ebenezer, saying, Hitherto hath the Lord helped us" (1 Samuel 7:12).

In later years, as Samuel made his circuit to judge the people in various locations of Israel, he would pass by Mizpeh. We do not know how close he came to that stone of help, but whether it was close enough to touch or far enough away that he would simply see it on the horizon, it reminded him of what God had done for Israel. Though it served as a reminder for all of Israel, it was a personal stone of help that Samuel had erected. He could always look at it and reflect, I remember when God helped us there. We did what God said to do, and God gave the victory.

We will never forget that spot. I like the idea that God can help us. I like the idea that God can give us reminders of when and where He has helped us in the past. From year to year there is a "circuit" that each of us will travel, and along the way, we will have memorials that we can look to.

If I were to take you on a circuit past some of my spiritual memorials and places where God has helped me, I would start by heading northeast from Jos, Plateau state a city made popular by ethno-tribal religious cruel attacks and civil crisis where I worked and lived with my foremost family, and Kaduna, Kaduna state where I grew up down to western Nigeria, Lagos. That is where eitherto God had helped me sojourned. I could take you to the spot where, I have a memorial there. Another place of remembrance on my spiritual circuit is a two-story apartment building where I was living as a undergraduate student in Ilorin, Kwara my state of origin, at the time of my early days in ministry and University.

That is a memorial in my life: the place where God helped me to realize that I wanted nothing to do with the indecision elements of adolescent life.

I have another memorial in Lagos, adventurous times of itinerant ministry and several months of struggling financially to obtain victory. However, There is a landmark in that I eventually got my first international book published by prophetic evangelist Dr. Debbie Wright, Ohio based Publisher. It was a memorial, a stone of help. God helped me there. He gave me what stood like mountain. I got breakthrough after a few breakdown disappointments and been misunderstood and dubbed.

I have another memorial at a spot in the tabernacle at redemption camp and prayer city respectively where I had received definite instructions on what next to do and overcome challenges. During a teaching on entire sanctification, I sensed that God was sanctifying me right there as I listened to the message. That is a memorial! When I go into the faith tabernacle, I can look over at that spot and remember what God did for me there. Back behind the Canaan land campground restaurant is another spot I look to as a "stone of remembrance." Justification forgives past sins and gives one power to go and sin no more. Salvation took away my temper and the profanity and a whole lot of other things. I believe God does that as I praised the Lord with my head down on my arms, lost in prayer, I suddenly found myself speaking in a language I had never been taught, and I realized God had just baptized me with the Holy Ghost and with fire. And I look back to that moment as a memorial to the fact that God helped me.

That is what an Ebenezer is. It does not have to be a physical stone: it is simply a place of help. It is a time in your life, a spot, a physical location where you looked up to God and said, "God help me." And He did! That fact makes such an impact that you hearken back to it later and remember that God helped you there.

Having a place of help also means you have had a place of desperation. We do not typically ask for help when it is not needed. On that journey of life, you will encounter places where you need divine help and so will I. We have the promises of God's Word that His help is available. Later, we will look back and say with authority, "I can tell you that I had help from Heaven. I have an Ebenezer in that place." In one sense, we do not really want an Ebenezer, but we need them. We need the knowledge that God has stepped in and provided the assistance that our situation demanded. We could not resolve that hard place through our own efforts, but we found that we could rely on God. He met us there, at our point of weakness and need. We want to be like the Psalmist, who said: "I will lift up mine eyes unto the hills, from whence cometh my help. My help cometh from the Lord, which made heaven and earth" (Psalm 121:1-2). Consider that as you move along through the circuit of your life this year. If God made Heaven and earth—and He did—you can be sure that you will not encounter anything too difficult for Him to resolve or to provide help for if He chooses not to resolve it.

The Psalmist said in the same psalm: "He that keepeth thee will not slumber." God is available to offer help, strength, and encouragement any time of day or night. He is never busy. He will never fail to answer our call. He will not look at who is calling and say, "Later." No, He will be there in our moment of need! He is our help. The psalm concludes, "The Lord shall preserve thy going out and thy coming in from this time forth, and even for evermore." What a wonderful promise! If you are facing a situation that you cannot handle, why not erect an Ebenezer today? Go to your knees and look to God. Ask Him to flood your heart with grace and with comfort and with strength. God will do it! If you have not experienced this great salvation yet, ask God's forgiveness for your past sins, and He will forgive you. If you have been saved but have not yet experienced entire sanctification, consecrate your life to Him.

You do not need to go through life struggling with a carnal nature. Life will bring enough temptations and outer circumstances that assault you without you also having to deal with your own carnality. God will eradicate that carnal nature through sanctification. If you have been sanctified, ask Him to fill you with the Holy Ghost Whatever your need is, God sees and knows. Ask for His help and receive it!

Is It Convenient? In a society geared toward instant gratification, it can be easy to slip into the same mentality when it comes to serving God.

We live in a time of convenience. Our society is acclimated to quick fixes, instant gratification, and on-demand convenience. We have fast food, quick lube for our cars, e-mail and text messaging for instant communication, and ATM and on-line banking so we do not have to go to the bank and stand in line. Everything is geared toward convenience. Convenience has also reached into the modern church. Most of us in our country freely drive to services, rather than walk in hiding. We sit in comfortable pews, the building is climate-controlled, and there is no obvious persecution. Some churches are so convenient that a person does not even need to go, but can stay at home and listen or watch. The Bible can be obtained on a CD or mp3, so it can be heard without reading. Never has the Gospel been more easily accessible than it is for us. This is not necessarily bad. However, we need to guard against thinking it is a convenient Gospel, that we can take it or leave it depending upon our feelings and schedules of the moment.

A desire for convenience

Wanting a convenient Gospel is not a new attitude. Paul the Apostle was put in prison for the cause of Jesus Christ. He was falsely accused, and in time, brought before Felix, the governor. Paul presented the Gospel to Felix, and it appears that he listened to what Paul had to say. However, he deferred Paul's case until a later time. Then the Bible says that after certain days, Felix "sent for Paul, and heard him concerning the faith in Christ." God's Word was going forth to Felix for a second time, because Paul "reasoned of righteousness, temperance, and judgment to come."

Paul preached salvation to him, and the Bible says that Felix trembled, which in the original language means to be terrified. Felix was convicted of his sins; the Holy Spirit spoke to his heart and caused him to tremble. But sadly, his response was, "Go thy way for this time; when I have a convenient season, I will call for thee" (Acts 24:25). Felix wanted to consider the matter on his own terms and in his own time. The Bible indicates that Felix called for Paul often and communed with him, but we never read that he trembled or felt such a strong call from God as he had before. Two years later, when Felix was relieved of the governorship, he left Paul bound as a prisoner.

The dictionary says *convenience* is "that which gives ease; that which is suited to wants; freedom from difficulty; easily accessible." Many today want the Gospel to be convenient. The attitude of those who are not serving God may be: When I can hear it on my own terms, I will listen.

When I get my life together, then I will come to Christ. When it is convenient, I will call on God. Christians may think: When it is convenient I will read my Bible, or seek the Lord and pray more. When it is convenient, I will come to church. When it is convenient, I will share the Gospel with others. When it is convenient, I will apologize and make things right with fellow believers.

Where is the sacrifice in these attitudes? There may be many who are searching for an easy way to Heaven, an undemanding salvation, a way that does not require commitment or sacrifice. But Jesus did not preach a convenient Gospel; He did not preach one of ease or one without sacrifice. He said, "If any man will come after me, let him deny himself, and take up his cross, and follow me" (Matthew 16:24), and, "Strive to enter in at the strait gate" (Luke 13:24). He instructed, "Yet a little while is the light with you. Walk while ye have the light, lest darkness come upon you" (John 12:35), and, "He that shall endure unto the end, the same shall be saved" (Matthew 24:13). That sounds like sacrifice and effort!

Consider the outcome

Consider the outcome if Philip would have said it was too inconvenient for him to leave a revival and go out into the desert. Would he have shared the Gospel with a man who was hungry for God? As the Good Samaritan walked down the road, what if he had said it was too inconvenient for him to stop and help a man? Would there have been any to give aid, since two men had already passed by? If Peter had said it was too inconvenient for him to leave his prayer time and go speak to Cornelius and those at his house, how would the Gospel of Jesus Christ have been opened to the Gentiles? If someone had decided it was too inconvenient to tell you about Jesus, where would you be? This matter of convenience is serious business; souls are at stake. A convenient time is not promised to any of us.

Matthew 25 gives the account of the ten virgins. Five of them did not take the time to get the full supply of oil; perhaps it was inconvenient. The other five made the effort. What does the parable tell us? When the bridegroom came, the five foolish virgins went searching for oil, but it was too late, because when they returned, the door of opportunity was closed.

An opportunity to prepare

May God help us all to take advantage of the opportunities that we have to prepare to meet Him! Like Felix, many people have heard messages on righteousness and salvation.

Sadly, many have said they would wait for a more convenient time, that they want the Gospel in their own way. They presume that they will have another opportunity to seek God. Yet how will they know when it is their convenient time? Will bells and whistles go off? Will there be all sorts of noise and flashing lights like a game show? Will a sign drop down which says, "This is your convenient time"? In my years as a preacher, I saw literally hundreds of people who had stepped into eternity unexpectedly.

They thought they were going to be alive the next day, but they were not. Untold numbers will be in a lost eternity lamenting that they did not find a convenient time to turn to God. They will mourn the fact that they did not take advantage of the opportunities that were presented to them.

There is absolutely no better time to seek God than now. The Bible says, "Now is the accepted time; behold, now is the day of salvation" (2 Corinthians 6:2). There are souls out in our world who need the Lord. There was a young man in our neighborhood who I tried to minister to and mentor. He was in and out of prison. At times he seemed to be doing well, and then I'd see him with a bottle of alcohol in one hand.

Periodically the Lord would lay a burden on my heart, and I would go around town looking until I found him. I'd invite him so we could talk, and I would challenge him about what he knew of the Gospel. We would pray together, but then in a while he would end up back in prison, saying, "If I had just listened to you!"

One day he made a profound statement that will forever remain in my mind. He said, "I was always taught how to accept Jesus as Savior, but never taught how to make Him Lord of my life." This man had been taught a convenient Gospel, not one of sacrifice and commitment where God has His will in the life. I tried to share the Gospel some more with him and prayed with him. Eventually he said he felt he had the victory and that he was going to move out of our neighborhood. For about a year, I lost track of him.

Then God brought him to my mind, and I felt a renewed burden for him and began to pray for him again. One day I went to the grocery store by our house and ended up looking all over the store for a specific item. I was frustrated at the delay in finding it. Then when I was ready to go, the line at the check-out stand was backed way up. When I finally got through, I hurriedly headed for the door. Just as I got there, this man walked into the other door. When he saw me, he let out a yell and gave me a big hug. He said, "I am so glad to see you! I want to let you know that I've been clean for a year. I'm a fulltime student at the University College." He was still saved! Thank God, this man found out how to make Jesus the Lord of his life.

Share it with others: God is looking for people who will take the time and inconvenience to share the Gospel with others.

He wants people to make a full commitment to Him. Let us make sure that we do not take the Gospel for granted or try to make it into a convenience Gospel. It is a precious Gospel that has been carefully preserved for us down through the years. We ought to treasure it, and not just assume it is always going to be available. Jesus could return at any moment. We want to be vibrantly alive and walking close to God, consistent in our determination to serve Him. Make this your moment to yield yourself completely to God.

Have you ever wondered what the Bible means when it says that David "encouraged himself in the Lord his God" (1 Samuel 30:6)? Difficult times come to everyone—saved or unsaved—but the Christian's response to trials should be markedly different from that of an unbeliever.

How do you respond to troubles in your life? Let's consider David. The first part of this verse says that David was "greatly distressed"—and with good reason. He had been fleeing for his life from King Saul for a number of years and had six hundred men with him who were rebels against Saul's rule. After fleeing from place to place, this group of soldiers and their families had finally found refuge in Ziklag with the Philistines—longtime enemies of Israel.

When the Philistines prepared to fight with the Israelites, the king included David's men as part of his army, but later sent them away at the prompting of his fellow warlords.

David and his men returned to Ziklag, only to find the city burned and their wives and children taken captive by the Amalekites. In the midst of his personal grief (his family, too, had been taken), David began to hear rumors of mutiny among his men and once again feared for his life.

What was David's response to all of this mounting tragedy? 1 Samuel 30 tells us that he and the people that were with him "wept until they had no more power to weep" (verse 4).

But David "encouraged himself in the Lord his God" (verse 6), "enquired at the Lord" (verse 8), and then, with the Lord's blessing, took action and "recovered all that the Amalekites had carried away."

How did a man who was in the depths of grief bring himself to the point where he was able to get clear direction from the Lord and then lead a group of several hundred men—some of whom wanted to kill him—into battle? What exactly does 1 Samuel 30:6 mean when it says that David "encouraged himself in the Lord his God"?

I like to think he sang some of his psalms. He had written a number of them by then. Maybe Psalm 7," . . . My defence is of God, which saveth the upright in heart . . ." or Psalm 31, ". . . Be of good courage, and he shall strengthen your heart, all ye that hope in the Lord . . ." Music can be a powerful source of encouragement. I have found this in my own life as well.

I have a playlist on my iPod called "Promise Songs." These are the songs I listen to over and over when I face the challenges of life. Some were direct promises from the Lord and became spiritual landmarks in my life. Others I have found and purchased for future times when I would need to "encourage myself." Somehow, when combined with a prayer, they never fail to revive my confidence in the Lord and His care for me.

Spiritual songs reassure me that "the God on the mountain is still God in the valley," and "no doubt it'll be alright."

BEARING SPIRITUAL FRUITS

In John chapter 15, Jesus used a fruit-producing vine as an illustration for His disciples. This was one of the few topics He discussed with them between their observance of the Passover in the Upper Room and His prayer in the Garden of Gethsemane. Jesus wanted His disciples to produce spiritual fruit, and He considered this so important that it was one of the last things He talked about with them before His death.

In this spiritual parallel, Jesus identified Himself as the Vine and made it known that He is the source of life for the branches—those who are united with Him. He told them, "I am the true vine, and my Father is the husbandman. Every branch in me that beareth not fruit he taketh away: and every branch that beareth fruit, he purgeth it, that it may bring forth more fruit" (John 15:1-2). We can observe from this statement that if a branch is in the vine, it *is* producing fruit. The gardener (or husbandman) sees to that. If you are "in the Vine" spiritually, you can count on the fact that you are producing fruit. You do not have to be a "super Christian." Jesus said as long as you are connected to Him, you are producing. If you are saved, your life is producing fruit, and it is pleasing to the Lord. Notice that purging, or pruning, is part of how the gardener tends to his vines. In order for those trees to produce the fruit we wanted, it was important for them to be correctly trimmed. Spiritually, there are times when the Lord must cut something from our lives in order for us to produce more fruit.

We should remember His purpose in doing so and submit ourselves to Him, knowing that ultimately we will benefit from the pruning process. We want to produce fruit, so the purging will be worth it in the end.

Jesus went on to tell His disciples, "Now ye are clean through the word which I have spoken unto you. Abide in me, and I in you. As the branch cannot bear fruit of itself, except it abide in the vine; no more can ye, except ye abide in me" (verses 3-4).

When Jesus said that the disciples were "clean," he used the same word that He used when instructing them in the ordinance of foot washing. At that time, Jesus indicated that they were not all clean because Judas, who shortly would betray Him, was among them (see John 13:10-11). By this time, Judas had departed and Jesus stated that all of the remaining disciples were clean, and therefore were able to produce spiritual fruit. The experiences of salvation, entire sanctification, and the baptism of the Holy Spirit are wonderful, and they bring about that connection with the Vine and enable us to begin producing spiritual fruit. But, as Jesus admonished in verse four, in order to continue producing, we must "abide," or remain connected to the Vine.

Ever since the Lord saved me, I deeply appreciate what God did for me back then, but I must maintain my Christian walk. The vine is the source of life. It is only by staying attached to the vine that branches have life and the ability to produce fruit. Jesus said, "He that abideth in me, and I in him, the same bringeth forth much fruit: for without me ye can do nothing" (verse 5). It is not a case of producing smaller fruit, or less of it. Jesus made it clear that without His life flowing through us spiritually, there will be *no* spiritual fruit produced.

Some people try to produce spiritual fruit on their own. They suppose that if they attend church, try to be honest, do good deeds, and live the best life they can live, that will be enough. Those are all good things to do, but it takes more than that— we need to be attached to the Vine! Vines without branches do not produce fruit, and branches without vines do not produce fruit. Fruit is produced when we abide in Him and He abides in us. The Lord gives us the life and power we need to produce fruit.

Jesus went on to describe the tragic results of not being connected to the Vine. He said, "If a man abide not in me, he is cast forth as a branch, and is withered; and men gather them, and cast them into the fire, and they are burned" (verse 6).

A couple of years ago, we had a great storm. It was quite devastating and many branches of trees around our city broke off because of the weight of the wind pressure. Branches that are broken off the vine wither away. They no longer produce fruit. They are dead. Eventually, those dead branches need to be cleared away and burned. So it is spiritually. There will come a day when the Lord will return for those who are in the Vine and bearing fruit.

At that time, the branches that have been broken off and withered will be cast off forever. We don't want that to happen to anyone! Nor does the Lord want that to happen. He wants us all to be attached to the Vine, full of life and producing good fruit. Jesus explained to His disciples the result of spiritual fruit-bearing, telling them, "Herein is my Father glorified, that ye bear much fruit" (verse 8). The fruit of a garden is the glory of the farmer who planted it, tilled it, fertilized it, pruned it, and carefully tended it. You know someone is a good farmer if his land produces much fruit. And the same is true in this spiritual parallel: God is glorified when individuals come into a right relationship with Him and begin producing much fruit in their spiritual lives.

Loving others, responding to those in need, and praying for the spiritually lost are examples of bearing fruit. These evidences of our connection with Christ will be a natural and spontaneous result of that connection, rather than something we try to do in our own strength. Another example is sharing our testimony. If we are abiding in the Vine, we have a testimony, and God is glorified when we share it. The gift of the Holy Spirit empowers us to be better witnesses for the Lord, and helps us produce even more fruit and give more glory to the Father.

The Lord expects much fruit of us. God, the Husbandman, is coming around and inspecting His branches. He is anticipating the fruit.

Are you doing all you can to be a fruitful branch? Are you abiding in Jesus and allowing the Gardener to prune you? Are you showing the Lord that you are His disciple by bearing fruit? You can be! The Lord will bless your life and use you for His glory if you will only let Him!

TO GET YOUR POSESSION YOU DON'T HAVE TO GET POLLUTED

POLLUTION IS nearly everywhere. Men have devised ways of trying to control pollution and to clean up the polluted areas. Even on the church premises, there are trash containers on one corner and more trash containers on another corner. This is because we want to keep down the pollution. If someone puts things out of place, sooner or later another person will come by and put something else out of place. Before long the area will be cluttered and polluted.

Christians need to guard their hearts. Proverbs 4:23 says, "Keep thy heart with all diligence." Spiritual pollution is all around us. The government has taken the Bible and prayer out of our schools. And the schools have been infested with guns, and drugs, and teenage pregnancy. Any time God is removed from an establishment, the door is open for the devil to enter. The church needs to be fervent in prayer.

There are so many dangers all around us. The worst pollution man can come into contact with is pollution in his heart. Even after we are saved, we must guard our hearts. When Satan brings harmful things to us, we have to fight them off and ask the Blood of Jesus to cover us. We cannot allow them to enter our hearts.

If trash were everywhere in the community, it would be because littering had been allowed. Just so, if our hearts are polluted, it is because we have allowed it to happen. Our power is limited, but God's power is unlimited. God deals in things that seem impossible. God deals with nothing. When He spoke things into existence, there was nothing. God just said, "Let there be . . ." and it happened. That is power! That is the kind of God I want to know. With that power, God can speak to the leper and change his spots.

He can take a drunkard, clean him up, and make him a preacher. He can take a jailbird, clip his wings, and he won't go back to jail anymore. He can take a wino and remove the wine bottle from his hand. He can take the dope addict and clean up his veins. The power of God is awesome. With that kind of power, God can keep Christians from the pollution of the world. But we must ask Him to do it, are you going to say with your whole heart give me this mountain?

We must allow Him to control our lives, and not allow the enemy to pollute our hearts. **Keeping your thoughts pure is the ultimate Pollution Solution.**

ARE YOU COMMITTED?

Often "commitment" is not a popular word in our society, but we need commitment in the Gospel. Jesus said, "If any man will come after me, let him deny himself, and take up his cross daily, and follow me" (Luke 9:23). That means if we are going to follow Christ, there is going to be a cross in our lives. The Apostle Paul was committed. He was sold out for Jesus, and he told people about the Gospel wherever he went. Not everybody liked or accepted his commitment. Once, forty people agreed together that they would not eat or drink until they had killed him. Why? Paul was so committed that he was a threat to the enemy. Are we that committed? We have the Gospel today because someone was committed. Someone said yes to the Lord and meant it and we know the truth of the Gospel.

Make a Commitment: Seasons of Life Serve One Another

It is going to take denying ourselves to serve God. If we have to stand alone, we still need to stay committed. In these last days, we are going to need prayer; we are going to need Holy Ghost power to stand for Christ. God will give us all that if we are committed to Him. Christians, on your journey there are seasons. The Bible says, "To every thing there is a season, and a time to every purpose under the heaven" (Ecclesiastes 3:1). Sometimes circumstances in our lives seem to be very out of place, and we may fail to understand what is going on.

However, we must remember that all seasons have a beginning and an end, and the Almighty God has charge of every event and happening in our lives. If we are living according to God's Word, the things that God allows to confront us are meant to be stepping stones to help us reach the inheritance He has for us. At times we may have a season where we feel that we are at the bottom. Even then, we can know that God has already set the limits and the boundaries of the season. Whatever we are experiencing, God is watching. He will help us.

A story is told about an old man who had four sons. At different times he called them individually and sent them about five miles down a path to look at a pear tree. He sent one in the wintertime, another in the springtime, the third in the summertime, and the fourth son in the fall.

In a year's time, when the sons came back to their father, the first son said the tree was dry, and any foliage on it was rotted and hanging down. The second son said, "No, the tree looked nice and beautiful. It had little buds on it and looked as if it wanted to sprout." The third son reported that the tree was full of life and had many blossoms. The fourth son said the tree was full of ripe fruit that looked so good. The father told them, "I know that you all disagree, but you all saw that tree at a different season in its life."

Maybe you are in a wintertime season in your life. Don't give up! If you leave God in a winter season of your life, you will miss the promise of spring, the beautiful summer, and the fulfillment of your fall. Trouble does not last forever; persevere through the difficulties, because better times are coming. Better days lies ahead, you will get your testimony after these trials.

One day, there is going to be a sound made—the sound of the great archangel. When the Trumpet sounds so Christ's Bride can be raptured to be with Him, those who are ready will be delivered from this life. That will be the greatest season of all. Now is the time to prepare for that day!

In a typical classroom setting in our day, when a new subject is to be introduced, the teacher will try to ascertain the prior knowledge of the students. The teacher may do this by asking them a question. Jesus asked His disciples a question that is recorded in John 13:12, "Know ye what I have done to you?" Jesus had taught His followers a whole lot of doctrine, but in the final hours of His life, He was introducing a new ordinance.

We read, "He riseth from supper, and laid aside his garments; and took a towel, and girded himself. After that he poureth water into a bason, and began to wash the disciples' feet, and to wipe them with the towel wherewith he was girded" (John 13:4-5). It was the custom of the Jewish people in those days to wash the feet of their guests so they would feel welcome.

This was the duty of a servant when the guests arrived. Yet, after supper, Christ, as the Master, humbled Himself to wash His disciples' feet. He was giving them an example, teaching them that they were to go out into the world to serve, and they were to serve in humility. He let them know that "the servant is not greater than his lord." If He, the Master, could wash the disciples' feet, they should wash one another's feet.

Jesus wanted the best for His disciples, and He wants the best for us as well. A whole lot of folks in the world today want to be happy; we want to live a happy life. Jesus was trying to let us know that the way to be happy is to be a doer of the Word, to live a holy life, and to be an example of the believers. If we do these things, we will be happy.

Walking With God . . . taking Godly Counsel

THE FIRST PSALM begins, "Blessed is the man that walketh not in the counsel of the ungodly." We want to be careful to seek our help in the right areas. The Bible says that when we have problems in our lives, we should seek out people who have promoted the Gospel and have stood through spiritual tests. Walking in the council of the ungodly will bring misery, but the man who does not do that is blessed. Verse 1 continues, ". . . nor standeth in the way of sinners." On our jobs, in school, around the marketplace, we must rub shoulders with sinners every day, but when it is time to relax, do we seek out and "stand" with those who do not serve God? Yes, we need to witness to those who are not Christians, when we can. I talk to people on the job about sports or other matters, but when the workday is over, I go home to my family. I do not choose to spend my free time fellowshipping with my ungodly co-workers.

That first verse concludes, ". . . nor sitteth in the seat of the scornful." As Christians, why would we want to be involved with a person who is always criticizing or degrading the Gospel? If we choose to "sit" there, to participate in the conversation of the scornful, they will bring us down. We want to take a stand and respond as God wants us to.

The second verse of Psalm 1 says, "But his delight is in the law of the Lord; and in his law doth he meditate day and night." At the end of the day, if you work like I do, you will be looking for your recliner. Yet, even as we relax, we need to delight ourselves in the law of the Lord. Sometimes it is important to pull away from the television screen, even if a favorite team is playing! If we love God, we will read His Word. We need to pick up the Book regularly and see what God has in store for our lives.

When I was young, my father would say, "Men ought always to pray." After I was older and had a job, I wondered, Since I am obligated to give a ten-hour day on this job, how can I get down on my knees and pray all day? But as I read the Bible, it came to me: build an altar in your heart. Build an altar in your mind. We need to meditate on God's Word day and night. We cannot meditate on God's Word if we do not know what is in it. We can meditate if we read it last night, and if we read it this morning. What is the promised result if we do so? "Whatsoever he doeth shall prosper" (Psalm 1:3). In Christ we can receive joy and peace and happiness in this present world and then the glory of Heaven.

WHAT DOES IT MEAN to walk with God? You might have walked with the rich. You might have walked with the well-to-do. You might have walked with the unfortunate, but if you haven't walked with God, you haven't walked at all. The Bible says, "And Enoch walked with God and he was not; for God took him" (Genesis 5:24). Man is made to walk and talk with God. Man was created and placed in the Garden of Eden, and God came down in the cool of the day and walked with him. God walked and talked with Adam many times in the garden. But after he sinned, Adam covered himself and hid among the trees. You cannot cover sin. It has to be confessed and repented of.

God meant for us to walk and talk with him in this life. I don't know how we can get out of this life and into Heaven without walking and talking with our Maker. We don't know our way out. But if we walk and talk with God, He knows the way. Enoch walked with God, and God took him. Genesis 6:9 says, "Noah walked with God," and God gave him the blueprint letting him know how to build the ark for the saving of his family. God told Abraham, "Walk before me, and be thou perfect" (Genesis 17:1). I can just see Abraham when he prayed. He knew his nephew Lot was down in that wicked city of Sodom. Abraham went before God and said, "If You can find fifty righteous, will You spare the city?" Then, in case fifty could not be found, Abraham prayed right on, and Lot's life was spared because of Abraham's intercession.

Are you walking with God? God means for us to walk with Him, talk with Him. The only way we can find joy in this life is to walk with God. He is coming for those who are ready and walking with Him. I don't know the way out of this world, but God does. If we walk with Him, He will someday take us to Heaven. However, before the roll is call up yonder He will take away every giants and give us our possessions here on earth, He promised giving to his children all the hidden treasures of the heathen

Checking Your Load!

A preacher's job is to show you the way of God's salvation. You alone must make the decision to ask Jesus to come and dwell in your heart. That is the rule God has laid down. Our responsibility to God does not end when we back up to the dock and load on salvation. No, we do not get saved and just fly off to Heaven. Between conversion and Heaven, some real living goes on, and Jesus expects us to carry the load faithfully until He calls us Home. To do that, we must continually check our loads. Paul said, "Examine yourselves, whether ye be in the faith; prove your own selves" (2 Corinthians 13:5).

We must watch that we secure the load well. If the load is placed on the Tail gate, when we hit the bumps and climb the hills, we may lose our cargo. Get a good grip on salvation. Get it all the way in and fasten it down. Don't just come to the altar to pray and let somebody pat you on the back and say, "You've got it!" Instead, pray until you feel a change inside. Pray until God regenerates your heart. Check your load and be sure you have the goods. Be sure you are saved and that it is working in your life. If we have real salvation, pure religion, undefiled before God, it will see us through this world. It will keep us steady. If you start feeling shaky, you had better check your load, be sure you still have it, and that your salvation didn't fall by the wayside. There is a devil out there, and he will take your salvation in a moment if given the opportunity.

In chapter 25 of the Book of Matthew we find the parable of the ten virgins. We are told that five of them were wise and five were foolish. They were to wait for the bridegroom with their lamps burning. But when at midnight the cry rang out, "Behold, the bridegroom cometh; go ye out to meet him" (Matthew 2 5:6), the lamps of the foolish virgins were not burning anymore. They begged the wise to give them some of their oil, but it was not something they could share. The foolish virgins had not bothered to check their load. When the flames failed and darkness replaced the light, they knew they were caught unprepared.

They were concerned about the state of their cargo, but it was too late for them. While they ran to find more oil, the bridegroom came, the wise entered in, and the foolish virgins were left out in the cold. When you backed up to the dock of Christianity, did you load on salvation? Did you pray until Christ came in and His Spirit bore witness with your spirit that you were a child of God? One of the things I learned when I was taking driving classes was that every morning you check the oil and the water. The fuel speaks for itself. I encourage you every day to pray through, know where you are, know that you are still saved, that you are still sanctified, and that the fire of the Holy Ghost is burning in your soul.

Be sure there is no envy or strife in your heart. Daily living can bring that to you, even between brethren. The devil tries to brew up contention between church people. Don't let it stay there! The Bible says, "Anger resteth in the bosom of fools" (Ecclesiastes 7:9). If something aggravates you, pray it through. Whether a Christian or a sinner is responsible for it, pray it through. If you don't like what the pastor says, pray it through. Don't be caught too late like those foolish virgins. Check your load now while the door of mercy is yet ajar.

If you are saying to the lord 'Give me this mountain' 'It is vital to make sure your relationship with God is up to date. checking your thoughts.

The price that was paid for us to possess our possessions was the highest price that has ever been paid for anything. God wants us to realize that!

It is the Blood of Jesus Christ and because of that we can boast, without a shadow of a doubt, that we are His and that we are worth something. God was willing to pay the highest price ever for us. God was willing to let His Son go to the cross for us, willing to let the Blood flow from Jesus' side because He loves us. Money couldn't do it for you and me—Jesus Christ had to give His life. We can't get any more valuable than that! God knew from the beginning of time that He would have to give His only Son so that you and I might be able to enjoy salvation. When it came time for Jesus to give His life, He willingly came to the world, knowing that He would die for our sins. The price that was paid for us was the highest price that has ever been paid for anything.

God wants us to realize that! Think of how we cherish things that we deem as priceless. Undoubtedly, we do all we can to ensure that they are kept in good shape. If God has deemed us important enough to die for, we should cherish our salvation. We also need to show God that we appreciate the price He paid for us. To do this, we need not only to be saved, but to be sanctified holy and to receive the baptism of the Holy Spirit. And it doesn't stop there. If it means giving up worldly friends or questionable activities, we must do it. Whatever it takes to stay close to God, we need to do. We must never think of ourselves as being of little value.

Consider the price that was paid for us, and you will know how much God thinks we are worth! He gave His best that we might belong to Him.

Have you ever questioned how important you were? There are many people who don't think they are worth much, but we need to stop and recognize that we are worth something. In fact, in God's eyes, we are incredibly priceless. In 1 Peter 1:18-19 we read, "Forasmuch as ye know that ye were not redeemed with corruptible things, as silver and gold, from your vain conversation received by tradition from your fathers; but with the precious blood of Christ, . . ." We have been bought with a price. To this world, we may not look like much, but in God's sight we are very precious. God paid a premium price for us. The reason God paid such a price is because He saw something in us—He saw who we could be, not just who we were. There's a "red line" running through the people of God.

Let me close this chapter with the salutation and great revelation of Apostle Peter: 2 Peter 1:1-4. To those who have obtained like precious faith with us by the righteousness of our God and Savior Jesus Christ: Grace and peace be multiplied to you in the knowledge of God and of Jesus our Lord, as His divine power has given to us all things that pertain to life and godliness, through the knowledge of Him who called us by glory and virtue, by which have been given to us exceedingly great and precious promises, that through these you may be partakers of the divine nature, having escaped the corruption that is in the world through lust."

The price that was paid for us was the highest price that has ever been paid for anything. He did not spared His only begotten Son and therefore will freely give us all our request in accordance with His word just as He gave Caleb that mountain hill country, He will do for us today what He did in times past, He never changes and He is not man that would lie, God wants us to realize that!

CHAPTER FIVE

TAKING A CLOSER LOOK INTO THE MIRROR

Therefore, putting aside all filthiness and all that remains of wickedness, in humility receive the word implanted, which is able to save your souls. But prove yourselves doers of the word, and not merely hearers who delude themselves. For if anyone is a hearer of the word and not a doer, he is like a man who looks at his natural face in a mirror; for once he has looked at himself and gone away, he has immediately forgotten what kind of person he was. But one who looks intently at the perfect law, the law of liberty, and abides by it, not having become a forgetful hearer but an effectual doer, this man will be blessed in what he does. If anyone thinks himself to be religious, and yet does not bridle his tongue but deceives his own heart, this man's religion is worthless. Pure and undefiled religion in the sight of our God and Father is this: to visit orphans and widows in their distress, and to keep oneself unstained by the world. James 1:21-27.

Then Joseph could not control himself before all those who stood by him, and he cried, "Have everyone go out from me." So there was no man with him when Joseph made himself known to his brothers. He wept so loudly that the Egyptians heard it, and the household of Pharaoh heard of it. Then Joseph said to his brothers, "I am Joseph! Is my father still alive?" But his brothers could not answer him, for they were dismayed at his presence. Then Joseph said to his brothers, "Please come closer to me." And they came closer. And he said, "I am your brother Joseph, whom you sold into Egypt. "Now do not be grieved or angry with yourselves, because you sold me here, for God sent me before you to preserve life. "For the famine has been in the land these two years, and there are still five years in which there will be neither plowing nor harvesting. "God sent me before you to preserve for you a remnant in the earth, and to keep you alive by a great deliverance. "Now, therefore, it was not you who sent me here, but God; and He has made me a father to Pharaoh and lord of all his household and ruler over all the land of Egypt. "Hurry and go up to my father, and say to him, 'Thus says your son Joseph, "God has made me lord of all Egypt; come down to me, do not delay.

GENESIS 45:1-9.

Do you know that Joseph emphasized his dreams of future grandeur beyond just relating it to his family? How hard-hearted would Joseph's brothers have to have been in order to sell their blood brother into slavery? Did you know that the same dreams that caused Joseph trouble as a youth served his best interest and stabilized his faith through the dark, difficult years of imprisonment? These are a few of the things we will examine about Joe and a couple of others in this chapter. (the likes of Moses/Zippo rah, king David, Queen Esther, Prophets Elijah, Elisha and Balaam)

Joseph carries forward another generation. When Moses recorded Israel's history in the book of Exodus, years after Jacob's and Joseph's lifetimes, Joseph's story received the most thorough treatment. Joseph was a dreamer. Early in life these dreams caused him trouble, but later his dreams encouraged him to maintain his integrity and holiness, helping him through trouble. He eventually even interpreted dreams for others. Joseph knew the power of a dream. However, **Joseph's Dreams Went to His Head** In his youth Joseph became proud. He allowed his dreams to make him believe he was better than his brothers. Joseph's father questioned his favorite son, because Joseph seemed to believe he was superior even to his parents.

As you know Joseph had a dream, and when he told it to his brothers, they hated him all the more. He said to them, "Listen to this dream I had: We were binding sheaves of grain out in the field when suddenly my sheaf rose and stood upright, while your sheaves gathered around mine and bowed down to it." His brothers said to him, "Do you intend to reign over us? Will you actually rule us?" And they hated him all the more because of his dream and what he had said.

Then he had another dream, and he told it to his brothers. "Listen," he said, "I had another dream, and this time the sun and moon and eleven stars were bowing down to me." When he told his father as well as his brothers, his father rebuked him and said, "What is this dream you had? Will your mother and I and your brothers actually come and bow down to the ground before you?" His brothers were jealous of him, but his father kept the matter in mind. (Genesis 37:5-11)

The Hebrew form of the word translated "told" in verse 5 is an accentuated form of the verb. In the Hebrew language, a grammatical addition to a verb changes the nuance to a stronger form with the same meaning. For example, that same grammatical addition makes the verb *kill* become "slaughter." In Joseph's case, *told* becomes "told with emphasis" or "bragged." In other words, young Joseph did not just tell his brothers about his dreams, he told them with apparent boasting. This paints a different picture than if Joseph had humbly related his dreams in a neutral manner. Joseph had not yet learned God's purpose for dreams.

Dreams give hope, focus, and direction for our energies. Energy without a dream is frantic and meaningless activity. Dreams hold us on target, inspire us to action. Dreams give us healthy ambition and motivate us. Dreams are not given to us by God to inflate our egos, but to encourage us to accomplish things for Him. Dreams are often from God, as were these two of Joseph's. But dreams are not always from God; sometimes they are the product of human imagination. It is far better to adopt a "wait and see" attitude toward dreams than to become puffed up and proud because of them. Let's learn from Joseph's error. Even if our dreams are from God, humility is the wiser attitude as we wait to see if the dream is from God or not. Give God your dreams, and if He gives them back to you, they are yours; if He does not, they never were. When dreams get in our spirit, they can do us good and lead us forward, but when they go to our heads, they can become big problems for others and for ourselves.

Joseph's Brothers Sold Him into Slavery

While running an errand for his father, Joseph approached his brothers. As he did, they plotted against him. "Here comes that dreamer!" they said to each other. "Come now, let's kill him and throw him into one of these cisterns and say that a ferocious animal devoured him. Then we'll see what comes of his dreams." When Reuben heard this, he tried to rescue him from their hands. "Let's not take his life," he said. "Don't shed any blood. Throw him into this cistern here in the wilderness, but don't lay a hand on him." Reuben said this to rescue him from them and take him back to his father. So when Joseph came to his brothers, they stripped him of his robe—the richly ornamented robe he was wearing—and they took him and threw him into the cistern. The cistern was empty; there was no water in it. As they sat down to eat their meal, they looked up and saw a caravan of Ishmaelites coming from Gilead. Their camels were loaded with spices, balm and myrrh, and they were on their way to take them down to Egypt. Judah said to his brothers, "What will we gain if we kill our brother and cover up his blood? Come, let's sell him to the Ishmaelites and not lay our hands on him; after all, he is our brother, our own flesh and blood." His brothers agreed. So when the Midianite merchants came by, his brothers pulled Joseph up out of the cistern and sold him for twenty shekels of silver to the Ishmaelites, who took him to Egypt. (Genesis 37:19-28)

The story of Joseph includes a vicious betrayal by blood brothers. Those who sold Joseph into slavery were not his enemies or even strangers; they were his family. Later in the narrative the brothers reflected on their betrayal. They said to one another, "Surely we are being punished because of our brother. We saw how distressed he was when he pleaded with us for his life, but we would not listen; that's why this distress has come on us" (Genesis 32:21). Joseph's character was about to be tested. He was a teenager when these developments occurred, and not until he was thirty years of age did he become prime minister of Egypt. With this incident, thirteen years of character development began for seventeen-year-old Joseph. When reverses occur, do not assume all is lost. God is at work—working on you, perhaps.

Joseph Succeeded in Management and Resisted Temptation

Satan will try to kill, steal, and destroy your dream. You will be tested as you wait on God to fulfill your dream. Joseph's trust in God, after his character was refined, made him a loving son, magnanimous brother, and powerful national leader. Joseph's God, coupled with faith, morality, and character on Joseph's part, led him to success and the fulfillment of his dreams.

When enduring the temptation of Potiphar's wife, Joseph gave her a wise response: "How then could I do such a wicked thing and sin against God?" (Genesis 39:9). Joseph would not compromise his morality. Now Joseph had been taken down to Egypt. Potiphar, an Egyptian who was one of Pharaoh's officials, the captain of the guard, bought him from the Ishmaelites who had taken him there. The Lord was with Joseph so that he prospered, and he lived in the house of his Egyptian master. When his master saw that the Lord was with him and that the Lord gave him success in everything he did, Joseph found favor in his eyes and became his attendant. Potiphar put him in charge of his household, and he entrusted to his care everything he owned. From the time he put him in charge of his household and of all that he owned, the Lord blessed the household of the Egyptian because of Joseph. The blessing of the Lord was on everything Potiphar had, both in the house and in the field. So Potiphar left everything he had in Joseph's care; with Joseph in charge, he did not concern himself with anything except the food he ate. Now Joseph was well-built and handsome, and after a while his master's wife took notice of Joseph and said, "Come to bed with me!" But he refused. "With me in charge," he told her, "my master does not concern himself with anything in the house; everything he owns he has entrusted to my care. No one is greater in this house than I am. My master has withheld nothing from me except you, because you are his wife. How then could I do such a wicked thing and sin against God?" And though she spoke to Joseph day after day, he refused to go to bed with her or even be with her. One day he went into the house to attend to his duties, and none of the household servants was inside. She caught him by his cloak and said, "Come to bed with me!" But he left his cloak in her hand and ran out of the house. When she saw that he had left his cloak in her hand and had run out of the house, she called her household servants. "Look," she said to them, "this Hebrew has been brought to us to make sport of us! He came in here to sleep with me, but I screamed. When he heard me scream for help, he left his cloak beside me and ran out of the house." She kept his cloak beside her until his master came home. Then she told him this story: "That Hebrew slave you brought us came to me to make sport of me. But as soon as I screamed for help, he left his cloak beside me and ran out of the house." (Genesis 39:1-18)

If men and women of God will keep their faith focused on the fulfillment of their God-given dreams, it will help them through temptations. Satan can only kill, steal, and destroy when we yield to his temptations. Knowing that sin is against the God we love gives us power to resist.

God Protected Joseph and Gave Him More Success in Prison

The bible does not say that Potiphar was angry *with Joseph*, just that he was angry. Potiphar would have known all too well the nature of his own intimate relationship with his wife. He knew his wife's moral level and was also aware of Joseph's high moral character. If Potiphar had believed Joseph were guilty of his wife's accusation, he would have had Joseph killed. Since Potiphar only put Joseph in prison, we may conjecture that Potiphar knew Joseph was innocent. Joseph's reputation was already at work for him. Maybe the prison bars were not so much intended to keep Joseph in, but to keep Potiphar's wife out. When his master heard the story his wife told him, saying, "This is how your slave treated me," he burned with anger. Joseph's master took him and put him in prison, the place where the king's prisoners were confined. But while Joseph was there in the prison, the Lord was with him; he showed him kindness and granted him favor in the eyes of the prison warden. So the warden put Joseph in charge of all those held in the prison, and he was made responsible for all that was done there. The warden paid no attention to anything under Joseph's care, because the Lord was with Joseph and gave him success in whatever he did. (Genesis 39:19-23)

Joseph's reputation for morality saved him. As a Christian of influence in the body of Christ, you too will experience accusations. The best defense is holiness, morality, ethical behavior, trustworthiness, and honesty. Arm yourself with these in advance, as Joseph did.

Joseph Developed Further and Even Served Others in Prison: We might think that Joseph had already endured enough, been tested sufficiently, and proven himself true. But

God was not finished developing him. Some time later, the cupbearer and the baker of the king of Egypt offended their master, the king of Egypt. Pharaoh was angry with his two officials, the chief cupbearer and the chief baker, and put them in custody in the house of the captain of the guard, in the same prison where Joseph was confined. The captain of the guard assigned them to Joseph, and he attended them. After they had been in custody for some time, each of the two men—the cupbearer and the baker of the king of Egypt, who were being held in prison—had a dream the same night, and each dream had a meaning of its own. (Genesis 40:1-5)

When his fellow prisoners asked for an interpretation of their dreams, Joseph could easily have responded by saying, "Ha! Dreams. They don't mean anything." But he did not. Joseph knew dreams could have meanings, and he interpreted their dreams for them. The king's cupbearer received a good interpretation for his dream. When the chief baker saw that Joseph had given a favorable interpretation, he said to Joseph, "I too had a dream: On my head were three baskets of bread. In the top basket were all kinds of baked goods for Pharaoh, but the birds were eating them out of the basket on my head." "This is what it means," Joseph said. "The three baskets are three days. Within three days Pharaoh will lift off your head and impale your body on a pole. And the birds will eat away your flesh." Now the third day was Pharaoh's birthday, and he gave a feast for all his officials. He lifted up the heads of the chief cupbearer and the chief baker in the presence of his officials: he restored the chief cupbearer to his position, so that he once again put the cup into Pharaoh's hand—but he impaled the chief baker, just as Joseph had said to them in his interpretation.

The chief cupbearer, however, did not remember Joseph; he forgot him. (Genesis 40:16-23) This further delay would have been a difficult test for Joseph. He was in Egypt because his brothers had sold him, in prison on false charges, forgotten by a prison mate whom he had helped. Would it ever end? Yes, it would. Two years later, when Pharaoh had a dream that no one could interpret (or because the meaning was so bad that no one had the courage to interpret it), the stage was set. Joseph had been humbled, mellowed, tried, tested, and proven. He was ready. If Joseph had not endured until this juncture, he would not have been able to seize the opportunity that came his way in a timely manner.

What events surround you today? What is happening in your neighborhood, village, city, and nation? What opportunities might the Lord be preparing for you at the same time He is preparing you for them? Remember Joseph and stay faithful.

In God's Time Joseph Received a Life-Changing Opportunity Sovereign opportunities are providentially arranged. No human has the power to appear to another in a dream. No one could make Pharaoh have a certain kind of dream. No one can know the future or declare what will be and then make it happen the way God can. Christians who follow Joseph's model also follow the God Joseph trusted.

Then Joseph said to Pharaoh, "The dreams of Pharaoh are one and the same. God has revealed to Pharaoh what he is about to do. The seven good cows are seven years, and the seven good heads of grain are seven years; it is one and the same dream. The seven lean, ugly cows that came up afterward are seven years, and so are the seven worthless heads of grain scorched by the east wind: They are seven years of famine. "It is just as

I said to Pharaoh: God has shown Pharaoh what he is about to do. Seven years of great abundance are coming throughout the land of Egypt, but seven years of famine will follow them. Then all the abundance in Egypt will be forgotten, and the famine will ravage the land. The abundance in the land will not be remembered, because the famine that follows it will be so severe. The reason the dream was given to Pharaoh in two forms is that the matter has been firmly decided by God, and God will do it soon." (Genesis 41:25-32)

Joseph told the king the meaning of the dream. His assignment was fulfilled. But Joseph did not stop there. He went beyond the requested interpretation of the dream and counseled the king regarding what to do about the problem. Joseph had an answer for a question that had not yet occurred to Pharaoh. Have you learned to anticipate questions and have an answer ready? This is a fine mark of a leader—whether in the military, academia, business, church leadership, or even the family. It is one thing to evaluate, analyze, or articulate the nature of a problem. It is quite another to be prepared to offer a concrete, practical, and workable solution.

Joseph did not have much time to develop a plan, but he seized the moment and rose to the occasion. He suggested the administrative strategy that would guide the Egyptian commodities policy for the next fourteen years, including the food crisis that loomed ahead. He was ready. Joseph suggested to the king:

"And now let Pharaoh look for a discerning and wise man and put him in charge of the land of Egypt. Let Pharaoh appoint commissioners over the land to take a fifth of the harvest of Egypt during the seven years of abundance. They should collect all the food of these good years that are coming and store up the grain under the authority of Pharaoh, to be kept in the cities for food. This food should be held in reserve for the country, to be used during the seven years of famine that will come upon Egypt, so that the country may not be ruined by the famine."

The plan seemed good to Pharaoh and to all his officials. So Pharaoh asked them, "Can we find anyone like this man, one in whom is the spirit of God?" Then Pharaoh said to Joseph, "Since God has made all this known to you, there is no one so discerning and wise as you." (Genesis 41:33-39)

Joseph's hour had arrived. Glory, he's about to get what has stood before him for years like mountain, his hour of revelation and glorification had now come. He had been humbled and stretched as he waited on God through discouraging trials. Now he had the wisdom needed for that hour. He was ready. Will you be ready when your hour arrives?

Joseph Was not Vindictive, but Recognized God's Providence

Forgiveness is a mark of greatness. The foolish always try to prove they are right, seek to be vindicated, and desire to be recognized or honored. The mellowed and humbled Joseph was no longer bragging about his dreams and proudly proclaiming his superiority. He was kind, loving, and understanding. Those are the marks of great character. When famine overtook the land of Canaan, Jacob sent his sons to Egypt to buy food on two different occasions. Joseph recognized them both times, but did not immediately reveal that he was their brother. Then Joseph could no longer control himself before all his attendants, and he cried out, "Have everyone leave my presence!" So there was no one with Joseph when he made himself known to his brothers. And he wept so loudly that the Egyptians heard him, and Pharaoh's household heard about it. Joseph said to his brothers, "I am Joseph! Is my father still living?" But his brothers were not able to answer him, because they were terrified at his presence. Then Joseph said to his brothers, "Come close to me." When they had done so, he said, "I am your brother Joseph, the one you sold into Egypt! And now, do not be distressed and do not be angry with yourselves for selling me here, because it was to save lives that God sent me ahead of you. For two years now there has been famine in the land, and for the next five years there will be no plowing and reaping. But God sent me ahead of you to preserve for you a remnant on earth and to save your lives by a great deliverance. "So then, it was not you who sent me here, but God. He made me father to Pharaoh, lord of his entire household and ruler of all Egypt. Now hurry back to my father and say to him, 'This is what your son Joseph says: God has made me lord of all Egypt. Come down to me; don't delay. You shall live in the region of Goshen and be near me—you, your children and grandchildren, your flocks and herds, and all you have. I will provide for you there, because five years of famine are still to come. Otherwise you and your household and all who belong to you will become destitute.'" (Genesis 45:1-11)

Joseph recognized that God had worked providentially through the betrayal of his brothers, the temptation by his boss's seductive wife, the unjust prison years, and his successful administrative years as Egypt's prime minister. God can use those who recognize His handiwork. Those who blame others and carry grudges are not good tools in God's hands. Those whose character is a reflection of His compassionate, forgiving, and gracious heart, those who are easy to get along with and are easily entreated, are those who best represent Him. Those are the tools He uses the most. Strive to be that kind of tool in God's hands.

A Lesson Regarding Being as Opposed to Position

I wonder if Jesus had Abraham's descendants in mind when He said, "The last shall be first, and the first last" (Matthew 19:30). Abraham's son Isaac was elevated above Ishmael, the older. Although Jacob was Isaac's second-born, he became greater than his brother Esau. In the next generation, Jacob's eleventh son became ruler of the family. And Joseph's second-born, Ephraim, was elevated above his older brother, Manasseh. Now Israel's eyes were failing because of old age, and he could hardly see. So Joseph brought his sons close to him, and his father kissed them and embraced them. Israel said to Joseph, "I never expected to see your face again, and now God has allowed me to see your children too." Then Joseph removed them from Israel's knees and bowed down with his face to the ground. And Joseph took both of them, Ephraim on his right toward Israel's left hand and Manasseh on his left toward Israel's right hand, and brought them close to him. But Israel reached out his right hand and put it on Ephraim's head, though he was the younger, and crossing his arms, he put his left hand on Manasseh's head, even though Manasseh was the firstborn. Then he blessed Joseph and said, "May the God before whom my fathers Abraham and Isaac walked faithfully, the God who has been my shepherd all my life to this day, the Angel who has delivered me from all harm—may he bless these boys. May they be called by my name and the names of my fathers Abraham and Isaac, and may they increase greatly on the earth." When Joseph saw his father placing his right hand on Ephraim's head he was displeased; so he took hold of his father's hand to move it from Ephraim's head to Manasseh's head. Joseph said to him, "No, my father, this one is the firstborn; put your right hand on his head." But his father refused and said, "I know, my son, I know. He too will become a people, and he too will become great. Nevertheless, his younger brother will be greater than he, and his descendants will become a group of nations." He blessed them that day and said, "In your name will Israel pronounce this blessing: 'May God make you like Ephraim and Manasseh.'" So he put Ephraim ahead of Manasseh. (Genesis 48:10-20)

Let no man or woman called and chosen by God regret, fret, or in any way concern him or herself with position or sequence among siblings within his or her family. God looks at the character of a person, not the position. Character is superior to position any day. Be what God wants you to be and He will use you how He wants to use you. "Who are you?" is a more important question than "Where are you?" "What is your character?" is a greater issue than "What is your rank?" The answer to "What are you?" is far more important than the answer to "What is your title?"

Joseph Forgave Those Who Had Treated Him Unfairly

After their father, Jacob, was no longer present to keep the peace among the family, the older brothers felt it necessary to guarantee their safety before the unjustly treated and offended Joseph. Joseph's brothers had witnessed their father's deep, ongoing, excessive grief over the "death" of Joseph. Perhaps they had not forgiven themselves. That could be part of the reason they fabricated a story to protect themselves. When Joseph's brothers saw that their father was dead, they said, "What if Joseph holds a grudge against us and pays us back for all the wrongs we did to him?" So they sent word to Joseph, saying, "Your father left these instructions before he died: 'This is what you are to say to Joseph: I ask you to forgive your brothers the sins and the wrongs they committed in treating you so badly.' Now please forgive the sins of the servants of the God of your father." When their message came to him, Joseph wept. His brothers then came and threw themselves down before him. "We are your slaves," they said. But Joseph said to them, "Don't be afraid. Am I in the place of God? You intended to harm me, but God intended it for good to accomplish what is now being done, the saving of many lives. So then, don't be afraid. I will provide for you and your children." And he reassured them and spoke kindly to them. (Genesis 50:15-21)

Joseph had already put any idea of revenge so far out of his mind that he was grieved that his brothers even thought he might still carry a grudge. In character he was head and shoulders above his brothers. Someone who carries grudges is small in character. People who are big in character release those who have injured them. How you treat those who treat you well does not reveal much about your character. How you treat those who cause you damage is a true test of your character.

Joseph Looked Forward to God's Future for Israel: By faith Joseph anticipated God's eternal purpose for the nation of Israel just as his father, Jacob, had. We may deduce this through the instructions Joseph gave his family regarding what to do with his body. His last wish was forward—looking. Joseph stayed in Egypt, along with all his father's family. He lived a hundred and ten years and saw the third generation of Ephraim's children. Also the children of Makir son of Manasseh were placed at birth on Joseph's knees. Then Joseph said to his brother Israelites, "I am about to die. But God will surely come to your aid and take you up out of this land to the land he promised on oath to Abraham, Isaac and Jacob." And Joseph made the Israelites swear an oath and said, "God will surely come to your aid, and then you must carry my bones up from this place." (Genesis 50:22-25)

The sovereignty, greatness, wisdom, and excellence of our God is shown in many ways, and human history is one of them. The unfolding of the trans-generational plan of God for the nation of Israel is impossible to explain any other way than the direct work of God among people. How else could prophets have predicted millenniums ago that the nation of Israel would once again be gathered to its own land after centuries of dispersion? The events in the Holy Land since 1948 are a fulfillment of God's plan for His people. Jacob and Joseph wanted to be buried there and instructed their families to take their remains back there. No other rationale can be given than that they saw into the future and knew God had a plan for their family to become a nation. As you read the Hebrew prophets, notice how often they refer to the restoration and re-gathering of God's people Israel to their Promised Land. Watching the unfolding history of Israel today enables us to know what time it is in God's plan for the nations. We are indeed living in the last days. Jesus will soon return to earth and set up His kingdom. Those who treasure this hope and look to the future with expectation share in the spirit and blessing of Jacob and Joseph. The prophets Ezekiel and Daniel also saw clearly into the distant future and recorded for us the fulfillment of God's glorious plan for the human race. A strong eschatology (the doctrine of future things) is a good basis for the Christian's hope. It is also a firm foundation for character development. The Christian with a clear sense of what God is doing in the world has kingdom-related motivation that favorably impacts his or her life, behavior, ministry, and leadership.

Beloved, What unfair frame-ups similar to Joseph's have you experienced, and how is God using them to develop you? Can you identify any way(s) in which you can serve others while you are in "prison" developing yourself for God? Does Joseph's steadfastness during his prison years have any lesson(s) for you as you seek God and wait for Him to use you more influentially? Can you see the greatness in Joseph's character in the noble way in which he forgave his brothers? How will you forgive those who have hurt you? Have you ever been distressed over your position when you should have been concerned about what kind of character you were developing and who you were becoming? What are you doing to make certain that you are forward-looking and expectant rather than backward-looking and despondent?

MOSES THE PROPHET OF LIBERATION:
THUS SAYS THE LORD LET MY PEOPLE GO

The LORD said, "I have indeed seen the misery of my people in Egypt. I have heard them crying out because of their slave drivers, and I am concerned about their suffering. So I have come down to rescue them from the hand of the Egyptians and to bring them up out of that land into a good and spacious land, a land flowing with milk and honey—the home of the Canaanites, Hittites, Amorites, Perizzites, Hivites and Jebusites. And now the cry of the Israelites has reached me, and I have seen the way the Egyptians are oppressing them. So now, go. I am sending you to Pharaoh to bring my people the Israelites out of Egypt." But Moses said to God, "Who am I, that I should go to Pharaoh and bring the Israelites out of Egypt?" And God said, "I will be with you. And this will be the sign to you that it is I who have sent you: When you have brought the people out of Egypt, you will worship God on this mountain." Moses said to God, "Suppose I go to the Israelites and say to them, 'The God of your fathers has sent me to you,' and they ask me, 'What is his name?' Then what shall I tell them?" God said to Moses, "I AM WHO I AM. This is what you are to say to the Israelites: 'I AM has sent me to you.'" God also said to Moses, "Say to the Israelites, 'The LORD, the God of your fathers—the God of Abraham, the God of Isaac and the God of Jacob—has sent me to you.' This is my name forever, the name by which I am to be remembered from generation to generation. Exodus 3:7-16

Do you know that our source of information about Moses is Moses himself? And he tells us the bad as well as the good. Did you know that Moses made a serious error that cost him his opportunity to lead the Israelites into the Promised Land? Are you aware that Moses tried several times to get God to change His position on the issue of his entry into Canaan, all to no avail? These lessons are coming up as we look closely in to lives and times of the great liberation legendary leader Moses.

Moses was the first leader of the nation of Israel. His life was a mixture of successes and disappointments. His successes greatly outnumbered his failures, yet because of his mistakes he did not experience all the privileges he might have otherwise enjoyed. The lives of Abraham, Moses, Joshua, David, and Elijah all contain lessons about how to lead God's people. Each of these men had a failure that limited his usefulness to God. We can learn from both their successes and their failures.

In this chapter, rather than look at all of Moses' dramatic, influential, and illustrious life, we will draw important lessons by examining just one of his failures and its unfortunate consequences.

Moses Models Transparency and Tells It Like It Is: Moses himself wrote the story of his anger in the wilderness of Zin. He was willing to tell of his weaknesses and failures just as readily as he told of his great accomplishments. Moses did not paint an idealistic picture of himself. He did not avoid the narratives that show his vulnerability. Yet he is still highly honored by Jews and Christians as one of God's great leaders. The works of God through us do not depend on our being perfect. The fact that God skillfully uses flawed human tools shows us more about God and His greatness than it does about any requirement of strength or wisdom necessary in the man or woman God uses. In telling the full story, Moses gives us hope that even though we have faults and weaknesses, God can use us.

Many Christians believe they cannot let other people, especially unbelievers, see any weaknesses or faults in their lives. They believe self-disclosures will make people turn away from them and from God if they find out Christians are less than perfect. This contributes to a misunderstanding of the grace of God. The people Christians know may begin to think that God demands perfection and will not tolerate any weakness or failure. As a result, they think that God will disqualify them as Christians if they do something wrong. Or they may consider themselves second—or third-rate Christians. People need to know that failure is a normal part of our human existence and that God understands that. He is willing to forgive and help us continue growing to maturity.

When a Christian fails in some way, he or she should not attempt to hide from other people the fact that he or she is weak. If we admit our weaknesses and failures within the context of demonstrating God's grace for a repentant sinner, people will take courage that God will still love and forgive them if they fail. For a Christian to publicly show vulnerability and weakness helps our hearers see that we recognize our imperfections. Admitting our sins creates an atmosphere in which others may feel more willing to admit theirs. Rarely will anyone be discouraged by our confessions; more likely they will appreciate our honesty. Naturally, we should not be too explicit when confessing our weaknesses. We should not appear to be relishing or enjoying the memory of a sin or failure. Let's avoid making sin seem attractive or interesting.

Human Beings Have Great Needs: In the first month the whole Israelite community arrived at the Desert of Zin, and they stayed at Kadesh. There Miriam died and was buried. Now there was no water for the community, and the people gathered in opposition to Moses and Aaron. (Numbers 20:1-2) All human beings are needy. That is why God called us to minister to others. He selects and uses specific human "tools" to meet the needs of His people. When the people we serve irritate us, we should remember that if they were perfect they would not need us; God would not have called us to assist them. Because people have needs, we have opportunities to be useful. The man or woman of God, as a tool in the hands of God, can be used to effectively meet other people's needs. God could meet their needs directly, but He often uses a human instrument to do it. This is cause for joy in being useful rather than a reason for complaint on our part. We should be honored to experience the joy of usefulness and service.

The people of Israel had a genuine need. They were thirsty and wanted water. People today are also thirsty—thirsty for the water of life, which is Jesus. Even years after someone begins drinking of the water of salvation, the man or woman of God still longs to drink the waters of God. Our thirst continues and even grows the longer we walk with God. David said, "As the deer pants for streams of water, so my soul pants for you, my God. My soul thirsts for God, for the living God. When can I go and meet with God?" (Psalm 42:1-2). Isaiah said, "Come, all you who are thirsty, come to the waters; and you who have no money, come, buy and eat!" (Isaiah 55:1). Jesus said, "Let anyone who is thirsty come to me and drink. Whoever believes in me, as Scripture has said, rivers of living water will flow from within them" (John 7:37-38). John gives the invitation in Revelation 22:17, "Let those who are thirsty come; and let all who wish take the free gift of the water of life." The thirsty Israelites symbolize thirsty humanity. God has called us to serve others the water of life. We should never tire of meeting people's needs or complain about having to serve them. We are vessels taking the true water—Jesus—to them. When people have needs, God can minister through us. That is our calling. At times we may become tired and impatient with people, as Moses apparently did. But let us not forget to be instruments in God's hands, wherever and whenever the need arises.

Humans Quarrel with and Oppose the Persons Best Able to Help Them: They quarreled with Moses and said, "If only we had died when our brothers fell dead before the Lord! Why did you bring the Lord's community into this wilderness, that we and our livestock should die here? Why did you bring us up out of Egypt to this terrible place? It has no grain or figs, grapevines or pomegranates. And there is no water to drink!" (verses 3-5) The thirsty Israelites complained to Aaron and Moses about their thirst. This illustrates the human tendency to blame others when problems occur. The instruments God chooses to minister to people often receive a misguided, unkind, and undeserved backlash as people resist God in their resentment of His authority. People want to be in control of their situations; they want to be their own gods, but they cannot be. They express their anger at God toward His chosen leaders, as though they would like to bring those people down.

You and I will sometimes be mistreated by those we are trying to help. Understanding this dynamic will help us exercise patience with God's people. Some will oppose us, but we are not the problem if we are walking in obedience to God's leading. The accusations made by the Israelites in verses 4 and 5 are unfair. The people wanted to be free from slavery in Egypt, but when faced with the difficulties of life in the desert, they were quick to blame Moses and Aaron. We are channels of God's solutions. Yet we are only one of the tools God uses to solve the problems of others.

The Bible says no weapon formed against us will prevail (Isaiah 54:17). No matter how often people oppose you, if you are obeying God, He will defend you. If you take matters into your own hands and try to vindicate yourself, more serious problems will arise. Time and time again throughout the travels to Canaan land, God defended Moses when his followers complained. But in the wilderness of Zin, Moses took the matter into his own hands. And we can learn from the sad outcome. Moses taught the people, "Do not seek revenge or bear a grudge against anyone among your people, but love your neighbor as yourself. I am the Lord" (Leviticus 19:18).

But Moses forgot what he himself had taught. Just before Israel crossed into Canaan, Moses said, "It is mine to avenge; I will repay" (Deuteronomy 32:35). In Romans 12:19 Paul quotes Moses when he says, "Do not take revenge, my dear friends, but leave room for God's wrath, for it is written: 'It is mine to avenge; I will repay,' says the Lord." David allowed God to defend him (1 Samuel 26:9-11). Moses began well, but he reacted the wrong way.

The Success of God Pivots on Three Things

Moses and Aaron went from the assembly to the entrance to the tent of meeting and fell facedown, and the glory of the Lord appeared to them. (verse 6) As recorded in this verse, Moses did three things right. He is a good and duplicable model on each of these three behaviors. We too can do all three of these things. We just must decide that they are worth doing.

Moses left the people and went to God in prayer.

"Moses and Aaron went from the assembly to the entrance to the tent of meeting." If we stay in the arena of activity with people and try to pacify or deflect their anger, answer their questions, or solve their problems by our own strength, wisdom, or ability, we will fail. We must sometimes get away from people in order to get alone with God. We don't remain away from them, nor do we avoid them endlessly. We must be approachable and available. But unless we sometimes get away from them and spend time alone with God, we will never obtain the help we and those we serve need from God. Even Jesus did this many times (Mark 1:35).

Moses expressed his humility and dependence on God.

Moses "fell facedown." The human face is a symbol of our identity; it is how others recognize us. God has created each of our faces differently. Orientals go to great lengths to "save face" and to help others do the same. But far from seeking to save his own face—maintain his own reputation—Moses got on his face before God. God knows each of our faces. God knew Moses' face and talked to him face to face. "Since then, no prophet has risen in Israel like Moses, whom the Lord knew face to face" (Deuteronomy 34:10). Yet in the above narrative Moses has his face to the ground. This is a posture of humility and desperation and is a model for intercessors today as well.

Moses saw the glory of the Lord. "The glory of the Lord appeared to them." God's glory is not always displayed in flashing colors and bright beams. Sometimes the glory of God is soft, subdued, and subtle. Elijah knew the glory of God in the cave when he heard the still, small voice of the Lord after the wind, earthquake, and fire had come and gone. If we want to see the glory of God, we must let Him show us whichever aspect of His glory He chooses to reveal at any given time. It is better to seek Him than to seek His glory, but in seeking Him we may see His glory. When we follow this pattern— leave people temporarily, fall on our faces before God, and pray faithfully until we see the glory of God—we will be able to minister to His people, love the unlovely, and lead God's people in God's paths God's way. Our love for God's people may wane in the process of ministry to them. But we are their fellow-servants and servants of God and must never lose our sense of His glory. It is He whom we serve. He is the Source and End of all that we do.

God Gave Moses the Solution: The Lord said to Moses, "Take the staff, and you and your brother Aaron gather the assembly together. Speak to that rock before their eyes and it will pour out its water. You will bring water out of the rock for the community so they and their livestock can drink." (verses 7-8) God gave Moses specific directions. He directed him to take his staff and speak to the rock. Many times in Scripture we find God giving humans practical instructions. Two other good illustrations of this are David at Ziklag (1 Samuel 30:6-8) when God told him to pursue the Amalekite raiding party, and Jehoshaphat when he moved into battle formation and then the sun reflected on the water, providing a miraculous deliverance (2 Kings 3:17-18). We need practical solutions to ministry problems and we also need personal comfort. God is a master at giving us both. God revealed His glory to Moses, then gave him specific instructions as to what to do. He will do the same for you.

Moses Followed God's Instructions: Moses took the staff from the Lord's presence, just as he commanded him. (verse 9). Moses started well. He took the staff and began to do what God said to do. What went wrong? How is it that Moses, the meekest man on earth besides Jesus Christ, lost control of his emotions and became angry and resentful? Starting well is not enough. We must begin and end correctly.

Moses Became Angry with God's People: He and Aaron gathered the assembly together in front of the rock and Moses said to them, "Listen you rebels, must we bring you water out of this rock?" Then Moses raised his arm and struck the rock twice with his staff. (verses 10-11a). In both Leviticus and Deuteronomy Moses teaches against revenge and grudges. Yet in between those two books lies the book of Numbers, which records Moses' fleshly response of anger with God's people. Moses:

(1) called the Israelites rebels.
(2) included himself in the miracle: "Must *we* bring you water?" (emphasis mine)
(3) did not speak to the rock but struck it. Twice.

Bible archeology teaches us that in that area of wilderness a crust can develop on the surface of the earth that makes the dirt hard and waterproof. The water is held inside the earth by the crust on the surface. Moses spent forty years in that desert; he knew how to find and release the water. By striking the rock, Moses resorted to a human ploy rather than just speaking to the rock and allowing God to receive all the glory. Moses struck another rock some forty years before when people needed water. Exodus 17:5-6 tells us, "The Lord answered Moses, ' . . . I will stand there before you by the rock at Horeb. Strike the rock, and water will come out of it for the people to drink.' So Moses did this in the sight of the elders of Israel." On that occasion, Moses did the right thing to strike the rock. This time, however, it was a flagrant disobedience to specific instructions. There is rich symbolism in these stories.

First Corinthians 10:4 tells us that rock represented Jesus, symbolizing His being smitten on the cross for our sins that we may receive His water of life. He died once, and that was enough to give the water of life to all the thirsty of the world. He did not have to die twice. From the one-time crucified Jesus flows the water of life to quench the spiritual thirst of all humanity. Jesus is the Rock of our salvation, the Rock that is our firm foundation, the Rock that is a shelter in the time of storm, the Rock in whose shadow humans find protection, comfort, and refreshment. Moses did not have to strike the rock at all, not even once. He had only to speak to it. In the same way, we do not strike the Rock. Simply speak to Jesus and you will be nourished.

Even after just having spent time in God's presence, seeing His glory, and receiving His detailed and specific instruction, Moses gave in to his emotions. He expressed his anger in ways that did not honor God or reverence His holiness. Moses' actions were irreverent; he did not treat God respectfully. Moses' anger and lack of self-control greatly dishonored and displeased God. And there were consequences to Moses' actions. Even though God did not immediately remove him from leadership, Moses was severely reprimanded by God. Even so, God remained faithful to Moses, as shown in this word to Joshua: "As I was with Moses, so will I be with you; I will never leave you or forsake you" (Joshua 1:5).We do not know if Moses' anger was influenced by God's anger at the complaint of the people. But even if Moses discerned that God was angry, it was not his prerogative to show anger, especially when He had clearly instructed him what to do.

Samuel was angry with the people of God when they wanted a king. But God said, "Give them a king." (I Samuel 8:22). God was more gracious than either Moses or Samuel. He can be angry with His people; we should not.

Though God's Tool Was Faulty, God Still Cared for His People's Needs: Water gushed out, and the community and their livestock drank. (verse 11b).In spite of Moses' sin, God still gave the people the water they needed. Moses failed, but God did not. The human instrument took revenge, but God showed mercy. Moses entertained an ego-related desire for vindication and revenge. God cared for His people and met their needs. God's provision is more about what He does than what His instruments do.

When God continues to do His good work through His chosen servants for His people, that is not necessarily an indication that the human instrument is doing everything correctly. Do not assume that God using you means you can relax and stop growing spiritually. God gave the Israelites water through a miracle produced by Moses' rod striking the rock twice—not because Moses did it right but in spite of the fact that he did it wrong. Moses erred greatly in becoming angry and departing from the instructions God gave him to speak to the rock. But God still met the needs of the people.

God Pronounced an Irrevocable Punishment on Moses: But the Lord said to Moses and Aaron, "Because you did not trust in me enough to honor me as holy in the sight of the Israelites, you will not bring this community into the land I give them." (verse 12)

We prefer to emphasize grace, mercy, love, forgiveness, and the encouraging aspects of God's character. Yet to have the whole picture of who God is and how He operates, we need to remember that He also has a firm side. He has authority. He is sovereign. We are to fear and respect Him, and remain cautious in our strict obedience to His every command and instruction. Moses disobeyed God and thus dishonored Him before the people he was leading. God wanted to bring water from the rock without it being struck. That would have brought greater glory to God than Moses striking the rock.

Paul cautioned his readers, "Consider therefore the kindness and sternness of God; sternness to those who fell, but kindness to you, provided that you continue in his kindness" (Romans 11:22). We often take courage from the fact that God keeps His promises of reward, comfort, blessing, healing, and forgiveness, and it is right that we do that. However, He also keeps His promises of judgment, and we may experience the consequences of the mistakes we make for a long time. God is gracious and we experience favor, but we dare not ignore His sternness. But the Lord said to Moses and Aaron, "Because you did not trust in me enough to honor me as holy in the sight of the Israelites, you will not bring this community into the land I give them." (verse 12).This sobering judgment from God is even more serious when we look at Moses' speech as the Israelites were about to enter the Promised Land: At that time I pleaded with the Lord: "Sovereign Lord, you have begun to show to your servant your greatness and your strong hand. For what god is there in heaven or on earth who can do the deeds and mighty works you do? Let me go over and see the good land beyond the Jordan—that fine hill country and Lebanon."

But because of you the Lord was angry with me and would not listen to me. "That is enough," the Lord said. "Do not speak to me anymore about this matter. Go up to the top of Pisgah and look west and north and south and east. Look at the land with your own eyes, since you are not going to cross this Jordan. But commission Joshua, and encourage and strengthen him, for he will lead this people across and will cause them to inherit the land that you will see." (Deuteronomy 3:23-28)

Later in that same speech, Moses said to Israel: The Lord was angry with me because of you, and he solemnly swore that I would not cross the Jordan and enter the good Land the Lord your God is giving you as your inheritance. I will die in this land; I will not cross the Jordan; but you are about to cross over and take possession of that good land. Be careful not to forget the covenant of the Lord your God that he made with you; do not make for yourselves an idol in the form of anything the Lord your God has forbidden. For the Lord your God is a consuming fire, a jealous God. (Deuteronomy 4:21-24) Moses remembered the strictness of God because of his own experience and reminded the Israelites that God has a stern side too. Then Moses climbed Mount Nebo from the plains of Moab to the top of Pisgah, across from Jericho. There the Lord showed him the whole land—from Gilead to Dan, all of Naphtali, the territory of Ephraim and Manasseh, all the land of Judah as far as the Mediterranean Sea, the Negev and the whole region from the Valley of Jericho, the City of Palms, as far as Zoar. Then the Lord said to him, "This is the land I promised on oath to Abraham, Isaac and Jacob when I said, 'I will give it to your descendants.' I have let you see it with your eyes, but you will not cross over into it." And Moses the servant of the Lord died there in Moab, as the Lord had said. (Deuteronomy 34:1-5).Moses had a long and successful career, but it could have been even longer and more successful. You too can have a rich, enduring, and effective ministry if you carefully obey every leading, instruction, and command of God. God keeps His promises.

The People's Quarrel Was with the Lord, Not Moses: These were the waters of Meribah, where the Israelites quarreled with the Lord and where he was proved holy among them. (verse 13).Moses and Aaron bore the brunt of verbal abuse from the Israeli people. Verse 3 says, "They quarreled with Moses." But verse 13 says, ". . . where the Israelites quarreled with the Lord and where he was proved holy among them." Two things are important for us in this verse: (1) The people's quarrel was not just with Moses; it was a complaint against God; (2) God was proved holy by the judgment He pronounced. The first lesson is easy to understand. God's ministers can take great comfort from knowing that the complaints people have are not just against them but are also against God. Stay on God's side in a quarrel. He will defend you. The second lesson is more subtle. Moses did not enter the Promised Land. By giving Moses a judgment for his disobedience that limited his ministry, God's holiness was maintained. If God allowed us to disobey and yet He continued to bless our ministry without measure, where would His holiness be? Where is the high standard of conduct for God's people if they can disobey and still have unhindered and lasting ministry? Moses' error and God's judgment teach us to be careful to obey fully, willingly, and if possible, cheerfully. Let's go all the way to the Promised Land.

MEET Mrs, ZIPPORAH MOSES

Did you know that Moses left Egypt two times, once out of intense fear and once out of great faith? Has it ever occurred to you that God may have used Moses' conversations with his Midianite wife, Zipporah, to encourage him? Are you aware that Moses may have written the book of Genesis while in Midian? Did you know that the value of Zipporah's actions, which saved Moses' life on the way to Egypt, are lost to most Bible readers because of what she said about Moses? What part did Zipporah play in the secret drama of Moses' restoration on the back side of the desert? Let us take a closer look at this fascinating woman. Zipporah has been largely overlooked by scholars who study Bible characters. Even when her story is examined, she has often been misunderstood. Many feel she is either an unimportant Bible character or an example of a problematic wife. Careful observation of the Bible, however, reveals that she was likely a wise, courageous, perceptive, influential, and supportive wife.

Three Verses Are Enough: Most of our opinions about Zipporah are based on an incident that occurred as she traveled with her husband, Moses, and their two sons on the road from Midian to Egypt. Correctly interpreted, this incident provides an insight into the nobility of her character. Not long after Moses' experience with the burning bush, he asked his father-in-law, Jethro, for permission to return to Egypt. Then Moses went back to Jethro his father-in-law and said to him, "Let me return to my own people in Egypt to see if any of them are still alive." Jethro said, "Go, and I wish you well." Now the Lord had said to Moses in Midian, "Go back to Egypt, for all those who wanted to kill you are dead." So Moses took his wife and sons, put them on a donkey and started back to Egypt. And he took the staff of God in his hand. The Lord said to Moses, "When you return to Egypt, see that you perform before Pharaoh all the wonders I have given you the power to do. But I will harden his heart so that he will not let the people go. Then say to Pharaoh, 'This is what the Lord says: Israel is my firstborn son, and I told you, "Let my son go, so he may worship me." But you refused to let him go; so I will kill your firstborn son.'" (Exodus 4:18-23).Traditionally, Bible scholars display a negative impression of Zipporah because of what she said to Moses on that trip to Egypt: "Surely you are a bridegroom of blood to me" (Exodus 4:25). But if we look at the complete story in context and what she *did,* we must reach another conclusion. In a time of Moses' weak faith and disobedience to the command of God to circumcise Israel's sons, Zipporah actually saved her husband's life. At a lodging place on the way, the Lord met Moses and was about to kill him. But Zipporah took a flint knife, cut off her son's foreskin and touched Moses' feet with it. "Surely you are a bridegroom of blood to me," she said. So the Lord let him alone. (At that time she said "bridegroom of blood," referring to circumcision.) (Exodus 4:24-26).In those three verses we see enough of Zipporah's action to judge her character and appreciate the role she played in Moses' life.

The bible continues: The Lord said to Aaron, "Go into the wilderness to meet Moses." So he met Moses at the mountain of God and kissed him. Then Moses told Aaron everything the Lord had sent him to say, and also about all the signs he had commanded him to perform. Moses and Aaron brought together all the elders of the Israelites, and Aaron told them everything the Lord had said to Moses. He also performed the signs before the people, and they believed. And when they heard that the Lord was concerned about them and had seen their misery, they bowed down and worshiped. (Exodus 4:27-31)

Aaron went to meet Moses at the same time Moses was traveling toward Egypt with his family. They met at the mountain of God. But the two brothers would never have met had Zipporah not saved Moses' life by her brave actions. Commentators often say that Zipporah went back to her father then, but the Bible does not say that here.

Moses Fled from Egypt the First Time in Fear, not Faith

Forty years earlier, a younger, less cautious, more presumptuous Moses attempted to deliver the Israelite slaves in his own strength. At that time Moses had not yet had his own personal encounter with God. He did not attempt to rescue all the Israelites, but he saved at least one Hebrew slave who was being mistreated by another. One day, after Moses had grown up, he went out to where his own people were and watched them at their hard labor. He saw an Egyptian beating a Hebrew, one of his own people. Glancing this way and that and seeing no one, he killed the Egyptian and hid him in the sand. The next day he went out and saw two Hebrews fighting. He asked the one in the wrong, "Why are you hitting your fellow Hebrew?" The man said, "Who made you ruler and judge over us? Are you thinking of killing me as you killed the Egyptian?" Then Moses was afraid and thought, "What I did must have become known." When Pharaoh heard of this, he tried to kill Moses, but Moses fled from Pharaoh and went to live in Midian, where he sat down by a well. (Exodus 2:11-15)

Moses was no longer the man he used to be. He was not the self-confident deliverer he had imagined himself to be just days earlier. He had run for his life. Neither was he yet the controlled and certain man who watched God perform many mighty miracles in effecting Israel's escape from Egypt. The book of Hebrews tells us that Moses left Egypt by faith. But his departure by faith was the second time he left Egypt. This first time, he was running for his life. He had been trying to save Israel by his strength, not by his faith in God. And his strength had proven inadequate. He arrived in Midian alone and despondent.

Moses had thought he was a deliverer and he eventually became one, but when he reached Midian he had no desire to be a national deliverer. He was only willing to deliver seven pretty shepherdesses from some unfair and aggressive shepherds. One of those shepherdesses was the woman God chose to be his wife. Now a priest of Midian had seven daughters, and they came to draw water and fill the troughs to water their father's flock. Some shepherds came along and drove them away, but Moses got up and came to their rescue and watered their flock. When the girls returned to Reuel their father, he asked them, "Why have you returned so early today?" They answered, "An Egyptian rescued us from the shepherds. He even drew water for us and watered the flock." "And where is he?" he asked his daughters. "Why did you leave him? Invite him to have something to eat." Moses agreed to stay with the man, who gave his daughter Zipporah to Moses in marriage. (Exodus 2:16-21)

After he married Zipporah, the name Moses gave their first son does not suggest either hope for the future or despair because of the past. It is a neutral name, merely relaying the idea that he was living in a foreign land. "Zipporah gave birth to a son, and Moses named him Gershom, saying, 'I have become a foreigner in a foreign land'" (Exodus 2:22). The Bible does not say how much time passed before the second son was born, but it does say that Moses took his *sons* with him when he returned to Egypt with Zipporah, (Exodus 4:20).

Some couples compete. Some argue; others fight. Some develop even warmer and more mature relationships than the good ones with which they began. The Bible does not tell us the nature of the rapport between Moses and Zipporah. Were they friends? We don't know, but it appears they had a good bond. Throughout the years of shepherding, family times, and life in the desert together, Moses and Zipporah undoubtedly discussed their varying cultural backgrounds. How many nights might they have watched the stars and Moses told her of God's promise to Abraham, his ancestor, and that Abraham's descendants would be like the stars—innumerable? Moses would have told her about Abraham's call, name change, and travels, and Isaac's disputes with the residents of Canaan over the issue of the wells Isaac had dug and the local people claimed for themselves. He would have told of Jacob and Esau, Jacob's travels to Paddan Aram, Jacob's wives and children. About Joseph being sold as a slave and rising to the prime minister's position, and the migration of the entire family of Jacob from Canaan to Egypt. The years of Israeli slavery, his own experiences in the court and family of Pharaoh, and his own failed attempt to deliver the Israelite slaves with his own strength. They spent four decades discussing all of this. We only need to read Genesis to guess what they might have talked about since all of that happened before Moses left Egypt and fled to Midian. Did Moses write Genesis in the desert after leaving Egypt? He had the time, but did he have the faith? Possibly Zipporah was inspired by the stories Moses' told of his heritage. Could that have motivated her to defend her husband as he returned to Egypt? Perhaps Jethro was also inspired. We don't know what god Jethro represented. Perhaps he maintained his career as priest and changed his god. Did Jethro know the genuine God before Moses arrived? Was he, like Abimelek, Melchizedek, and Job, a non-Jewish believer in the true God? We know that he eventually believed in the real God. Did Jethro's daughter, Moses' wife, have anything to do with her father's change in faith?

Moses Resisted God's Plan for His Return to Egypt to Deliver Israel

After forty years of shepherding in the wilderness of Midian, Moses encountered the voice of God in a bush that burned but was not consumed. The continual burning of the bush was a miracle. There God told Moses His name: "I am who I am" (Exodus 3:14). He promised Moses favor. He gave him the miraculous sign of the staff turning into a snake and back into a staff. God gave him the amazing sign of a hand becoming leprous and then clean again. The conversation between God and Moses was long and detailed. Yet all the while Moses resisted God. Then he complained about his inability to speak: Moses said to the Lord, "Pardon your servant, Lord. I have never been eloquent, neither in the past nor since you have spoken to your servant. I am slow of speech and tongue." The Lord said to him, "Who gave human beings their mouths? Who makes them deaf or mute? Who gives them sight or makes them blind? Is it not I, the Lord? Now go; I will help you speak and will teach you what to say." But Moses said, "Pardon your servant, Lord. Please send someone else." (Exodus 4:10-13).The narrative makes it clear that Moses was not eager to return to Egypt. He felt incapable. Yet centuries later, Stephen testified before the Sanhedrin: At that time Moses was born, and he was no ordinary child. For three months he was cared for in his parents' home. When he was placed outside, Pharaoh's daughter took him and brought him up as her own son. Moses was educated in all the wisdom of the Egyptians and was powerful in speech and action. (Acts 7:20-22). According to Stephen, Moses was "powerful in speech and action," yet at the burning bush Moses claimed he was slow of speech. What made the difference between the fearful, hesitant Moses and the confident, brave man who eventually challenged Pharaoh and demanded that he let Israel go? What brought this uncertain, cautious man out of his pit into faith and trust in God again? Moses had arrived in Midian apprehensive and discouraged, and forty years later he appears to have still been negative. What changed? It would be an exaggeration to say that Zipporah, the faith-filled wife of Moses, made all the difference—that because of her support, this frightened, timid shepherd morphed into a mighty man of courage. But the role Zipporah filled, the support she demonstrated, the courage she displayed, the knowledge she had of Israeli tradition, and the faith she placed in Moses and Moses' God certainly would have been a positive contribution to the restoration of his confidence and therefore a major factor in the success of Moses' public life. She stepped in at a crucial juncture and God used her. As the couple traveled back toward Egypt, the reluctant Moses did not act like a deliverer. He had resisted God's call and the burning bush and failed to circumcise at least one of his sons. If Zipporah had not saved him he would have died.

What Really Happened on the Road to Egypt: We do not know how long Moses was in Midian before he married Zipporah or how long they were married before they had children. It appears that Zipporah circumcised at least one of their sons on the way to Egypt, because when God had Moses pinned down on the point of circumcision she put the foreskin of one son at Moses' feet. The image of Zipporah as a supportive wife comes into focus when we view Zipporah's *action*, not just her words. But Zipporah took a flint knife, cut off her son's foreskin and touched Moses' feet with it. "Surely you are a bridegroom of blood to me," she said. (Exodus 4:25)

With her husband pinned down and his life threatened, Zipporah had the perception, discernment, wisdom, and courage to pull out a knife, require at least one of her possibly grown sons to expose his genitals, and cut off his foreskin. This would have been a bloody and painful experience for both mother and son, whatever their ages. She saw the death threat to Moses, and because she believed in the value and validity of his mission, she acted out her faith. They had not casually decided to visit Egypt for a pleasant vacation. Zipporah was drawn by the history of Moses' people, by Abraham, Isaac, Jacob, and Joseph's confidence in a miracle-working God, the true God. This assignment to Egypt was to be another in a series of great moves of God among His people. God had spoken to her husband in a burning bush and he had signs to prove God was with him. Together they were on an important and godly undertaking. Off went the clothes. Out came the knife. Off went the foreskin. Onward went the travelers. If you are married to a Christian leader, support your spouse. Lend the support he or she needs from time to time. If you and your spouse are both spiritual leaders, each of you can be supportive of the other, and your partnership will prove both strong and fruitful. Cast your vision so your spouse catches it, believes in what you are doing, and supports you. Take time to inspire your spouse with your dreams. Even the great Moses needed a Zipporah. Encouragement is valuable. Earn it. And give it liberally.

Zipporah's Role as Informant to Jethro

Moses' second son's name was Eliezer, which means "God is my helper." Moses stated, "My father's God was my helper; he saved me from the sword of Pharaoh" (Exodus 18:3-4). Eliezer's name gives glory to God. He was born later—perhaps after Moses, though still in Midian, had regained some of his optimism. The Bible does not clearly state how many years passed during the time of the ten plagues, or when or from where Zipporah left with her two sons to return to Jethro. But at some point Moses sent her away. She later came back to Moses and the recently delivered Israelites in the wilderness, along with her father, Jethro, and her sons, Gershom and Eliezer. Most Bible commentators claim that Zipporah returned to

Midian during the chaos of the plagues in Egypt. It is more likely that she returned to her father in Midian after the exodus from Egypt. During the narrative of the plagues, there is no mention that Zipporah left. Zipporah's departure from Moses is recorded after the exodus occurred. Now Jethro, the priest of Midian and father-in-law of Moses, heard of everything God had done for Moses and for his people Israel, and how the Lord had brought Israel out of Egypt. After Moses had sent away his wife Zipporah, his father-in-law Jethro received her and her two sons. One son was named Gershom, for Moses said, "I have become a foreigner in a foreign land"; and the other was named Eliezer, for he said, "My father's God was my helper; he saved me from the sword of Pharaoh." (Exodus 18:1-4) Zipporah would be the most likely person to have been the informant for her father. "Jethro, the priest of Midian and father-in-law of Moses, heard of everything God had done for Moses and for his people Israel, and how the Lord had brought Israel out of Egypt" (Exodus 18:1). How did he hear these wonderful words? Zipporah could only relate this to her father as a firsthand eyewitness if she had gone to and remained in Egypt with her husband throughout the months of the plagues. Jethro heard of all that God had done. I can think of no more likely newscaster than the woman whom Jethro had given to Moses, the woman who heard the stories of the patriarchs, who believed in Moses' God, and who believed in Moses. Zipporah supported her man by relaying to her father the multiple mighty miracles God worked through him. Wives, support your husbands. All men have feet of clay, and we all have times of weakness and discouragement. Your man may now be more like the defeated and terrified Moses who just arrived at Midian, or the hesitant Moses who moved cautiously toward Egypt, than the brave Moses who left Egypt walking through the Red Sea on dry ground. In any case, you have an opportunity to further the work of the Lord by partnering with your husband, believing in him, supporting him, praying for him, and encouraging him. Husbands, share your ministry dreams with your helpmate in such a way that she will believe in your God and in the validity of your ministry. If your wife is a minister, support her in her role as a spiritual leader. Protect her and provide for her the leadership God gives you in His Word as she cooperates with your leadership in the family. Support the man or woman of God in your family—that is the lesson we learn from Zipporah.

Moses wrote, "For this reason a man will leave his father and mother and be united to his wife, and they will become one flesh" (Genesis 2:24). The way Zipporah responded to Moses makes it apparent that Moses believed what he wrote. Enough of human history had occurred by Moses' time that he could assess the disadvantages of emotionally bonding with other family members, neighbors, business associates, or friends more than with one's wife. He knew the value of "leaving" father and mother and uniting with one's wife. Whether geographically or just emotionally, the husband and wife who recognize this principle and unite with each other experience many enormous personal benefits. Zipporah was blessed with a husband who understood and practiced this. By her supportive behavior, Zipporah indicates that she did too. God's Word upholds the primacy of the marital relationship over all others. Sociologists call it the husband/wife social dyad. Scripture clarifies its great worth. If we appreciate, defend, and prize it, we will enjoy it immensely. We do not quickly associate learning about romance and teamwork in marriage with the story of Moses the law-giver. But these reflections on Zipporah enable us to consider the romances Moses recorded in Genesis: Adam and Eve, Abraham and Sarah, Isaac and Rebecca, Jacob and Rachel, and, after escape from seductive temptations, Joseph's eventual marriage at age 30 to Asenath, the daughter of Potiphera the priest of On. Moses and Zipporah were a successful ministry team, bonded emotionally, and they maintained a friendly relationship. We have reason to believe Mo and Zip got on well together.

Was Zipporah Moses' Cushite Wife? Years after the exodus and many adventures in the wilderness, an incident occurred between Moses and his siblings, Miriam and Aaron, over his Cushite wife. Was this wife Zipporah or another woman? The Bible does not say. Here is what the Bible does say: Miriam and Aaron began to talk against Moses because of his Cushite wife, for he had married a Cushite. "Has the Lord spoken only through Moses?" they asked. "Hasn't he also spoken through us?" (Numbers 12:1-3) At least three possibilities exist: 1. Zipporah died and Moses remarried, this time to a Cushite (an African of Ethiopia). 2. Moses married a second wife in addition to Zipporah. 3. Zipporah had all along been a Cushite who lived in Midian.

Let's briefly explore these possibilities: **1. Zipporah died and Moses remarried, this time to a Cushite:** If this were the case, Miriam and Aaron would have exhibited small character to oppose Moses on the basis of his wife. That smallness in their character could, however, explain why God so quickly and decisively defended Moses and, in doing so, indirectly defended the Cushite wife as well. This part of the story would then uphold the idealism of predominance of the marriage relationship.

2. Moses married a second wife in addition to Zipporah: Miriam and Aaron may have been opposed to Moses having a second wife who, incidentally, was a Cushite. The Scripture does not say whether they opposed Moses because his Cushite wife was a Cushite or because she was a second wife. Many godly people in Israel, both before and after Moses, had more than one wife. It is therefore doubtful that Moses' siblings opposed him because the Cushite was a second wife. The skin of a Cushite was black. Is it possible that Miriam and Aaron were opposed to Moses because he married a second wife and because she was black woman? In either case, God defended Moses—and the wife. In either case the moral to be learned would be solidarity in marriage.

3. Zipporah was a Cushite who lived in Midian: It is possible that Jethro and his family were Cushites who lived in Midian. Then the Cushite wife God defended when He defended Moses would be Zipporah from Midian, the daughter of Jethro, the priest of Midian. When Zipporah rejoined Moses at the Israeli camp in the wilderness, her successful role as wife, confidant, supporter, and helper to Moses may have aroused jealousy in Aaron and Miriam. Once Moses had his wife with him again, he no longer leaned emotionally on his sister and brother. Zipporah was a thinking person who had ideas of her own, which she shared with her husband. Resuming her constructive involvement in his career, she no doubt made suggestions and gave advice, based on her experience as a desert shepherdess, that proved to be a greater help than Moses' sister and brother could provide. God defended Moses' wife against the verbal attacks of Moses' siblings, and Moses remained on the side of his spouse. Your spouse needs your unconditional support too. You are one with your spouse, not your siblings. How many painful family arguments could be avoided if we understood this biblical principle? Unfortunately, the mountain before some especially preachers is their spouse who have become thorns in the flesh and instrument of Satan to hinder the fulfillment of divine mandate given to the minister.

BALAAM: A PROPHET WITH DIVIDED ALLEGIANCE

"How shall I curse whom God has not cursed? And how can I denounce whom the LORD has not denounced?" As I see him from the top of the rocks, And I look at him from the hills; Behold, a people who dwells apart, And will not be reckoned among the nations. "Who can count the dust of Jacob, Or number the fourth part of Israel? Let me die the death of the upright, And let my end be like his!" Then Balak said to Balaam, "What have you done to me? I took you to curse my enemies, but behold, you have actually blessed them!" He replied, "Must I not be careful to speak what the LORD puts in my mouth?" Numbers 23:8-12.

Beloved, do you know that the story of Balaam gives practical evidence for the reality of the invisible spiritual war that is going on all around us? Were you aware that Balaam did what God said, but since his heart was not in it, he fell into a trap? Do you realize that Balaam represents those of us who say and even do the right thing, but don't obey from our hearts?

Balaam symbolizes what happens when our ministry motives get tangled with carnal desires. The Bible is realistic, and though socioeconomic and geopolitical realities may differ from generation to generation, human nature does not. The lessons we learn from this man's story are as relevant now as when Moses first recorded the interlocking of Balaam's failure with developments within Israel. The present generation of God's ministers needs a serious review of the warnings to be gleaned from Balaam's experience. Balaam saw the spirit world with remarkable clarity but was blind to his own incorrect impetus. The extreme measures he took in pursuit of his personal goals differ from any Christian minister's materialistic motivations only in degree; a lesser form of Balaam's rationale may be lurking unknowingly in any of us.

The Spiritual Battle Is Real

"Whenever the ark set out, Moses said, 'Rise up, Lord! May your enemies be scattered; may your foes flee before you.' Whenever it came to rest, he said, 'Return, Lord, to the countless thousands of Israel'" (Numbers 10:35-36). Why did Moses concern himself with this kind of routine spiritual warfare? The story of Balaam provides part of the answer to that question. Then the Israelites traveled to the plains of Moab and camped along the Jordan across from Jericho.

Now Balak son of Zippor saw all that Israel had done to the Amorites, and Moab was terrified because there were so many people. Indeed, Moab was filled with dread because of the Israelites. The Moabites said to the elders of Midian, "This horde is going to lick up everything around us, as an ox licks up the grass of the field." So Balak son of Zippor, who was king of Moab at that time, sent messengers to summon Balaam son of Beor, who was at Pethor, near the Euphrates River, in his native land. Balak said: "A people has come out of Egypt; they cover the face of the land and have settled next to me. Now come and put a curse on these people, because they are too powerful for me. Perhaps then I will be able to defeat them and drive them out of the land. For I know that whoever you bless is blessed, and whoever you curse is cursed." The elders of Moab and Midian left, taking with them the fee for divination.

When they came to Balaam, they told him what Balak had said. "Spend the night here," Balaam said to them, "and I will report back to you with the answer the Lord gives me." So the Moabite officials stayed with him. (Numbers 22:1-8)

Understanding the "other side"—the unseen enemy activity that is the background behind the visible drama—helps us better understand the nature of the battle. Here we see the causes for one of Israel's sins and the plague that broke out in the camp as a result. The story of Balak and Balaam reveals their roles in the seduction of Israel. If we did not know about Balak and Balaam, we would not have the richer picture of the spiritual battle behind the moral battle. In the spiritual battle, blessings and cursings have some effect, but sin matters even more. At the end of Balaam and Balak's eventual strategy to oppose Israel by enticing Israel to sin, Balak fought a partially successful battle. Because of Phinehas, God's people were spared an even worse plague. Balaam's curses from the mountains around the Israeli camp did not entirely destroy Israel. But enticing Israel to sin was, tragically, an effective plan. Israel's own sin did to Israel what Balaam's curses could not do. What a devilishly cunning battle strategy.

Balaam's Outward Start Was Right—But What of His Heart?

God came to Balaam and asked, "Who are these men with you?" Balaam said to God, "Balak son of Zippor, king of Moab, sent me this message: 'A people that has come out of Egypt covers the face of the land. Now come and put a curse on them for me. Perhaps then I will be able to fight them and drive them away.'" But God said to Balaam, "Do not go with them. You must not put a curse on those people, because they are blessed." The next morning Balaam got up and said to Balak's officials, "Go back to your own country, for the Lord has refused to let me go with you." So the Moabite officials returned to Balak and said, "Balaam refused to come with us." (Numbers 22:9-14).God's first word to Balaam was a statement of His will. "Don't go." This is comparable to a conversation God had with Moses. God had promised Abraham He would make a great nation of his descendants. This was God's original and unchanging plan, and Moses knew it. So Moses was able to resist temptation when God tested his moral character by offering to destroy the Israelites and make of Moses' descendants a great nation.

Balak was not pleased with Balaam's refusal. He sent more officials to persuade him to come. This time, as Balaam prayed, Jehovah God gave him permission to go, but he had to do only what God told him to do. Unlike Moses, Balaam did not discern the difference between what God *says* and what God *intends*. It is possible that Balaam was experiencing an inner struggle, seeking both to obey God and to gain the monetary reward Balak was offering. Or Balaam's obedience may have been only outward as he inwardly looked for an opportunity to receive Balak's reward. Balaam did not have the same discernment Moses had. If he had, he probably would not have taken the request back to God the second time. In going with Balak's envoy, Balaam evidently displeased God, even though Balaam's outward behavior conformed to what God instructed. "God was very angry when he went" (Numbers 22:22). God even used Balaam's donkey to communicate to Balaam His displeasure and a need for caution. Twice God told Balaam to go. But there is a difference between what God told Balaam the second time and what He really wanted. In this case Balaam did not discern the difference between what

God said and what God intended, as Moses had done. Do you know God well enough that He can speak to you in code form—a unique and personal way that only you and He know about—and you still understand His intent? Let us cultivate a close and trusting relationship with Him such that we know His will, and then do it.

Balaam Followed Through Correctly—At First

When Balak heard that Balaam was coming, he went out to meet him at the Moabite town on the Arnon border, at the edge of his territory. Balak said to Balaam, "Did I not send you an urgent summons? Why didn't you come to me? Am I really not able to reward you?" "Well, I have come to you now," Balaam replied. "But I can't say whatever I please. I must speak only what God puts in my mouth." Then Balaam went with Balak to Kiriath Huzoth. Balak sacrificed cattle and sheep, and gave some to Balaam and the officials who were with him. The next morning Balak took Balaam up to Bamoth Baal, and from there he could see the outskirts of the Israelite camp. Balaam said, "Build me seven altars here, and prepare seven bulls and seven rams for me." Balak did as Balaam said, and the two of them offered a bull and a ram on each altar. Then Balaam said to Balak, "Stay here beside your offering while I go aside. Perhaps the Lord will come to meet with me. Whatever he reveals to me I will tell you." Then he went off to a barren height. God met with him, and Balaam said, "I have prepared seven altars, and on each altar I have offered a bull and a ram." The Lord put a word in Balaam's mouth and said, "Go back to Balak and give him this word." So he went back to him and found him standing beside his offering, with all the Moabite officials. Then Balaam spoke his message: Balak brought me from Aram, the king of Moab from the eastern mountains.

"Come," he said, "curse Jacob for me; come, denounce Israel."
How can I curse those whom God has not cursed? How can I
denounce those whom the Lord has not denounced? From the
rocky peaks I see them, from the heights I view them. I see a
people who live apart and do not consider themselves one of
the nations. Who can count the dust of Jacob or number the
fourth part of Israel? Let me die the death of the righteous, and
may my final end be like theirs! Balak said to Balaam, "What
have you done to me? I brought you to curse my enemies, but
you have done nothing but bless them!" He answered, "Must
I not speak what the Lord puts in my mouth?" (Numbers
22:36-23:12)

Balaam's first message was a blessing, not a curse. Evidently
he gave God's whole message. Notice a phrase that is part of
Balaam's first blessing: "I see a people who live apart and do not
consider themselves one of the nations" (Genesis 23:9). This
was God's desire: that His people live apart from other nations
and be separated—holy—unto Himself. This is why Israel's
request for a king was so offensive to Samuel. They wanted to
be like other nations. That was one of Israel's gravest errors.

Satan is the god of this world. To be separate from the world
system—separated unto God—is a blessing. We have the
best there is when we have God. Why would we want to be
like other nations, like other people? Why are we so prone to
conform to the patterns, expectations, and value systems of the
world? Why are we so eager for acceptance with those in the
world's system? Let's live in the blessing God pronounced on
Israel through Balaam, the blessing of being separated from
the world and separated to God.

A Review of Balaam's Second through Seventh Prophecies

Balaam's second prophecy includes statements about God being unchangeable. "God is not a human that he should lie, not a human being, that he should change his mind. Does he speak and then not act? Does he promise and not fulfill? I have received a command to bless; he has blessed, and I cannot change it" (Numbers 23:19-20). These statements about the unchangeableness of God strike to the core of the issue before Balak—God had chosen to bless Israel, and God does not change His mind like humans do. The second prophecy is longer, fuller, and stronger in its expression of God's blessings than the first one. The third prophesy is still stronger and longer, revealing God's unchangeable intention to bless Israel. Balaam gave his fourth through seventh prophecies on his own initiative, without Balak's invitation. The fourth prophecy says Israel will crush her enemies, which included Moab. This would not have pleased Balak the king of Moab. Then he spoke his message: The prophecy of Balaam son of Beor, the prophecy of one whose eye sees clearly, the prophecy of one who hears the words of God, who has knowledge from the Most High, who sees a vision from the Almighty, who falls prostrate, and whose eyes are opened: I see him, but not now; I behold him, but not near. A star will come out of Jacob; a scepter will rise out of Israel. He will crush the foreheads of Moab, the skulls of all the people of Sheth. Edom will be conquered; Seir, his enemy, will be conquered, but Israel will grow strong. A ruler will come out of Jacob and destroy the survivors of the city. (Numbers 24:15-19)

The fifth prophecy said Amalek would be destroyed. "Then Balaam saw Amalek and spoke his message: 'Amalek was first among the nations, but they will come to ruin at last'"

(Numbers 24:20).The sixth prophecy said the Kenites would be destroyed. "Then he saw the Kenites and spoke his message: 'Your dwelling place is secure, your nest is set in a rock; yet you Kenites will be destroyed when Ashur takes you captive'" (Numbers 24:21-22).

The seventh prophecy said ships from Cyprus would also be destroyed. "Then he spoke his message: 'Ah, who can live when God does this? Ships will come from the shores of Cyprus; they will subdue Ashur and Eber, but they too will come to ruin'" (Numbers 24:23-24).

As chapter 24 concludes, Balaam returned home, evidently without any reward, and Balak moved on. "Then Balaam got up and returned home, and Balak went his own way" (Numbers 24:25).

Here it appears that Balaam obeyed God at every step. However, from other Scriptures that we are about to look at, it becomes evident that Balaam did not obey from his heart. That was a problem for him. Apparently there was a darker side of Balaam and his involvement in what happened. The king of Moab did not try to curse Israel anymore, but changed his strategy drastically by inviting Israel to sacrifice to their gods and engage in sexual immorality.

Moab Seduces Israel with Serious Consequences to Israel

After Balaam returned home, the Moabite women enticed Israeli men to their idolatrous sacrifices and sexual promiscuity. "While Israel was staying in Shittim, the men began to indulge in sexual immorality with Moabite women, who invited them to the sacrifices to their gods. The people ate the sacrificial meal and bowed down before these gods. So Israel yoked themselves to the Baal of Peor. And the Lord's anger burned against them" (Numbers 25:1-3).

So offensive was this and so dangerous to Israel that Moses took drastic and radical measures. He told Israel's judges to kill Israel's leaders publically in order to turn away God's anger.

The Lord said to Moses, "Take all the leaders of these people, kill them and expose them in broad daylight before the Lord, so that the Lord's fierce anger may turn away from Israel."

So Moses said to Israel's judges, "Each of you must put to death those of your people who have yoked themselves to the Baal of Peor." (Numbers 25:4-5)

Phinehas is one of the heroes of this story because he stopped the plague. Zimri, an Israelite, took Kozbi, the daughter of Zur, a tribal chief of the Midianites, into the tabernacle. While they were having sex, Phinehas, the son of Aaron, killed them both with the same plunge of one spear. Twenty-four thousand Israelites had already been killed in the plague before Phinehas stopped it with his brave, bold, and righteous act.

The Numbers narrative of this event does not include Balaam. But as we will see, he was involved. He counseled Balak to have the Moabite women seduce Israel's men, and Israel's sin blocked the blessings and protection of God, bringing down the curse of a plague on Israel—the same Israel that Balaam had not been able to curse effectively. The enemy cannot touch us; we bring tragedy on ourselves by our sin.

Numerous Other Biblical References Fill in the Gaps

Throughout the Bible, many other references to the story of Balaam and Balak round out the narrative and thereby fill in the blanks between Numbers chapters 24 and 25. These other Bible writers tell of Balaam giving moral lessons—or rather immoral lessons. Each reference adds another insight into Balaam's serious error.

Moses reports that Israel later took vengeance in Midian and killed Balaam. "They also killed Balaam son of Beor with the sword" (Number 31:8). Joshua reports, "In addition to those slain in battle, the Israelites had put to the sword Balaam son of Beor, who practiced divination" (Joshua 13:22).

The explanation for killing Balaam is given in Numbers 31:16. Moabite women enticed Israel to sin; they "followed Balaam's advice."

From Moses' explanation in Deuteronomy, it seems Balaam may have wanted to pronounce curses, but God would not let him. Regarding the Moabites he said, "For they did not come to meet you with bread and water on your way when you came out of Egypt, and they hired Balaam son of Beor from Pethor in Aram Naharaim to pronounce a curse on you. However, the Lord your God would not listen to Balaam but turned the curse into a blessing for you, because the Lord your God loves you. Do not seek a treaty of friendship with them as long as you live" (Deuteronomy 23:4-6).

Joshua spoke for God and explained spiritual warfare in his famous farewell speech near the end of his life. "When Balak son of Zippor, the king of Moab, prepared to fight against

Israel, he sent for Balaam son of Beor to put a curse on you. But I would not listen to Balaam, so he blessed you again and again, and I delivered you out of his hand" (Joshua 24:9-10).

Nehemiah explained why Ammonites and Moabites were not allowed in the assembly. "No Ammonite or Moabites should ever be admitted into the assembly of God because they had not met the Israelites with food and water but had hired Balaam to call a curse down on them. (Our God, however, turned the curse into a blessing.)" (Nehemiah 13:1-2).

Micah reminded his generation of God's righteousness in the Balaam/Balak incident. "My people, remember what Balak king of Moab plotted and what Balaam son of Beor answered. Remember your journey from Shittim to Gilgal, that you may know the righteous acts of the Lord" (Micah 6:5).

Peter says that Balaam was already sinning before he went to Balak, even before his verbal exchange with the donkey. Balaam "loved the wages of wickedness" and was insane to pursue his course. He evidently only reluctantly obeyed God in delivering the prophecies God gave him to bless, not curse, Israel. Peter says, "They have left the straight way and wandered off to follow the way of Balaam son of Bezer, who loved the wages of wickedness. But he was rebuked for his wrongdoing by a donkey—and animal without speech—who spoke with a human voice and restrained the prophet's madness" (2 Peter 2:15-16).

Jude describes sinful people who reject God's way by using three examples from the Old Testament. "Woe to them! They have taken the way of Cain; they have rushed for profit into

Balaam's error; they have been destroyed in Korah's rebellion" (Jude 11, emphasis mine).

John says in Revelation, "There are some among you who hold to the teaching of Balaam, who *taught Balak to entice the Israelites into sin* so that they ate food sacrificed to idols and committed sexual immorality" (Revelation 2:14, emphasis mine).

We can summarize Balaam in this way: 1.Although Balaam appeared to fear Jehovah God, he also practiced divination, which is forbidden to God's people. 2.He probably in his heart wanted to curse Israel, just as Balak wanted to.3.He was motivated by financial gain.4.He taught Balak to entice the Israelites into sin.5.Israel put Balaam to death for his part in this story.

Based on the colorful but sad story of Balaam, we reach twelve concrete conclusions:-

1. The lessons we are to learn from Balaam's sin are pervasive throughout the Bible. God wants us to be duly warned about the possibility of Christian service being sidetracked by the love of money.

2. Jesus was serious when He said, "You cannot serve both God and money" (Matthew 6:24).

3. Balaam helps us see the extremes of evil to which one will stoop when motivated by the love of money. The love of money truly is the root of all kinds of evil (1 Timothy 6:10).

4. Not everyone who speaks the truth about God and His people is a sincere follower of God's will. It is possible to have a great difference between your message, which can be very good, and the intents of your heart, which can be very evil. For a time you may be able to fool people, but God will eventually expose you. "Be not deceived: God cannot be mocked. People reap what they sow" (Galatians 6:7).

5. God may mercifully use an unusual method to attempt to get our attention, to try to stop us from going against His will. We must learn to distinguish between adversity that we should prayerfully overcome and cautions that God graciously gives us for our protection and good.

6. Sin gives the enemy room to work against us. Balak scored a certain though limited victory. Stay pure so you can fight successfully.

7. Psychologists say we find what we are looking for—we find evidences that support what we believe. We may notice verses in the Bible that affirm our desire for financial prosperity yet overlook the references to a simple lifestyle or to Balaam and his sin of using spiritual gifts for monetary gain.

8. Balaam's obedience may have been only outward as he inwardly looked for an opportunity to receive Balak's reward.

9. Sexual temptations (1) are spiritually motivated by the enemy, (2) may succeed when other temptations do not, and (3) will ruin your ministry.

10. We do not need to fear anyone's curse. God can turn curses into blessings.

11. Spiritual warfare is a reality. God needs influential Christians who will discern the battle lines, enter into spiritual war, and gain victories over a clever enemy. What would have happened had Moses not been doing spiritual warfare all those years?

12. Our own sin blocks God's blessings and protection far more than our enemy's cursings.

KING DAVID: A MAN AFTER GOD'S HEART

David asked the men standing near him, "What will be done for the man who kills this Philistine and removes this disgrace from Israel? Who is this uncircumcised Philistine that he should defy the armies of the living God?" They repeated to him what they had been saying and told him, "This is what will be done for the man who kills him." When Eliab, David's oldest brother, heard him speaking with the men, he burned with anger at him and asked, "Why have you come down here? And with whom did you leave those few sheep in the desert? I know how conceited you are and how wicked your heart is; you came down only to watch the battle." "Now what have I done?" said David. "Can't I even speak?" He then turned away to someone else and brought up the same matter, and the men answered him as before. What David said was overheard and reported to Saul, and Saul sent for him. David said to Saul, "Let no one lose heart on account of this Philistine; your servant will go and fight him." Saul replied, "You are not able to go out against this Philistine and fight him; you are only a boy, and he has been a fighting man from his youth." But

David said to Saul, "Your servant has been keeping his father's sheep. When a lion or a bear came and carried off a sheep from the flock, I went after it, struck it and rescued the sheep from its mouth. When it turned on me, I seized it by its hair, struck it and killed it. Your servant has killed both the lion and the bear; this uncircumcised Philistine will be like one of them, because he has defied the armies of the living God. The LORD who delivered me from the paw of the lion and the paw of the bear will deliver me from the hand of this Philistine." Saul said to David, "Go, and the LORD be with you."

Then Saul dressed David in his own tunic. He put a coat of armor on him and a bronze helmet on his head. David fastened on his sword over the tunic and tried walking around, because he was not used to them.

"I cannot go in these," he said to Saul, "because I am not used to them." So he took them off. Then he took his staff in his hand, chose five smooth stones from the stream, put them in the pouch of his shepherd's bag and, with his sling in his hand, approached the Philistine.

Meanwhile, the Philistine, with his shield bearer in front of him, kept coming closer to David. He looked David over and saw that he was only a boy, ruddy and handsome, and he despised him. He said to David, "Am I a dog, that you come at me with sticks?" And the Philistine cursed David by his gods. "Come here," he said, "and I'll give your flesh to the birds of the air and the beasts of the field!" David said to the Philistine, "You come against me with sword and spear and javelin, but I come against you in the name of the LORD Almighty, the God of the armies of Israel, whom you have defied. This day the LORD will hand you over to me, and I'll strike you down and cut off your head. Today I will give the carcasses of the Philistine army to the birds of the air and the beasts of the earth, and the whole world will know that there is a God in Israel. All those gathered here will know that it is not by sword or spear that the LORD saves; for the battle is the LORD's, and he will give all of you into our hands." As the Philistine moved closer to attack him, David ran quickly toward the battle line to meet him. Reaching into his bag and taking out a stone, he slung it and struck the Philistine on the forehead. The stone sank into his forehead, and he fell facedown on the ground. So David triumphed over the Philistine with a sling and a stone; without a sword in his hand he struck down the Philistine and killed him.

David ran and stood over him. He took hold of the Philistine's sword and drew it from the scabbard. After he killed him, he cut off his head with the sword. When the Philistines saw that their hero was dead, they turned and ran. Then the men of Israel and Judah surged forward with a shout and pursued the Philistines to the entrance of Gath and to the gates of Ekron. Their dead were strewn along the Shaaraim road to Gath and Ekron. When the Israelites returned from chasing the Philistines, they plundered their camp. David took the Philistine's head and brought it to Jerusalem, and he put the Philistine's weapons in his own tent. 1 Samuel 17:26-54

Beloved, do you know that David lived, grew up, and developed a relationship with the Lord in obscure sheep fields? How do you suppose he cultivated an ability to trust in and focus on God by watching sheep? Could the sheep he led have taught him not to fight back or seek revenge?

David was gifted, perhaps a genius. He was a musician, poet, athlete, military strategist, ethicist, statesman, leader, and king.

He is one of the most prominent figures in the history of the world and the most famous ancestor of Jesus, who is called the Son of David. No Bible character offers such a full range of human successes and failures as David.

The highlights of David's life are recorded in 1 Samuel 16 through 1 Kings 2:11 and in 1 Chronicles 10:14 through 29:30. There we learn that this man after God's own heart (1 Samuel 13:14) allowed sin in his sons without correcting them. That he loved God passionately yet had an affair with a married woman. That he was a loyal soldier and beloved military leader who betrayed one of his finest warriors and closest friends.

David's life falls into three phases: his years of preparation for leadership, the successful years of his reign, and the years of difficulty following his moral failure. Fewer chapters record his successful years than record the events of his preparatory or difficult years. We often think that as soon as David got past his training under the discipline of Saul, his successful kingly career began and continued for a long time. But Scripture indicates his successful years were limited and that trouble, adversity, and embarrassment awaited him in his latter years as a result of his moral failure, not correcting his sons, and trusting in the flesh.

Obscurity Is No Problem for God

When Samuel visited Jesse's home in search of the next king for Israel, Jesse overlooked David. If this is any indication of the family's posture toward David, it is clear that the family had little regard for the youngest son. Assuming that David wrote the 116th Psalm, he refers favorably there to the formative example of his mother. "Truly I am your servant, Lord; I am your servant, as was my mother before me; you have loosed my bonds of affliction" (Psalm 116:16). Though disregarded by his father and his brothers (who followed Jesse's example), David was nevertheless encouraged by his mother's love for God.

We do not know how many years (or how many months in each year) David spent alone, watching the sheep. His references in the psalms to his sheep-watching responsibilities suggest that shepherding was a major part of his young life. In any event, he used those hours well, worshipping, developing the performing arts in his musical abilities, and practicing with his sling, killing a bear and a lion. Most important, he used the contemplative opportunity to develop his personal philosophy of life (Psalm 23). In the lonely valleys near Bethlehem, God built Israel's most famous and beloved king.

David was like Moses as a leader-in-training. Moses was banished from the king's court and fled for his life. David was disregarded by his family and assigned to watching the sheep. Both leaders developed while watching sheep in obscurity and in due time were discovered and brought into public leadership. You may think you live in obscurity and no one knows you even exist. That is a wonderful place to be, because God knows exactly where you are. Be content, and do not waste the valuable training time God is giving you for contemplation, prayer, and self-development. Obscurity is not a problem for God. If you sulk in your obscurity you may remain there. Instead seek God and prepare yourself for greater service. God found Moses, and God found David. He will find you too.

Jesse neglected David, but God helped Samuel find him (1 Samuel 16). "For the eyes of the Lord range throughout the earth to strengthen those whose hearts are fully committed to him" (2 Chronicles 16:9). While you're waiting for Him to discover you, what are you doing to develop yourself?

The Basis for Confidence

Jesse sent his son David with instructions to take food supplies to his soldier brothers serving in Saul's army. When he arrived, his brothers scorned him rather than welcoming him. "When Eliab, David's oldest brother heard him speaking with the men, he burned with anger at him and asked, 'Why have you come down here? And with whom did you leave those few sheep in the wilderness? I know how conceited you are and how wicked your heart is; you came down only to watch the battle'" (1 Samuel 17:28). David was not discouraged by this treatment, however. He pursued his interest in the battle, Goliath, and God's reputation.

Later, as David approached the giant, Goliath cursed him by his gods. David ignored the giant's disdain and his slanderous remarks, and replied with his own mature statement of his philosophy of war: You come against me with sword and spear and javelin, but I come against you in the name of the Lord Almighty, the God of the armies of Israel, whom you have defied. This day the Lord will deliver you into my hands, and I'll strike you down and cut off your head. This very day I will give the carcasses of the Philistine army to the birds and the wild animals, and the whole world will know that there is a God in Israel. All those gathered here will know that it is not by sword or spear that the Lord saves; for the battle is the Lord's and he will give all of you into our hands. (1 Samuel 17:45-47)

Goliath was formidable, but David placed his faith in God and His power, and he won the victory. David's God-focused philosophy of war was right on target. It enabled him to fight successfully for many years.

Submitting to God's Training Program

Saul secretly anointed David to become king. Soon after that, God began the developmental process through which He prepared David. At Saul's invitation, David became Saul's harpist and began to observe life at the king's court. After returning to his home, presumably because of Israel's war with the Philistines, David's father sent him to his brothers at the battlefront with cheese and foodstuffs.

Jealous Saul was a difficult mentor. David escaped the king's spear twice and his army twice. But through adversity after adversity at the hand of Saul, David learned to not fight back. He refused to oppose God's anointed. David fled from Jerusalem when his son Absalom, an illegitimate and self-proclaimed leader, entered the city. He left his home rather than see a civil war destroy Jerusalem. Even against the silly and powerless fool Shimei, David would not fight (as recorded in 2 Samuel 16:10-14).

The imprecatory Psalms, which include cursing against enemies, are sometimes misunderstood. But when we realize that David trusted God to defend him rather than taking revenge himself, we can appreciate the high ethical standard David maintained. David, the ethicist, held to a higher level of behavior than Moses had taught. Moses only instructed that one should limit one's vengeance to repaying in kind the treatment of the original offender. If we do not fight for ourselves but rather let God do our fighting for us, we will have learned a valuable lesson from David.

David Was a Wise Leader of Soldiers

David's victory over Goliath catapulted him into a successful military career. He had victories everywhere he turned. "David was so successful that Saul gave him a high rank in the army" (1 Samuel 18:5). "In everything he did he had great success, because the Lord was with him" (1 Samuel 18:14). "David met with more success than the rest of Saul's officers, and his name became well known" (1 Samuel 18:30).

Later, at Nob, as he fled from Saul, David sought direction from God, relying on the priests there to assist him. "Ahimelek inquired of the Lord for him" (1 Samuel 22:10). Saul learned of the priest's assistance and became extremely angry. Ahimelek responded to Saul, "Was that day the first time I inquired of God for him? Of course not!" (1 Samuel 22: 15). Saul had eighty-five priests killed that day. This did not stop David from inquiring of the Lord often. Because he habitually sought the Lord, God gave David military intelligence for his protection many times. At Keilah, as he continued to flee from Saul, "he inquired of the Lord saying, 'Shall I go and attack these Philistines?'" (1 Samuel 23:2). "Once again David inquired of the Lord" (1 Samuel 23:4). "Again David asked, 'Will the citizens of Keilah surrender me and my men to Saul?' And the Lord said, 'They will'" (1 Samuel 23:12). David was protected time and time again.

When David became king, the Philistines invaded Israeli territory, "so David inquired of the Lord, 'Shall I go and attack the Philistines? Will you deliver them into my hands?'" (2 Samuel 5:19). The Philistines attacked again, "so David inquired of the Lord, and he answered, 'Do not go straight up, but circle around behind them and attack them in front of the poplar trees. As soon as you hear the sound of marching in the tops of the poplar trees, move quickly, because that will mean the Lord has gone out in front of you to strike the Philistine army'" (2 Samuel 5:23-24).

Little wonder David could say, "With your help I can advance against a troop; with my God I can scale a wall" (2 Samuel 22:30). David's guiding principle of continually inquiring of the Lord, coupled with his faith in God as the source for military victories, was the reason for his repeated successes. What if you and I were to apply that policy to the work we do for God? What difference would it make in our homes, businesses, careers, churches, communities, nations?

David's Heart Was toward God

One has only to read David's psalms to find ample poetic evidence of his strong desire for the Lord. The celebrative manner in which David directed and participated in the procession to Jerusalem with the ark is just one example of his public and private passion for God (2 Samuel 6:1-11). David was not ashamed of his zeal for the Lord, as evidenced by his scorning the ridicule that his wife, Saul's daughter, gave to him. "David said to Michal, 'It was before the Lord, who chose me rather than your father or anyone from his house when he appointed me ruler over the Lord's people Israel—I will celebrate before the Lord. I will become even more undignified than this, and I will be humiliated in my own eyes. But by these slave girls you spoke of, I will be held in honor'" (2 Samuel 6:21-22).

David's penitence after his sin with Bathsheba and against Uriah also reveals David's love for God.

Against you, you only have I sinned and done what is evil in your sight; so you are right in your verdict and justified when you judge . . . . Cleanse me with hyssop, and I will be clean; wash me, and I will be whiter than snow. Let me hear joy and gladness; let the bones you have crushed rejoice . . . . Create in me a pure heart, O God, and renew a steadfast spirit within me. Do not cast me from your presence or take your Holy Spirit from me. Restore to me the joy of your salvation and grant me a willing spirit, to sustain me . . . . You do not delight in sacrifice, or I would bring it; you do not take pleasure in burnt offering. My sacrifice, O God, is a broken spirit; a broken and contrite heart you, God, will not despise. (Psalm 51:4, 7-8, 10-12, 16-17) Let us too have a heart toward God.

Beginning Well Is not Enough

David was Israel's greatest king and the founder of the dynasty in which Jesus Christ was born, yet only ten chapters record David's triumphant years. For sixteen chapters he was in training, for ten chapters he was a triumphant king, and these are followed by fourteen chapters that record his sin, its consequences, and his constant struggle against various difficulties until he died. David had three major strengths that were offset later in life by three major failures. If he had used any one of his strengths, he could have avoided all three of the following failures:

1. *David did not correct his children*. David was soft on the sin in his own family. He failed to discipline his sons, three of whom most certainly should have been punished: Amnon, Absolom, and Adonijah. Amnon raped his sister Tamar. Absalom revolted against his father and tried to take the entire kingdom. When David did nothing about it, Joab took matters into his own

hands, killed Absalom, and eventually rebuked David. Just prior to David's death, Adonijah also tried to usurp the throne. Scripture says, "His father had never rebuked him by asking, 'Why do you behave as you do?'" (1 Kings 1:6). David did not discipline his sons; Israel suffered shame as a result.

2. *David sinned with Bathsheba and murdered Uriah.* Some Bible scholars believe that when David sinned with Bathsheba, he should not have been in Jerusalem in the first place, but rather on the battlefield. As a soldier and leader of soldiers, the sin of David murdering one of his mighty men is unconscionable.

3. *David showed his dependence on human strength by numbering his army, contrary to God's Word.* David's final mistake was to trust in the power of his own army rather than trust in God. God had told Israel through Moses not to count soldiers, which was a way of expressing the need to trust God, not the arm of flesh. Yet David insisted, against Joab's advice, on enrolling the fighting men.

David's major strengths that could have been utilized against those failures were: 1. *He believed in God for military victory.* Why did David not trust God for victory toward the end of his life? Earlier he had inquired of the Lord regarding military questions and gained numerous victories. Could God not give him further victories without relying on a strong army of many soldiers? Could God's strength in battle not also have helped David raise obedient children?

2. *He inquired of the Lord regarding military matters.* Why didn't David inquire of the Lord regarding his children's disobedience? Why not ask the Lord what to do with the problem of the woman in his neighborhood bathing within

view of the royal palace? Could he not have inquired of the Lord regarding the decision to number Israel's army?

3. *He had a passionate love for God.* If David loved God so intensely, why did he allow disobedience in his family? How could he have an affair with a neighbor's wife? How could he send Uriah to his death? How could he trust human military might and disobey God's command not to number his army?

It seems the older David grew, and the more comfortable he became as king, the more his moral and spiritual strength declined. His faith in God's power to deliver, his policy of regularly seeking God's counsel, and his love for God were in operation only selectively later in his life. This can be a lesson to help us avoid becoming too comfortable—and less dependent on God. David did not finish well. Will you?

FIRE BRAND PROPHET ELIJAH "THE GOD THAT ANWERS BY FIRE LET HIM BE GOD"

You may not feel like the mighty Elijah, but did you know that the Bible says Elijah was a human being just like we are? Were you aware that the prestigious and powerful Elijah was content with common things? What was Elijah really like? What do we need to know if we want to be an Elijah?

There are similarities between the spiritual condition of Israel in Elijah's day and that of our world today. We, like Israel, are under attack by a hateful spiritual enemy who wants to destroy us. Israel needed an Elijah; today's nations need men and women like Elijah.

Notice what Elisha did and said when Elijah, his mentor, was caught up into heaven: He picked up the cloak that had fallen from Elijah and went back and stood on the bank of the Jordan. Then he took the cloak that had fallen from him and struck the water with it. "Where is the Lord, the God of Elijah?" he asked. When he struck the water, it divided to the right and to the left, and he crossed over. (2 Kings 2:13-14)

Elisha asked, "Where is the Lord?" The answer is, "On His throne, listening to prayer, performing miracles, just as he has always been." The more important question is, "Where are the Elijahs of God?" Will you be one?

Elijah Was a Human Being Like Us

Elijah was one of the most powerful men in the Old Testament. His prayer life, miracles, and courage, and the powerful showdown in the contest with Baal and Asheroth in opposition to Yahweh on Mount Carmel, are recorded in some of the most picturesque literature in the Bible. He was a great man who did great things together with God.

If Elijah were different from us, we would be excused from doing or even trying to do what he did. The justification for not being as powerful an influence in our day as Elijah was in his day is effectively removed, however, by James 5:17, which says, "Elijah was a human being, even as we are." This statement challenges us. Since Elijah was like us, we could, and by implication should, do exploits like he did.

Elijah faced the same kinds of situations we face. I can imagine Elijah's little boy running to him, crying, "Daddy, Daddy, my puppy is lost. Where is he? How can I find him?" Or Elijah's wife coming to him, saying, "El, the water in the creek is so muddy I can't get the laundry clean. I wash and wash and the clothes get muddier and muddier. What can I do?" Or Elijah's neighbor demanding, "Elijah, your sheep are eating my grass. If you don't get them out of my field, I'm going to have one for dinner." Elijah had domestic challenges like ours, and he was a person like us. Yet he lived a godly life of prayer and spiritual accomplishment. We can too.

Here's the challenge, Even though you are a normal human being and have daily responsibilities, will you take time to be spiritual?

Elijah Was Not Enamored or Preoccupied with Earthly Finery

Second Kings 1:7-8 describes Elijah as "a man with a garment of hair and with a leather belt around his waist." Is it really important for us to know what kind of clothes Elijah had? No. But it is important that we understand what kind of character Elijah had. His clothes give us some indication of that. What he wore reflects his value system.

We find many references in the Old Testament to fine clothes. So we know they existed and that some people valued them.

Achan hid a pretty Babylonian robe taken from Ai in the floor of his tent along with stolen silver coins and a wedge of gold. He paid for that mistake with his life. It was not wrong to have nice clothes or even to value nice clothes. But it was wrong to steal them and pretend the theft had not happened. Achan would not have even been tempted with those clothes except that he valued them—too much. His strong desire for them was the deeper motivational problem that led to the sin of taking what Joshua had forbidden.

Gehazi had the same problem. He ran after Naaman's chariot and lied in order to receive exquisite Babylonian garments. His wrong value system led him into temptation.

Jacob gave Joseph a beautiful coat of many colors. This may have been unwise, because it set Joseph up to be a point of jealousy for his brothers. It would not have been wrong for Joseph to wear the gift, but according to the story, he bragged about his dreams, indicating that Joseph was self-impressed—perhaps, partly, because of his fine-looking garment.

Both Daniel and Mordecai were given royal robes to wear. But in neither of those cases did the clothes reflect the value system of the person wearing them. They were gifts given by someone else who valued them.

Wearing nice clothes is not wrong; we all ought to look our best for God's glory. After all, the Bible says that man looks on the outward appearance. (1 Samuel 16:7) The first impressions we give about ourselves are usually based on what people see. Our clothes are important statements about our tastes. However, we should not be preoccupied with finery. Elijah, had he chosen, could have made a priority of wearing long, flowing robes. Yet he was content with a garment of animal hair and a leather belt.

The Bible describes a position of balance in which our supply is adequate. Financial blessings do come to God's people—some more than others. Hard work, honesty, and clean habits, combined with avoiding the expenses of bad habits, give economic advantages to God's people. John wished blessings for his readers when he wrote, "I pray that you may enjoy good health and that all may go well with you, even as your soul is getting along well" (3 John 2). The Bible definition of *prosperity* is for the road to be open and smooth—for things to go well—which includes much more than just financial or material blessings. And the blessings God gives to those who tithe and give liberally to His work are well known.

Nevertheless, Jesus also taught the value of living simply. He said, "Do not store up for yourselves treasures on earth, where moth and rust destroy, and where thieves break in and steal." And, "No one can serve two masters. Either he will hate the one and love the other, or he will be devoted to the one and despise the other. You cannot serve both God and money" (Matthew 6:19, 24).

Paul wrote to Timothy about "false doctrines" believed by those who do "not agree with the sound instruction of our Lord Jesus Christ and godly teaching" (1 Timothy 6:3). Among the errors Timothy was to avoid was thinking that "*godliness is a means to financial gain*. But godliness with contentment is great gain . . . . For the love of money is a root of all kinds of evil" (verses 5-6, emphasis mine). Paul also warned the early Christians "not to be arrogant nor to put their hope in wealth, which is so uncertain, but to put their hope in God, who richly provides us with everything for our enjoyment" (verse 17). Some Christians today teach that we can use godliness or selected Bible practices to gain financially. This is not consistent with the teaching of the whole Bible and Paul calls it a false doctrine. We are to use money to serve God, not use God to serve money. Rejoice in what God gives you and don't be embarrassed about it. But neither be preoccupied with it or possessed by it. If you talk often about material possessions, that could be a signal that you value them too much. I see three problems with prosperity theology: 1. It causes those who prosper materially and financially to become proud and arrogant. Such arrogance hinders their ministries. 2. It causes those who do not prosper materially and financially to feel inferior or to lose confidence in their acceptance with God. This reduces or hinders their joy in ministry. 3. Prosperity theology is not consistent with the balanced teachings of the Bible.

Where are those who will not be caught up in the pursuit of financial prosperity, but rather seek first the kingdom of God? (Matthew 6:33)

Elijah Spent Much Time Alone with God

First Kings 17:1-5 says, "Now Elijah the Tishbite, from Tisbe in Gilead, said to Ahab, 'As the Lord, the God of Israel lives, whom I serve, there will be neither dew nor rain in the next few years except at my word.' Then the word of the Lord came to Elijah: 'Leave here, turn eastward and hide in the Kerith Ravine, east of the Jordan. You will drink from the brook, and I have ordered the ravens to feed you there.' So he did what the Lord had told him."

Even though Elijah faced domestic responsibilities at home, the time came when he needed to get away from normal daily activities in order to have an extended time alone with God. We do not know how much time passed between Elijah delivering his message to the king and his departure for the Kerith Ravine. But of the three and one-half years between Elijah's announcement and the contest on Mount Carmel, we might guess Elijah spent a number of months alone with God at Kerith.

I significantly increased the amount of daily time I spend in prayer. Since then I have experienced deeper insights into the truth of God's Word, greater liberty and authority in teaching and preaching, more opportunities to serve, teach, and preach, and increased fine-tuning of flawed character traits. When I pray more, God works more. I want God to work a lot in my life. So I will pray a lot in order to see God more involved. I have long said that the most important thing I do in any day is pray, but now I am practicing that. I spend more time in prayer than any other one thing I do each day. Have you discovered the value and productivity of spending lengths of time alone with God in prayer?

Elijah Discerned God's Plan and Prayed Accordingly

James 5:17b-18 says, "He prayed earnestly that it would not rain, and it did not rain on the land for three and a half years. Again he prayed, and the heavens gave rain, and the earth produced its crops."

The reason Elijah was so "powerful and effective" (James 5:16) in his prayer life was that he cooperated with God in prayer and prayed according to God's plan. He listened to God, who told him what He was planning to do, and Elijah prayed accordingly. Based on God's agenda, Elijah prayed that rain would not fall. That seems like a strange prayer. When we haven't had rain for a while, we usually pray *for* rain. What kind of prophet would pray that rain will *not* fall? A prophet who knows God's plan. God wanted to defame Baal, the Canaanite rain God. God's plan worked perfectly. The prophets of Baal could produce neither rain in the valleys nor fire on the mountain. When God's purpose in the drought was complete, and Elijah and God had everyone's attention, he prayed according to the next phase of God's plan—that rain *would* fall.

The second phase required Elijah to completely reverse his direction in prayer. What kind of prophet would pray one way one day and then pray exactly the opposite the next day? A prophet who knows how to move with God through the phases and stages of His plan, a prophet who partners with God and prays according to God's plan. In each instance, Elijah was following God's agenda for that specific time. The wisdom of God is far superior to the ideas of men. This is why we should submit our wills to His and seek His plan. Some of us do the will of God—what God has shown us to do—too long. We have to be sensitive to changes in God's direction. We have no right to assume that we will always be where we are now or that we will always do what we are doing today. We must stay up-to-date with God. We should be ready, as Elijah was, to move to the next phase, pray a new way, and do new things whenever God directs a change.

What is God's plan for your community? For your church? For your family? For your career? What would happen if you began to pray according to God's plan? What would your church or community be like ten years from now if for the next ten years you prayed according to God's agenda? Mount Carmel illustrates the power that can be released in the heavens and in the affairs of humans when a person of God prays according to God's plan instead of only what human imaginations can produce. God is "able to do immeasurably more than we can ask or imagine" (Ephesians 3:20).

God is even more eager than you are for you to pray according to His agenda. He is searching for those who will be more concerned about His desires than their own. When we ask God to reveal His will to us so that we can pray in cooperation with it, He is very pleased. He wants us to know His will. Therefore, we ought to be either praying according to God's will or praying that we may know His will so that we can pray in agreement with it.

Will you find out what God wants to do through you, and then pray and move with God as His cooperative partner?

Elijah Publicly Challenged the Political and Religious Systems

In 1 Kings 18:19 Elijah challenged Ahab, "Now summon the people from all over Israel to meet me on Mount Carmel. And bring the four hundred and fifty prophets of Baal and the four hundred prophets of Asherah, who eat at Jezebel's table." The following story illustrates this kind of miracle can also happen now if we pray.

While serving as itinerary Missionary evangelist, once we were at a community where a witch doctor in that village who could cause a person to levitate. He had so much influence in the community that some Christians reverted to their superstitious ways and many nonbelievers were afraid to become Christians. To counter this, we became concerned and prayerful as I stirred the handful group of Christians and publicly announced during the crusade that the true God would hinder the witch doctor so that he could not cause a person to levitate. The Christians in the community joined as we prayed fervently. The villagers gathered around. When the witch doctor was unable to conduct his usual ceremonies, observers saw that God's power was superior to that of the evil spirits.

Bible character like Elijah's may seem long ago and far away. Yet what happened on Mount Carmel, and the powerful encounters that are recorded in the book of Acts, can still occur today for those who are willing to follow God closely. After spending months alone with God in prayer, Elijah had the courage to publicly confront the established religious system of his day. He had the daring to taunt the prophets of Baal while they prayed. He also had the confidence to pour scarce water on the sacrifice he was about to offer to God—three times! He had the nerve to order the 450 prophets of Baal and the 400 prophets of Asherah killed. After this he again ascended Mount Carmel and began to pray for rain.

At the end of the day everyone knew which god was the true God and that He was a God of might and power. All this was possible because God found a partner who allowed himself to be a vessel used by a mighty God.

Christians are not to put God to the test in unwise, humanly imagined contests. That is foolish and presumptuous. But Elijah was moving in the will of God and was led by God in this public demonstration of His superiority. When God leads us and gives us the courage, we too can bring glory to Him by moving obediently and boldly.

Will you take the time to find out what God wants to do and then publicly, obediently, and boldly represent Him?

Elijah Addressed Important National Issues

First Kings 18:18 says, "'I have not made trouble for Israel,' Elijah replied. 'But you and your father's family have. You have abandoned the Lord's commands and have followed the

Baals.'" Second Kings 1:3-4 says, "The angel of the Lord said to Elijah the Tishbite, 'Go up and meet the messengers of the king of Samaria and ask them, "Is it because there is no God in Israel that you are going of to consult Baal-Zebub, the god of Ekron?" Therefore this is what the Lord says: "You will not leave the bed you are lying on. You will certainly die!"'"

Elijah understood God's perspective about events of national importance to Israel. Elijahs today should prepare sermons with the Bible in one hand and the newspaper in the other. We need to know Scripture *and* what it says about current events. We must skillfully use the Bible so our sermons have the authority of "This is what the Lord says." But unless we are also reading the newspaper or listening to the news, we will not know the important issues of the day. We will not be giving the Holy Spirit an opportunity to lay the burden of His concerns about current events on our hearts.

Elijahs today need to know what is going on around them in their society and nation, and we need to be concerned about those issues. We need to know what God has to say about these concerns and be able to speak "the very words of God" (1 Peter 4:11). This will require constant prayer and Bible study along with keeping up on the news. You may need to spend time sharing these things in prayer and study together with other wise men and women of God—there is wisdom in doing so. If you want to be an Elijah in your area of ministry, be sure you have God's perspective on important issues facing you and the people around you. Then have the courage to speak out in the name of the Lord. Know the problems. Have an informed opinion. Be knowledgeable about how the Bible speaks to contemporary concerns. Then gather the courage to speak out from Scripture on meaningful subjects.

What do you think about Christians becoming involved in politics? What do you think of corruption in public administration? What is your position on single sex history education in public schools? How can your city and state convert the wealth from the precious stones, gold, silver, and copper in your mountains into roads, bridges, schools, and hospitals? Have you thought this through? Do you pray about these things? Do you discuss and study such issues with other men and women of God? Do you seek God's wisdom? Have you ever expressed your views to your public leaders?

Will you become aware of local, national, contemporary issues, find God's will in the matter, and speak out for Him with authority?

Elijah Received Encouragement from God in a Moment of Weakness

The excitement of Mount Carmel must have been tremendous. The fire coming down from heaven to consume the sacrifice, the slaying of 850 false prophets, the miraculous and timely rain, each would have made a powerful impression on any observer, but especially on Elijah. It was also emotionally and physically exhausting. How did Elijah handle the emotion of the next few days? Evidently his thoughts turned in upon himself, as he fled from a wicked and angry queen intent on killing him. The thrill of yesterday's excitement was gone.

Where was the strong spiritual leader Israel needed? Hiding in a cave.

First Kings 19:9-12 says: There he went into a cave and spent the night. And the word of the Lord came to him: "What are you doing here, Elijah?" . . . He replied, . . . "I am the only one left, and now they are trying to kill me too.' There was a powerful wind . . . but the Lord was not in the wind . . . . There was an earthquake, but the Lord was not in the earthquake. After the earthquake came a fire, but the Lord was not in the fire. And after the fire came a gentle whisper. When Elijah heard it, he pulled his cloak over his face and went out and stood at the mouth of the cave. Then a voice said to him, "What are you doing here, Elijah?"

When the congregation is gathered, the musical instruments are playing, the dancers are dancing, the tambourines are playing, and the crowd is worshipping with joy, it is easy to be caught up in the glory of the presence of the Lord. In such a spiritually buoyant atmosphere God's anointing sometimes enables preachers to teach far better than they would be able to if success depended just on their own knowledge and understanding or verbal and rhetoric skills. We rejoice in the glorious presence of God on Sunday morning.

But when Monday arrives our emotions often take a dive. Yesterday's excitement seems long ago and far away. People in ministry probably should not make any important career decisions on Mondays—when they are in an emotional cave.

We humans are not designed to fly high with emotional excitement day after day. We must be able to hear the encouraging voice of the Holy Spirit on Monday if we want to minister and be ministered to the following Sunday. Cultivate the ability to work your way through the valleys if you want to celebrate the joy of the Lord with God's people at church again. Give yourself time to recuperate after exhausting and emotionally draining times of spiritual work. Then you will be ready for the next opportunity. The Bible records how God spoke through winds at the Red Sea and on Pentecost, in earthquakes in front of Korah's tents and at Phillipi, and through fires on Mount Sinai and in the upper room. Elijah was able to discern which of the sounds he heard at the cave contained the voice of the Lord. This time in the cave, it was not in the wind, earthquake, or fire, but in a whisper. When Elijah heard the whisper, he went to the mouth of the cave and God spoke to him. Let us too listen for God's whispers.

Will you hear the voice of the Lord in the emotional valley that follows the mountaintop experience and hold steady through the emotional ups and downs of the Christian life?

Elijah Was Involved in International Developments

In 1 Kings 19:15-18, God said to Elijah, "Anoint Hazael king over Aram. Also, anoint Jehu son of Nimshi king over Israel, and anoint Elisha son of Shaphat from Abel Mehoiah to succeed you as prophet. Jehu will put to death any who escape the sword of Hazael, and Elisha will put to death any who escape the sword of Jehu. Yet I reserve seven thousand in Israel—all whose knees have not bowed down to Baal and all whose mouths have not kissed him."

You may think that not everyone can be involved in international ministry. Not so. God will use you differently than He used Elijah, but still your regular place of prayer can become your "World Center for International Intercession." Jesus told . . . a parable to show them that they should always pray and not give up. (Luke 18:1) If you remain in me and my words remain in you, ask whatever you wish, and it will be given you. (John 14:7)

You may ask me for anything in my name, and I will do it. (John 14:14) I tell you the truth, my Father will give you whatever you ask in my name. (John 16: 23).This is the confidence we have in approaching God: that if we ask anything according to his will, he hears us. And if we know that he hears us—whatever we ask—we know that we have what we asked of him. (1 John 5:14-15) The prayer of a righteous man is powerful and effective. (James 5:16) Rise up, O Lord! May your enemies be scattered; may your foes flee before you. (Numbers 10:35) They will never be silent day or night. You who call on the Lord, give yourselves no rest, and give him no rest until he establishes. (Isaiah 62:6-7) . . . to him who is able to do immeasurably more than all we ask or imagine. (Ephesians 3:20) Ask of me and I will make the nations your inheritance, the ends of the earth your possession. (Psalm 2:8) What is impossible with men is possible with God. (Luke 18:27) Bless me and enlarge my territory! Let your hand be with me. (1 Chronicles 4:10) I will not let you go unless you bless me. (Genesis 32:27)

Elijah, Daniel, Isaiah, and Jeremiah all had messages, not only for Israel but for other nations as well. Why should we pray just for our own country? Look at a globe or a world map, and make a list of the nations. In my weekly routine, I begin with Iceland and pray my way through every nation of North America, Central America, the Caribbean, South America, Africa, Europe, the Middle East, Asia, and the Pacific regions. I pray for the pastors, churches, missionaries, peoples groups, Christians, prisoners, prison keepers, educators, media, entertainers, and other types of persons in societies, tribes, and governments in each of those regions.

Regardless of the nation I am in at the time, I have a "World Center for International Intercession" as I walk on the early-morning streets of Africa's cities or quieter rural roads. You can have an international ministry too. Your job, health, age, or other factors and responsibilities may hinder you from physically going abroad, but prayer knows no boundaries. In prayer you can travel the world from nation to nation anytime you want to.

Will you look at the nations of the world and become a part of God's army of intercessors?

Elijah Trained Future Ministers and Mentored a Successor

First Kings 19:19-21 says, "Elijah went from there and found Elisha son of Shaphat . . . . Then he set out to follow Elijah and he became his attendant." Second Kings 2:3, 5 says, "The company of the prophets at Bethel came out to Elisha and asked . . . . The company of the prophets at Jericho went up to Elisha and asked . . ."

Even though Elijah was a busy prophet, he took the time to train a successor. He also spent time with groups of prophets at Bethel, Gilgal, and Jericho. Activities like this take time, but if we want to influence not only our generation but also the next one, we must make this investment. God's work is vast. We will possibly not finish the job while we are alive. We must deliberately allow the next cohort of ministers to stand on our shoulders and do a better job than we did. By being transparent we can help them avoid making some of the same mistakes we made. When we make fewer mistakes, the Holy Spirit can do His work better. As we mature in ministry we learn that we will not always be the "sage on the stage," but the time comes for senior ministers to be the "guides on the side."

Are you giving opportunities to those you are training? Is a desire to develop younger leaders reflected in your choice of leaders at home group meetings? Do you take time to mentor younger servants of the Lord so they can carry on the work in the next generation?

Elijah Was Worth Chariots and Horsemen: Second Kings 2:11-12 says, "As they were walking along and talking together, suddenly a chariot of fire and horses of fire appeared and separated the two of them, and Elijah went up to heaven in a whirlwind. Elisha saw this and cried out, 'My father! My father! The chariots and horsemen of Israel!' And Elisha saw him no more. Then he took hold of his own clothes and tore them apart."

Elisha was not merely saying that he *saw* chariots and horsemen. He was actually calling Elijah "the chariots and horsemen of Israel." What is the symbolism of Elijah being called chariots and horsemen? Here is my understanding. Chariots were powerful weapons of warfare in Elijah's day. Archers could shoot arrows and spearmen could throw spears from elevated positions safe within the protective sides of chariots. The chariots themselves were also weapons, to say nothing of the war horses out front, striking with powerful hooves. On the wheels of some chariots were blades capable of cutting down many foot soldiers. Elisha was implying that Elijah was a strong spiritual weapon for Israel.

How would we illustrate this today? One powerful modern weapon is the Patriot missile. This strictly defensive weapon can hit an incoming intercontinental ballistic missile while it is still in the air headed toward its target. God needs "chariots" (us) to be spiritual weapons much like a Patriot missile that can bring down the fiery darts of the enemy before they reach our nations. Today, as in Elijah's time, we are under attack by invisible forces of unrighteousness. These evil spirits intend the destruction of God's people and His church. These unseen spiritual forces are responsible for the blinding and binding of many non-Christians and even some believers. God needs men and women today who, like Elijah, will be powerful, effective weapons, rushing to the defense of all that is precious to God. The militant church must fight against the spirits of jealousy that breed discontent, lusts that urge people into various forms of perverse sexual sins or marital unfaithfulness, false religions that lure people into demon and devil worship, and other deceptive spirits that lead to witchcraft, materialism, atheism, and numerous doctrines of devils.

Will you do today for your nation what Elijah did in his day for his nation? Will you become a strong spiritual weapon that God can use to tear down the forces of unrighteousness? If you are willing to do the difficult spiritual work in the invisible realm, you will be doing the work of an Elijah. You too will be "chariots and horsemen."

Will you enter into an invisible spiritual war and bring destruction to those forces that are trying to destroy your nation? Will you be an Elijah today?

ELISHA: the double portion prophet

And it came about when the LORD was about to take up Elijah by a whirlwind to heaven, that Elijah went with Elisha from Gilgal. Elijah said to Elisha, "Stay here please, for the LORD has sent me as far as Bethel." But Elisha said, "As the LORD lives and as you yourself live, I will not leave you." So they went down to Bethel. Then the sons of the prophets who were at Bethel came out to Elisha and said to him, "Do you know that the LORD will take away your master from over you today?" And he said, "Yes, I know; be still." Elijah said to him, "Elisha, please stay here, for the LORD has sent me to Jericho." But he said, "As the LORD lives, and as you yourself live, I will not leave you." So they came to Jericho. The sons of the prophets who were at Jericho approached Elisha and said to him, "Do you know that the LORD will take away your master from over you today?" And he answered, "Yes, I know; be still." Then Elijah said to him, "Please stay here, for the LORD has sent me to the Jordan." And he said, "As the LORD lives, and as you yourself live, I will not leave you." So the two of them went on. Now fifty men of the sons of the prophets went and stood opposite them at a distance, while the two of them stood by the Jordan. Elijah took his mantle and folded it together and struck the waters, and they were divided here and there, so that the two of them crossed over on dry ground.

When they had crossed over, Elijah said to Elisha, "Ask what I shall do for you before I am taken from you." And Elisha said, "Please, let a double portion of your spirit be upon me." He said, "You have asked a hard thing. Nevertheless, if you see me when I am taken from you, it shall be so for you; but if not, it shall not be so." As they were going along and talking, behold, there appeared a chariot of fire and horses of fire which separated the two of them. And Elijah went up by a whirlwind to heaven. Elisha saw it and cried out, "My father, my father, the chariots of Israel and its horsemen!" And he saw Elijah no more. Then he took hold of his own clothes and tore them in two pieces. He also took up the mantle of Elijah that fell from him and returned and stood by the bank of the Jordan. He took the mantle of Elijah that fell from him and struck the waters and said, "Where is the LORD, the God of Elijah?" And when he also had struck the waters, they were divided here and there; and Elisha crossed over.

Elisha Succeeds Elijah Now when the sons of the prophets who were at Jericho opposite him saw him, they said, "The spirit of Elijah rests on Elisha." And they came to meet him and bowed themselves to the ground before him. They said to him, "Behold now, there are with your servants fifty strong men, please let them go and search for your master; perhaps the Spirit of the LORD has taken him up and cast him on some mountain or into some valley." And he said, "You shall not send." But when they urged him until he was ashamed, he said, "Send." They sent therefore fifty men; and they searched three days but did not find him. They returned to him while he was staying at Jericho; and he said to them, "Did I not say to you, 'Do not go'?" Then the men of the city said to Elisha, "Behold now, the situation of this city is pleasant, as my lord sees; but the water is bad and the land is unfruitful." He said, "Bring me a new jar, and put salt in it." So they brought it to him. He went out to the spring of water and threw salt in it and said, "Thus says the LORD, 'I have purified these waters; there shall not be from there death or unfruitfulness any longer.'" So the waters have been purified to this day, according to the word of Elisha which he spoke. 2 Kings 2:1-22.

Do you know that Elisha was a wealthy man, but gave up everything to become Elijah's protégé? Were you aware that Elisha began his new career as a humble servant?

What is your value system? What do you seek first? What do you like to talk about most? Who do you aspire to become? These are important questions if you want to be used of God.

Elisha is considered by many to be similar to Elijah, his mentor. Yet the differences between these two mighty men of God provide additional lessons from this unique Bible character.

Elisha Valued the Role of a Prophet

Elisha had been a successful career man, employer, and land baron.

Elijah went from there and found Elisha son of Shaphat. He was plowing with twelve yoke of oxen, and he himself was driving the twelfth pair. Elijah went up to him and threw his cloak around him. Elisha then left his oxen and ran after Elijah. "Let me kiss my father and mother good-by," he said, "and then I will come with you."

"Go back," Elijah replied. "What have I done to you?"

So Elisha left him and went back. He took his yoke of oxen and slaughtered them. He burned the plowing equipment to cook the meat and gave it to the people, and they ate. Then he set out to follow Elijah and became his servant. (1 Kings 19:19-21)

Elisha was plowing with twelve yoke of oxen. One man alone cannot drive twelve pair of oxen at the same time. Elisha had to have had at least eleven employees, each driving a pair of oxen. He also drove a pair himself; he was a "hands on" man. He was obviously a successful farmer.

When presented with the opportunity to serve as Elijah's assistant, he immediately accepted the task. He asked only that he might part properly from his parents. Elijah gave him permission and at the same time released Elisha from any obligation. "'Go back,'

Elijah replied. 'What have I done to you?'" (1 Kings 19:20). Elisha killed one pair of oxen, offered meat to everyone nearby, burned the plow, and began to follow Elijah.

Over the centuries, other men have left their careers to follow the Lord. Amos left his sheep, and Peter and John left their nets. Surely we can and should serve God in other careers, and whatever vocation God leads us to follow we ought to do it with all our hearts, and as unto the Lord (see Ephesisan 6:7).

Full-time Christian leaders are not the only ones who are serving the Lord and an eternal purpose. But they do have the distinction of giving their entire energies to an eternal cause. There is no greater work than to help depopulate hell and populate heaven. Elisha evidently understood this.

Elisha Served

"Then he set out to follow Elijah and became his servant" (1 Kings 19:21). It is one thing to become a servant and another thing to have a servant's heart and serve from the heart. Many servants are referred to in the Bible. Not all of them followed in their masters' footsteps. But Elisha did.

Later, Elisha had his own servant, Gehazi, but Gehazi did not pursue God under Elisha's leadership as Elisha had under Elijah's leadership. Gehazi's poor performance provides a stark contrast with Elisha, who served fully and sincerely.

Later, in Dothan, Scripture tells us Elisha had a servant. We do not know who that servant was. It could have been Gehazi. Or, if Gehazi had died by then, this could be someone else.

After being Elijah's faithful servant, Elisha was granted the position of leading prophet. Not all servants are promoted like that. Was Elisha given this honor because of his desire for prophetic ministry and the value he placed on spiritual realities?

Just being close to a great man or woman of God is not enough for you to become one yourself. Seeking the God of the mighty man is better than seeking the mighty man of God. Elisha served a mighty man, but his behavior, attitude, and later ministry show us that he also sought the mighty God. Later in the story, Elisha is introduced to Jehoshaphat as the one who served Elijah. Jehoshaphat asked, "Is there no prophet of the Lord here, through whom we may inquire of the Lord?" An officer of the king of Israel answered, "Elisha son of Shaphat is here. He used to pour water on the hands of Elijah." (2 Kings 3:11)

As Joshua worked for Moses, and as Elisha ministered to Elijah, so we are to serve Jesus. This is not an easy task. A serving heart does not come easily, but God can give one to us if we ask Him. We naturally want to follow our own ideas. But if we subdue our personal wishes and maintain a desire for the heart of a servant, God will help us.

Elisha Sought Spiritual Things

In those days, it was customary for each son in a family to receive an equal share of his father's possessions, except the oldest son, who accepted the responsibilities of leadership in the family. He inherited twice as much as the other children. When Elisha asked Elijah for a "double portion," he was not asking for twice what Elijah had. He was asking for a double portion of what he thought the other sons of the prophet would receive. He was not grasping for personal greatness in a selfish, ambitious, or egotistical sense. Elisha wanted to inherit the leadership and responsibility for the family of prophets. Elisha wanted spiritual leadership opportunities and was willing to accept the consequent responsibilities and obligations.

Elijah said to Elisha, "Tell me, what can I do for you before I am taken from you?" "Let me inherit a double portion of your spirit," Elisha replied. "You have asked a difficult thing," Elijah said, "yet if you see me when I am taken from you, it will be yours—otherwise, it will not." (2 Kings 2:9-10)

God honored Elisha's desire for spiritual things. Elisha was present when Elijah was taken, and he did receive a great anointing from God.

Elisha Called Down a Curse on the Youth Who Jeered at Him

From there Elisha went up to Bethel. As he was walking along the road, some boys came out of the town and jeered at him. "Get out of here, baldy!" they said. "Get out of here, baldy!" He turned around, looked at them and called down a curse on them in the name of the Lord. Then two bears came out of the woods and mauled forty-two of the boys. (2 Kings 2:23-24)

As soon as Elisha's career was launched and miracles began to happen, some boys came along and made fun of him. Elisha called down a curse on them and the boys were punished.

This curious story raises questions about the place of cursing, if any, in the life of the modern man or woman of God. If Elisha cursed those who ridiculed him, should God's servants today also do that? Several observations may help us understand Elisha's situation and enable us to judge for ourselves whether we should follow his example.

This incident happened early in Elisha's career and may not be the way he would have handled the problem after he had mellowed over time. Ministers tend to be less vindictive after years of experience has taught them how to deal better with people.

Another consideration is the age of these "boys." The Hebrew language indicates that they were not children of eight or nine years, but youths, probably teens or older. Their jeers would have stemmed not so much from childish immaturity as from a deliberate, thoughtful, and perhaps even hateful disrespect for the man of God. Elisha was dealing with a more serious situation than little boys innocently making fun of a bald man.

A more important factor to consider in determining the validity of calling down curses on people is the stage of ethical developments in Elisha's generation.

Prior to Moses, it was customary in most cultures to exceed an original offense with stronger, more severe retribution. Moses taught that revenge should be limited to the severity of the original offense. If someone takes your eye, take only an eye; if someone takes your oxen, take the same number of oxen. Perhaps Moses' progressive view will be more clear if we insert some words: "[only an] eye for [an] eye, [only a] tooth for [a] tooth, [only a] hand for [a] hand, [and only a] foot for [a] foot" (see Exodus 21:24). The one who inflicted the injury should suffer only the same injury (Leviticus 24:20). Revenge had to be controlled and limited.

Generations later, David carried ethical development forward a huge step by asking God to take revenge. He would not seek vengeance himself, but committed the punishment of his enemies into God's care. In the following imprecatory psalm, David prays for a curse on his enemies: Contend, Lord, with those who contend with me; fight against those who fight against me. Take up shield and armor; arise and come to my aid. Brandish spear and javelin against those who pursue me. Say to me, "I am your salvation."

May those who seek my life be disgraced and put to shame; may those who plot my ruin be turned back in dismay. May they be like chaff before the wind, with the angel of the Lord driving them away; may their path be dark and slippery, with the angel of the Lord pursuing them. Since they hid their net for me without cause and without cause dug a pit for me, may ruin overtake them by surprise—may the net they hid entangle them, may they fall into the pit, to their ruin.

Then my soul will rejoice in the Lord and delight in his salvation. My whole being will exclaim, "Who is like you, Lord? You rescue the poor from those too strong for them, the poor and needy from those who rob them." (Psalm 35:1-10)

Centuries later, Jesus taught us to not seek revenge at all. He said we are to "turn the other cheek." (Matthew 5:39) We are to give our shirt to the one who demands our coat (Luke 6:29). "If someone slaps you on one cheek, turn the other also. If someone takes your coat, do not withhold your shirt." (Luke 6:29). This was yet another big ethical improvement.

In the epistles, Paul raised the bar still further by teaching us to help our enemies recognize their error by proactively doing good things to those who do evil to us. "On the contrary: If your enemy is hungry, feed him; if he is thirsty, give him something to drink. In doing this, you will heap burning coals on his head" (Romans 12:20).

In the series of ethical progressions described above, Elisha lived between David and Jesus. He had the Psalms to guide his thoughts. He knew Moses' teachings not to be vindictive and David's instructions not to seek his own revenge. He committed the jeering youths to God, letting Him punish them. The expression "in the name of the Lord" tells us that God had already authorized this curse for His own purposes, and Elisha was merely acting as God's personal representative in this matter.

Elisha's behavior, even calling a curse down on the youths in the name of the Lord, was appropriate according to the ethical standard of his day and according to his perception of how God wanted to act in this situation. His behavior was "phase specific"; it was acceptable for that time.

Should God's servants today curse those who ridicule them? As Christians we are to follow the teachings of Jesus. He said: You have heard that it was said, "Love your neighbor and hate your enemy." But I tell you, love your enemies and pray for those who persecute you, that you may be children of your Father in heaven. He causes his sun to rise on the evil and the good, and sends rain on the righteous and the unrighteous. If you love those who love you, what reward will you get? Are not even the tax collectors doing that? And if you greet only your own people, what are you doing more than others? Do not even pagans do that? Be perfect, therefore, as your heavenly Father is perfect. (Matthew 5:43-48)

Love your enemies, do good to those who hate you. (Luke 6:27).

We also have the high standards outlined in Paul's writings:

Bless those who persecute you; bless and do not curse. (Romans 12:14) We work hard with our own hands. When we are cursed, we bless; when we are persecuted, we endure it. (1 Corinthians 4:12).

The Lord came to take away our curse, to set prisoners free of curses. To be like Him, we must follow His lead and do the same. We have a high standard to achieve. What may have been acceptable for Elisha in his day is not necessarily appropriate for us to do in ours. Let us behave and think the way God wants us to. The fact that a Christian would even *want* to call down a curse on someone brings that person's character into question.

If Elisha had lived after Jesus, his love for the Lord would have dictated different behavior than is understandable for the inexperienced prophet just beginning his career in the period of time in which he lived.

Elisha Was Not Enamored by Strong, Influential Political Figures

Naaman, commander of the army of the king of Aram, went to visit Elisha. "So Naaman went with his horses and chariots and stopped at the door of Elisha's house. Elisha sent a messenger to say to him, 'Go, wash yourself seven times in the Jordan, and your flesh will be restored and you will be cleansed'" (2 Kings 5:9-10).

Elisha did not even go out to meet the well-positioned, important Naaman, but sent Ghazi with a message for him. Contrast this behavior with the way he treated the members of the school of prophets when they asked him to accompany them to the Jordan. Elisha was available to the no-name people in the school of prophets, but not to Naaman. He had his priorities correct.

Do we overly enjoy the company of people of great magnitude? What opportunities might we be missing to teach, mentor, or help younger believers if we are busy trying to associate with important people?

Elisha Understood Cross-cultural Issues

In 2 Kings 5, Elisha actually gave Naaman permission to kneel in the house of a heathen god, Rimmon. After repeatedly urging Elisha to accept the gifts he offered, Naaman finally gave up and then made a strange request:

"If you will not," said Naaman, "please let me, your servant, be given as much earth as a pair of mules can carry, for your servant will never again make burnt offerings and sacrifices to any other god but the Lord. But may the Lord forgive your servant for this one thing: when my master enters the temple of Rimmon to bow down and he is leaning on my arm and I have to bow there also—when I bow down in the temple of Rimmon, may the Lord forgive your servant for this." "Go in peace," Elisha said. (2 Kings 5:17-19)

Why did Naaman want to escort his king into a heathen temple and not be guilty of idolatry? And how do we interpret Elisha's response? There is a significant lesson in the incident recorded in 2 Kings 5.

Elisha understood that the condition of the mind and heart is more important than the position of the body. For Naaman to bow outwardly when he was not really worshipping the false god spiritually was not a problem to God. "Go in peace," Elisha said. We can interpret this to mean, "Do your vocational duty, fulfill the responsibilities of your profession. I know you will not be really worshipping as you bow." Naaman would *bow* but he would not *worship*. Elisha knew the difference between an outward form of worship and the meaning any action had to the doer. God looks on the heart.

The reverse application of this principle can also be made. Not all people who raise their hands, dance, and sing in a Christian church service are really worshipping. We must have our minds and hearts focused on the Lord for true worship to occur. Let's use the atmosphere of praise to advantage but actually adore God from our hearts. Words, hands, and songs can help but they are not worship.

Elisha Presided Over a Flourishing School of Prophets

Student enrollment was evidently up and new buildings were needed. The success of the company of prophets under the leadership of Elisha is indicated in the following conversation between Elisha and his students:

The company of the prophets said to Elisha, "Look, the place where we meet with you is too small for us. Let us go to the

Jordan, where each of us can get a pole; and let us build a place there for us to meet." And he said, "Go." (2 Kings 6:1-2) Did the school of prophets flourish at this time because of Elisha's gifts? His leadership? His charismatic persona? Was it because Elisha had better people skills than the abrupt, outspoken Elijah demonstrated? Was Elisha a better administrator? These questions remain unanswered, but we know from the above verses that the school experienced growth under Elisha's leadership.

We also know that Elisha's students wanted him to join them as they sought to expand their school. Evidently Elisha was approachable. This may be a factor in why the school prospered during his years at the helm.

Elisha submitted to the request of the prophets. They went together to the Jordan. Then one of them said, "Won't you please come with your servants?" "I will," Elisha replied. And he went with them. They went to the Jordan and began to cut down trees. (See 2 Kings 6:3-4.)

Either the school of prophets or Elisha, or both, had a good reputation in the community. Is this another reason the school was flourishing.

Otherwise, no one would have loaned one of them a valuable ax.

And he went with them. They went to the Jordan and began to cut down trees. As one of them was cutting down a tree, the iron ax head fell into the water. "Oh no, my lord!" he cried out. "It was borrowed!" (2 Kings 6:4-5)

The world over, God is growing His church. People are getting saved. Congregations are being started and are growing. The number of believers needing to be discipled continues to increase. Pastors are being called and appointed. Some step into responsibility because there is no one else to do the work and still others start churches themselves.

The education of God's prophets was an important matter in the days of Samuel, Elijah, and Elisha, as it is for God's servants and ministers today. Formal studies (attending accredited classes at Bible institutes, Bible colleges, and seminaries), informal learning (such as in a conversation), and nonformal professional improvements (conferences and seminars) are all vital forms of education and training for pastors and Christian leaders. Accredited degrees for those prepared academically to pursue them, and basic training for beginner leaders, are both necessary.

Over the centuries it has not been the scholars from academia who have broadly influenced the common people and their societies to move toward God at the grass-roots level. Samuel, Elijah, and Elisha seem to have understood this. They were successful prophets themselves and they took time to develop and encourage others. Jesus trained fishermen and other non-clergy for ministry, side-stepping the entire Levitical system and Aaronic priesthood organizations of His day. Ezekiel and Jeremiah were both priests, but not one of Jesus' disciples had been a priest before becoming a follower. We don't usually think of "school" and "prophets" in the same sentence, but Samuel's, Elijah's, and Elisha's schools of prophets were not contradictions in terms. Some church leaders tend to choose either power or knowledge, but such a choice is not necessary. Christian leaders must balance spiritual power and education.

If you are a prayerful, anointed, and inspired man or woman of God, add information and knowledge to your power by studying. If you are the scholarly type or have already received theological training or ministry-related academic instruction, empower your information by getting on your knees before God.

When I conduct Leadership Empowerment Conferences in the cities of Africa, we teach participants both to pray and to study, to fast and to get an education, to get on their faces before God in extended times of pursuing His anointing, while disciplining themselves to study God's Word, to prepare themselves spiritually and to preach content-rich sermons. It is not enough to stand in front of the congregation, shout hallelujah, and aim for a strong emotional response. Neither is it enough to inform people with dry, unmoving, impractical, theoretical rhetoric. If ministers do not have both the power of God and good information in their public ministry, they will not experience their full potential. We do not have to choose between emotion, good content, and the anointing of the Holy Spirit; we can and must have all three.

I often went to the famous "prayer mountains" where many burdened brothers and sisters poured out their hearts in earnest prayer for their land and their churches. These prayer mountains are one important factor in the revival and growth of the church for the nations. Its important we value and seek education, and also recognize the power and results of prayer.

I have seen the move of the Holy Ghost in our Africa Leadership Advancement Empowerment Conferences, I have great conviction that pastors and leaders need to be trained while they remain on the job in their place of ministry. Too many times well-intentioned ministerial candidates go to the big city or a faraway country for theological education and never return to the places of ministry that desperately need them. Our Apostolic Leadership conferences are similar to what Samuel, Elijah, and Elisha did as they moved from Ramah to Gilgal and Jericho, teaching, mentoring, and discipling prophets in multiple locations.

Elisha Saw Clearly into the Spirit World

The king of Aram was unable to defeat the Israeli army because Elisha kept informing Israel's king of his enemy's campaigns. Knowing he must first deal with Elisha, the king of Aram sent his army to pursue him in Dothan. Elisha's servant was alarmed the next morning to see the army with horses and chariots surrounding the city. Understandably, he panicked. Then he [the king of Aram] sent horses and chariots and a strong force there. They went by night and surrounded the city. When the servant of the man of God got up and went out early the next morning, an army with horses and chariots had surrounded the city. "Oh no, my lord! What shall we do?" the servant asked. "Don't be afraid," the prophet answered. "Those who are with us are more than those who are with them." And Elisha prayed, "Open his eyes, Lord, so that he may see." Then the Lord opened the servant's eyes, and he looked and saw the hills full of horses and chariots of fire all around Elisha. (2 Kings 6:14-17)

Why was Elisha not afraid? Did he already see the superior number of heavenly forces? Did he not need to see it to know it was there? Even if Elisha knew this, he understood that the servant needed to see it in order to understand it.

How would our lives be affected if we could see the spirit world? What if we could see the enemy lurking at a distance and the superior number and power of the forces of righteousness defending, protecting, ready to rescue, present and prepared for battle? Each of us envisions spiritual realities differently. But whether we see them or not, we can know, as Elisha did, that the forces of righteousness are greater in quantity, strength, authority, and ability to win the fight.

Elisha Recognized the Ministry Value of Music—Elisha recognized the value of the ministry of music in creating a spiritual atmosphere.

Elisha said, "As surely as the Lord Almighty lives, whom I serve, if I did not have respect for the presence of Jehoshaphat king of Judah, I would not pay any attention to you. But now bring me a harpist." While the harpist was playing, the hand of the Lord came on Elisha. (2 Kings 3:14-15)

The word *music* appears in Today's New International Version of the Bible 128 times, *song* appears 110 times, *sing* 158 times, *sang* 21 times, *choir* 5 times, and *instrument* (referring to musical instrument or instruments) 23 times. These combined 445 references give us an idea of the importance of music to God's people. We have more reasons to sing than anyone else in the world.

Satan scores some victories when he robs Christians of their song. Satan also scores victories when he gets Christians to sing the wrong songs. The world is full of music stolen from God to use for evil purposes. Some music is sensual, sexual, satanic, or hateful. Other types of music promote violence or encourage various forms of an ungodly lifestyle. But music is a gift from

God to us. Let us sing of God and sing to God. When we give our voices back to Him in worshipful song, we rejoice before the Lord. In times of prayer, a song sung to the Lord has great power to uplift and edify.

The Bible in general, and the book of Psalms particularly, have numerous references to music. Here is one excellent example: It is good to praise the Lord and make music to your name, O Most High, proclaiming your love in the morning and your faithfulness at night, to the music of the ten-stringed lyre and the melody of the harp. For you make me glad by your deeds, Lord; I sing for joy at what your hands have done. (Psalm 92:14)

Paul instructed his readers to sing, "speaking to one another with psalms, hymns and songs from the Spirit. Sing and make music from your heart to the Lord" (Ephesians 5:19).

One dry day, Joram, the king of Israel, and Jehoshaphat, king of Judah, agreed to confederate with the king of Edom to attack Moab, which had rebelled against Israel. After a seven-day march through the desert of Edom, the combined armies ran out of water. Not a drop for either soldiers or animals. Jehoshaphat asked, "Is there no prophet of the Lord here, through whom we may inquire of the Lord?" An officer of the king of Israel answered, "Elisha son of Shaphat is here. He used to pour water on the hands of Elijah." Jehoshaphat said, "The word of the Lord is with him." So the king of Israel and Jehoshaphat and the king of Edom went down to him. (2 Kings 3:11-12)

Elisha asked a strange thing; he asked for a harpist. Then he focused his attention on God. "*While the harpist was playing,* the hand of the Lord came on Elisha" (2 Kings 3:15, emphasis mine). Through Elisha, the Lord showed the three kings that He would not only supply them with plenty of water, but that He would also enable them to defeat Moab.

When we are faced with impossible situations, we should calm ourselves, sing, worship, and allow the Lord to speak to us. Music is one of God's gifts to us. He knows we need to be uplifted; He created the unique combination of music and music appreciation so that could happen.

Christian leaders carry a heavy load with their concern for the work of God, the condition of their flocks, and efforts to rescue the lost sheep. Understandably, they will not feel light-hearted all the time. Neither is any Christian. But if we never sing, never rejoice before the Lord in private times of prayer and praise as well as in corporate worship, we will not fully realize the power of singing to the Lord.

QUEEN ESTHER—if I perish I perish !

Esther was an orphan who possessed a submissive, cooperative attitude. Did you realize that Esther's physical beauty was enhanced by her helpful attitude and concern for others? Do you understand how intelligent, clever, and wise Esther was?

Good literature includes subtleties that arouse the reader's curiosity. The book of Esther meets this criterion. The story has intrigue, a sinister plot, divine involvement, and deliverance throughout which numerous moral lessons are cleverly couched. Because we like adventure, action, drama, romance, plots and counter-plots, success stories, and justice, we enjoy the story of Esther.

King Xerxes ruled over the Medes and Persians' 127 provinces from Eastern Africa to India, but he could not rule his wife Vashti. She would not cooperate with him and it deeply angered him when she refused to display her beauty. When he ordered a kind of "beauty contest" to find a suitable replacement, Esther was among the candidates. The record states, "Now the king was attracted to Esther more than to any of the other women, and she won his favor and approval more than any of the other virgins. So he set a royal crown on her head and made her queen instead of Vashti" (Esther 2:17).

What qualities caused the king to be attracted to Esther? Though she was certainly blessed with physical beauty, we need to look deeper than that if we are to profit fully from this character study. Esther's lesson-packed action drama illustrates the power of submission over tyranny as displayed by her self-control, poise, courage, willingness to use the means at hand, and firm contention for justice.

Esther Was Submissive

Esther was beautiful both outwardly and inwardly. "Mordecai had a cousin named Hadassah, whom he had brought up because she had neither father nor mother. This young woman, who was also known as Esther, had a lovely figure and was beautiful. Mordecai had taken her as his own daughter when her father and mother died" (Esther 2:7).

Esther was obedient to her uncle. "Esther had kept secret her family background and nationality just as Mordecai had told her to do, for she continued to follow Mordecai's instructions as she had done when he was bringing her up" (Esther 2:20).

She learned at an early age the virtue and importance of obedience.

This trait of obedience, however, was not exercised exclusively toward her original mentor, Mordecai. A spirit of submission and cooperation had evidently become a part of who Esther was. This is shown by the fact that she maintained it in the king's harem. "When the turn came for Esther (the young woman Mordecai had adopted, the daughter of his uncle Abihail) to go to the king, she asked for nothing other than what Hegai, the king's eunuch who was in charge of the harem, suggested. And Esther won the favor of everyone who saw her" (Esther 2:15). The Bible says that obedience is beautiful. "Your beauty . . . should be that of your inner self, the unfading beauty of a gentle and quiet spirit, which is of great worth in God's sight" (1 Peter 3:3-4).

Imagine being in the dressmaker's shop, between the perfumed oil bath and the hair salon in the harem's central beautification district. Three ladies have been outfitted with new gowns by the chief dressmaker. When the first new addition to the harem looks at her new gown, her beautiful face contorts into an ugly frown. "I don't like this color," she complains. "It never looks good on me. Besides, the texture is too rough, and it doesn't slide freely on my hips and legs. This will never do."

The second "beauty" tries on her new gown, purses her lips in a sulk, and whines, "Well, this is the color I agreed to, but the dress is too tight around my shoulders and too loose around my hips. Why can't you get it right?"

A third young woman arrives. She smiles, greets the dressmaker, and waits her turn. When presented with her gown, she thanks him. When she emerges from the dressing room for his review, he says, "Oh, the waist is not quite right." "I am sure you can fix that with no difficulty," she replies. "You are a professional. I like the rest of it. You do a wonderful job of making us look good." Which of the three do you think was the most beautiful?

Imagine further that everywhere she went, whether she was eating in the dining room, receiving a pedicure and manicure at the beauty parlor, or getting her eyebrows trimmed and eyelashes curled, Esther's humble and gracious attitude brought respect and appreciation. Attitude is an important part of beauty.

Esther's submissive, obedient, and cooperative spirit is not to be mistaken for weakness or a lack of her own well-developed opinions. Esther had courage and a strong will, as is shown later in the story when she risks her life and states her case before the king. She even dared to accuse Haman, who was present at the time. Esther was no coward or silly beauty. She had courage and character. She knew how to be in command of her will for beneficial purposes. She exhibited power under control. Esther could have become conceited, demanding, and/or self-impressed, given that she was beautiful and found favor with everyone. She evidently resisted those temptations.

Esther Showed Concern for Others

One day, as Esther was going about her duties as the new queen, the eunuchs and her female attendants came and told her that her uncle Mordecai was outside the gates of the palace, grieving in sackcloth and ashes. With the favor she received, the attention from the king, involvement in the activities of the court, and the affairs of the ladies of the court, Esther could have become preoccupied with other matters than her cousin out by the gate. But when she heard about Mordecai, she not only cared, but "was in great distress" (Esther 4:4). She sent clothes for him to put on instead of his sackcloth, but he would not accept them.

Esther had no idea that the issue troubling her uncle would affect her too. For all she knew, Mordecai had a personal difficulty that he thought perhaps she could help him with.

When Esther's offer of new clothes did not console him, she "summoned Hathak, one of the king's eunuchs assigned to attend her, and ordered him to find out what was troubling Mordecai and why" (Esther 4:4-5). When he returned, he told Esther that Mordecai had learned of a wicked plan, devised by Haman, one of the king's top advisors, to exterminate all the Jews in the kingdom. This massive tragedy would mean an end to the entire nation of the Jewish people.

Mordecai instructed her to make a plea with the king for her people.

Esther sent this reply to Mordecai: "Go, gather together all the Jews who are in Susa, and fast for me. Do not eat or drink for three days, night or day. I and my attendants will fast as you do. When this is done, I will go to the king, even though it is against the law. And if I perish, I perish." (Esther 4:15-16).

Esther did not sidestep the problem or abdicate her responsibility. Rather, she complied with Mordecai's instruction, knowing it could mean her own death.

Esther Resisted the Temptations of the Successful

Problems often reveal one's character. When the pressure is on, the true nature of an individual is revealed more clearly than when life is moving along normally and all seems well. On the other end of the spectrum, however, is a different kind of temptation. Success also provides an opportunity to view one's character. Accomplishment corrupts some people, allowing for further development of arrogance, contributing to an inflated ego and a superiority complex.

Why must the man or woman of God be particularly concerned about this? John 15:7-8 says that Jesus wants us to be fruitful in our lives, our characters, and our ministries. This brings glory to God. As we abide in Christ we can ask God for fruitfulness and He will grant our request. But if our fruitfulness makes us successful in life, we will be tempted by pride.

Esther avoided that temptation. She provides for us a model of a person who, in spite of beauty and success, remembered her roots and struggled on behalf of her people.

Esther Fought Her Battle by Praying

Esther and her attendants did a difficult thing; they conducted a three-day absolute fast—going without food and water. She asked Mordecai and the Jews at Susa to do the same. Then she put her life on the line by appearing without invitation before the king. She prayed, but she also planned and developed a wise strategy.

Nowhere in this book are the words *pray*, *prayed*, or *prayer* to be found. If Esther and her friends fasted, didn't they also pray? Certainly. And if they fasted and prayed, to whom did they pray? God, of course. No prayers to Him are mentioned in Esther, but they are unquestionably implied.

This seems rather like real life. We don't see God. We can't hear the private prayers of others. Prayer, if done in secret as Jesus said, is invisible, as is the God to whom we pray. Yet the results of His involvement in response to prayer abound.

God's active presence in our lives can be just as pervasive as demonstrated in the story of Esther. Even if we do not talk a lot about our prayer lives, we can see that He is involved and that He provides "grace to help us in our time of need" (Hebrews 4:16).

On the third day Esther put on her royal robes and stood in the inner court of the palace, in front of the king's hall. The king was sitting on his royal throne in the hall, facing the entrance. When he saw Queen Esther standing in the court, he was pleased with her and held out to her the gold scepter that was in his hand. So Esther approached and touched the tip of the scepter. (Esther 5:1-2)

It is never wrong to pray about the evils in political arenas. Let us not ignore our moral obligation to prayerfully oppose evil wherever it exists in government or society. Out of supposed political correctness or social tolerance some Christians sidestep opportunities to be an influence. God is willing to be involved in geo-political conflict on the side of righteousness. The story of Esther illustrates that He recognizes the reality of evil and desires to help us be victorious over it.

God has political opinions. One side can be right and the other side wrong. And when politically correct but morally wrong policies, agendas, party platforms, and/or ethical issues become evident, they must be opposed by prayer. Do not be afraid to have a political opinion and to pray about it. If you know the mind of God and how to pray in a given situation you must oppose evil through prayer. You may not be a queen, but you, your family, and your loved ones will be affected by political outcomes.

How did God answer Esther's prayers? He arranged for Mordecai to overhear two men, Bigthana and Teresh, conspiring to assassinate the king. God then kept the king from sleeping one night so that the boring records in the archives were brought out and read to him. God led the scribe at that very time to read the particular section that brought Mordecai's good deed to light. He arranged for Haman to be waiting at the door to enter the king's room just after Mordecai's good deed was revealed. It is not hard to see God's hand in these events.

Esther Planned Carefully and Did Not Hurry

In addition to praying, Esther planned. While she and her people were fasting these three days, Esther was strategizing how she should approach the king with her request. More than likely, she consulted certain trusted advisors. Too many Christians, even leaders and ministers, believe the Holy Spirit only acts spontaneously. But there are times when we must plan ahead in order to do the right things God's way. Esther understood how important this was.

When Esther approached the king, he extended his scepter and Esther touched its tip, undoubtedly relieved that God had graciously brought her safe thus far. At this point, she could have immediately expressed her request. But wisely, she did not. Instead, she mentioned a banquet she had prepared for him and Haman even before she approached the king. That took planning and effort. The king was suitably impressed by her preparations.

God Answered Esther's Prayers Even Before She Prayed

Esther is not the only one in the story who prepared in advance. Years before this crucial moment in time, God arranged for Mordecai to overhear two men, Bigthana and Teresh, conspiring to assassinate the king. The night after Esther invited the king and Haman to her prepared banquet, God kept the king from sleeping, so the boring records in the archives were brought out and read to him. God led the scribe to read at that very time the particular section that brought Mordecai's good deed to light. He even arranged for Haman to be waiting at the door to enter the king's room just after Mordecai's good deed was revealed.

When the king asked his trusted advisor what should be done for a man who had served the king well, Haman proudly assumed he was that man. So he described in detail the most public honor he could think of. Imagine his distress when the king gave this very honor to Haman's enemy, Mordecai.

It is not hard to see God's hand in these events.

Esther Exercised Patience

At the banquet, Esther still declined the opportunity to express her complaint. The king and Haman went to the banquet

Esther had prepared. As they were drinking wine, the king again asked Esther, "Now what is your petition? It will be given you. And what is your request? Even up to half the kingdom, it will be granted."

Esther replied, "My petition and my request is this: If the king regards me with favor and if it pleases the king to grant my petition and fulfill my request, let the king and Haman come tomorrow to the banquet I will prepare for them. Then I will answer the king's question." (Esther 5:3-8)

Esther was no empty-headed, vindictive, or emotional woman. The issue at hand meant life or death to her people. Yet she declined the opportunity to immediately express her desire to the king. That required strength of character. She evidently understood human nature quite well and decided to show honor to the king before making her request.

This delay gave time for the king's curiosity to be fully aroused. First she postponed her answer until later that same day, when she had a chance to honor him at a banquet she had prepared. Then Esther again put off her response until yet another day and the next banquet. She showed patience and wisdom by requesting these delays. She also certainly had the attention of the king In our impatience, do we fail to honor God? Is our desire for hasty results motivated by faith or a lack of faith? God never seems to hurry and is never late. Could we learn to be more like Him on this point? Wise Esther seems to have known that taking a slower pace allows for more reflection and satisfactory results.

Esther Remained Objective

We have arrived at the pivotal part of the drama. Esther did not blink, flinch, or hold back. At the right time she spoke courageously. Notice how poised, measured, confident, yet entreating her words are. So the king and Haman went to Queen Esther's banquet, and as they were drinking wine on the second day, the king again asked, "Queen Esther, what is your petition? It will be given you. What is your request? Even up to half the kingdom, it will be granted." Then Queen Esther answered, "If I have found favor with you, Your Majesty, and if it pleases you, grant me my life—this is my petition. And spare my people—this is my request. For I and my people have been sold to be destroyed, killed and annihilated. If we had merely been sold as male and female slaves, I would have kept quiet, because no such distress would justify disturbing the king."

King Xerxes asked Queen Esther, "Who is he? Where is he—the man who has dared to do such distress would justify disturbing the king."

Esther said, "An adversary and enemy! This vile Haman!" (Esther 7:1-6)

Esther focused on protection of herself and her people, not on hatred of her enemy. First she tactfully asked for her people to be saved. Only when the king asked the identity of the man who had dared to do such a thing did she spring the trap on Haman.

Then Haman was terrified before the king and queen. The king got up in a rage, left his wine and went out into the palace garden. But Haman, realizing that the king had already decided his fate, stayed behind to beg Queen Esther for his life.

Then Haman was terrified before the king returned from the palace garden to the banquet hall, Haman was falling on the couch where Esther was reclining. The king exclaimed, "Will he even molest the queen while she is with me in the house?" As soon as the word left the king's mouth, they covered Haman's face. Then Harbona, one of the eunuchs attending the king, said, "A pole reaching to a height of fifty cubits stands by Haman's house. He had it set up for Mordecai, who spoke up to help the king."

The king said, "Impale him on it!" So they impaled Haman on the pole he had set up for Mordecai. Then the king's fury subsided. (Esther 7:6-10)

Esther did not back down even when the king commanded Haman to be hanged on the gallows he had built for Mordecai. Esther showed no weakness. At the crucial moment she spoke with undeniable courage.

Justice requires wisdom and firmness. Mercy at the right times can be a result of wisdom and strength. But, unfortunately, mercy is too often merely a result of weak character—unwillingness to uphold righteousness and preserve justice. Esther's firmness and consistency in maintaining justice in this instance are qualities to be admired and emulated.

Esther Boldly Pressed Her Advantage

The day after the king gave the estate of Haman to Esther, the drama continued. Esther again pleaded with the king, falling at his feet and weeping. She begged him to put an end to the evil plan of Haman the Agagite, which he had devised against the Jews. Then the king extended the gold scepter to Esther and she arose and stood before him. "If it pleases the king," she said, "and if he regards me with favor and thinks it the right thing to do, and if he is pleased with me, let an order be written overruling the dispatches that Haman son of Hammedatha, the Agagite, devised and wrote to destroy the Jews in all the king's provinces. For how can I bear to see disaster fall on my people? How can I bear to see the destruction of my family?"

King Xerxes replied to Queen Esther and to Mordecai the Jew, "Because Haman attacked the Jews, I have given his estate to Esther, and they have impaled him on the pole he set up. Now write another decree in the king's name in behalf of the Jews as seems best to you, and seal it with the king's signet ring—for no document written in the king's name and sealed with his ring can be revoked."

At once the royal secretaries were summoned—on the twenty-third day of the third month, the month of Sivan. They wrote out all Mordecai's orders to the Jews, and to the satraps, governors and nobles of the 127 provinces stretching from India to Cush. These orders were written in the script of each province and the language of each people and also to the Jews in their own script and language. Mordecai wrote in the name of King Xerxes, sealed the dispatches with the king's signet ring, and sent them by mounted couriers, who rode fast horses especially bred for the king.

The king's edict granted the Jews in every city the right to assemble and protect themselves; to destroy, kill and annihilate the armed men of any nationality or province who might attack them and their women and children, and to plunder the property of their enemies. The day appointed for the Jews to do this in all the provinces of King Xerxes was the thirteenth day of the twelfth month, the month of Adar. A copy of the text of the edict was to be issued as law in every province and made known to the people of every nationality so that the Jews would be ready on that day to avenge themselves on their enemies. (Esther 8:3-14)

God does not approve of personal revenge. We are to be forgiving. So how are we to interpret Esther's behavior? She requested permission for the Jews to defend themselves and plunder the property of their enemies. Was this act pleasing to God?

Centuries earlier, Saul had failed to press his advantage against King Agag, whom Saul was to destroy, and whom Samuel eventually had to kill. Haman was an Agagite, a descendent of this wicked king. Esther was not weak like Saul. She acted more decisively and wisely than he.

Corrective punishment to rid the earth of evil is not the same as personal revenge. Men and women of God must follow God's example in His love for justice, understand the rightness of justice, and uphold justice in the administrative affairs of our churches and ministries. Of course, we cannot approve of vengeance. Justice breeds respect for right and distaste for wrong, while personal payback elicits still more hatred.

The Bible Supports National Defense

God miraculously provided the means of self-defense for the Jews. In previous centuries He used judges, armies, and kings for this purpose. This time he used the king's edict. This would not have happened if God were not in favor of countries protecting themselves. National self-defense is not revenge; it is the attempt to stop the aggressor and prevent further evil.

Every country that maintains a strong military for national defense contributes to the prevalence of peace in the world. Evil nations do not attack strong nations. A strong defense, therefore, is a deterrent to war. Christians who are serving their nations as soldiers are not soldiering because they want war, but because they *do not* want war. They are defending their nations and families against aggressors who do not recognize the rights of free people.

If God were anti-military, John the Baptist would have spoken to the Roman soldiers of his day on that subject instead of merely instructing them to not complain about their wages. "Some soldiers asked him, 'And what should we do?' He replied, 'Don't extort money and don't accuse people falsely—be content with your pay'" (Luke 3:14).

In Esther's time, God did not destroy the enemies of the Jews with hailstones, lightning, or thunder. He gave them the means to defend themselves. God's answer to our prayer for protection may be to provide us with the ability to protect ourselves. There is nothing wrong with using the defensive measures He has given us.

Esther was a beautiful, wise, poised, self-controlled, intelligent, considerate, and firm young woman who kept her power under control, put her life on the line, and became a savior for her people. Could it be that God has given you similar traits "for such a time as this" (Esther 4:14)?

FRIENDS, IN CONCLUSION, I WANT TO BELIEVE ITS TIME FOR YOU TO GO ON YOUR KNEES AND DO SOME SPIRITUAL WARFARE PRAYERS TO TAKE WHAT BELONGS TO YOU AND RECOVER ALL THE ENEMIES HAS STOLEN, DECLARE COURAGEOUSLY WITH THE AUDACITY OF FAITH . . . GIVE ME THIS MOUNTAIN AND SURELY YOU GET ACCESS TO YOUR POSSESSIONS AND DEFEAT THE GIANTS.

ABOUT THE AUTHOR

APOSTLE of FAITH (Dr.) Abraham Peters is a multi-gifted preacher, distinguished author, erudite educator, consultant and counselor who addresses critical Issues affecting the full range of Human, social and spiritual development. The central theme of his message is leadership development by discovery of personal Destiny and purpose, Building capacity through training of trainers and the maximization of individual potential by transforming follower into efficient and effective leaders; Reviving the saints and Rescuing sinners, by taking God's word as shinning torch to the darkness in Communities around the world.

Revd DR, Abraham Peters is the provost of Apostolic Leadership Advancement Foundation International Academy (ALAFIA) Development Centre Inc. and the presiding pastor of Champions Apostolic Commission, TRINITY TABERNACLE aka the Transfiguration mountain, A Revival fire, Prayer and Missionary Movement International Inc. an itinerant squad, interdenominational evangelistic outreach and all encompassing network of ministries with the base in Jos, Nigeria. He has earned degrees as Epidemiologist and Public Health Consultant from the prestigious University of Ilorin, Nigeria and trained as a minister at the premiere Nigerian Baptist Theological Seminary Ogbomosho, Nigeria. Traveling extensively as a conference speaker, seminar and convention versatile teacher and workshop facilitator, Abraham displays multi-faceted approach to critical Issues affecting every area of human capital development, social and spiritual advancement as he addresses the wholistic aspects of health, family, business, mediation or conflict resolution and communal peace/ Justice, compelling negative Attitudinal change to positive completely, Educational and spiritual realms of life.

A very humble, indefatigable, vibrant evangelical. Erudite scholar and prolific author whose breakthrough books are noted for their crisp simplicity, Biblical balanced and practical principles. Some of his breakthrough books include.

—DIVIDENDS OF DIVINE—DIRECTION: Biblical insights on getting guidance and leading from God.

—GROWING UP TO GREATNESS: Biblical lessons for Christian growth and supernatural success.

—FOSTERING FAITH IN FAMILY FOUNDATIONS: Proven Biblical fundamentals for effective parenting, child training and Building Healthy Christian homes today.

—PRACTICAL-CHRISTIAN COMMITMENT: Biblical principles for fruitful and committed Christian living.

—FOOTPRINTS OF FAITH: Biblical insights on Abrahams Adventure to the promised land.

—BEAUTIFUL FOR SITUATIONS: Real true life experiences and Biblical response for lasting solution.

—UNDERSTANDING DIVINE VISITATION: Biblical exposition on preparing for God's Blessings.

DYNAMICS OF POSITIVE ATTITUDE,
THE FAIR HAVENS,
GIVE ME THIS MOUNTAIN,
MAKING THE MOST OF OPPORTUNITY,
JOURNEY FROM THE ALTAR,
ITS YOUR TIME,
BEYOND THE SHADOW OF DREAMS,
DYNAMICS OF DIVINE DIRECTION,
LORD TEACH US TO PRAY,

—THE ANSWER—Why some Christians suffer for long! A critical assessment of protracted crisis, in spite of prayers. And

—LEADERSHIP TOWARDS NATIONAL REFORMATION: REBUILDING THE BROKEN HERITAGE AND REGATHERING THE COVENANT PEOPLE . . . An indept case study of EZRA and Nehemiah's legendary Leadership lessons for today's leaders.

AB-Peters fully committed In training and teaching seminars, Revival deliverance sessions characterised with Apostolic/ Prophetic signs and wonders following, together with amazing testimonies as GOD confirms the words of his servant;he's a charismatic leader who minister with a sensitive heart and a global vision.

E-Mail: abrahampeters@rocketmail.com
GSM;+234 08036138392, +2348088592999,
+2348054711387, +2347066711387,